GRADE K

Scaffolded Strategies
HANDBOOK

Glenview, Illinois • Boston, Massachusetts • Chandler, Arizona • Upper Saddle River, New Jersey

Acknowledgments of third-party content appear on page 427, which constitutes an extension of this copyright page.

ISBN-13: 978-0-328-85169-0
ISBN-10: 0-328-85169-8

7 16

Table of Contents

Part 1 Unlock the Text

Table of Contents

Part 2 Unlock the Writing

Scaffolded Lessons for the Performance-Based Assessments

Scaffolded Lessons for the Writing Types

Part 3 Routines and Activities

Reading Routines

Foundational Skills Routines and Activities

Table of Contents

Writing Routines

Listening and Speaking Routines

Language Routines and Activities: Vocabulary and Conventions

Part 4 Unlock Language Learning

Anchor Text, Supporting Text, and Writing

Language Routines and Resources

Acknowledgments

About This Book

What is the Scaffolded Strategies Handbook?

The *Scaffolded Strategies Handbook* is a valuable resource that provides support at the module level for all learners. As part of an integrated reading and writing program, this handbook works in tandem with each unit of the *ReadyGEN™ Teacher's Guide* to help you guide students as they read and write about the texts within each module. It provides models of scaffolded instruction, useful strategies, and practical routines that you can employ during reading and writing to support

- English language learners
- struggling readers
- students with disabilities
- accelerated learners

It is intended that these lessons be used during small-group time with students that you determine need additional scaffolded instruction for any of the ReadyGEN texts or writing activities. Refer to this handbook during planning to determine which lessons will provide the most focused scaffolds for your students. You may use any or all of the lessons or lesson parts as dictated by the needs of your students. Keep in mind that this handbook is meant not only for the classroom teacher, but can be used by any support person working with the diverse student population in your school.

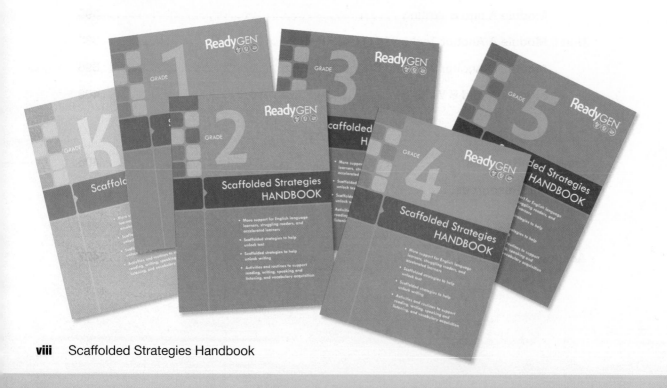

Using the Scaffolded Strategies Handbook

Part 1 Unlock the Text

Within Part 1 of this handbook, titled Unlock the Text, every anchor and supporting text in the ReadyGEN program is supported by research-proven scaffolds and strategies. Each lesson is divided into three parts:

- **Prepare to Read** This portion of the lesson provides more intensive readiness before reading. Students preview the text, activate background knowledge, and are introduced to troublesome vocabulary.

- **Interact with Text** Here, students do close reading and focus on stumbling blocks in the text.

- **Express and Extend** This section allows students to react to the text by discussing and writing about their ideas.

With every student text, qualitative measures of text complexity, such as those determined by the Common Core Learning Standards, are identified:

- Levels of Meaning
- Structure
- Language Conventionality and Clarity
- Knowledge Demands

Each of the three lesson parts is divided to address all of these qualitative measures. These become customized access points for your specific student populations, allowing all students to access and make sense of complex texts.

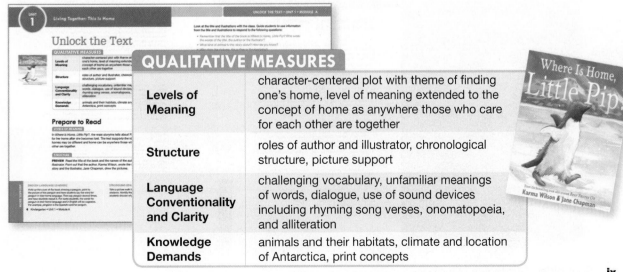

QUALITATIVE MEASURES

Levels of Meaning	character-centered plot with theme of finding one's home, level of meaning extended to the concept of home as anywhere those who care for each other are together
Structure	roles of author and illustrator, chronological structure, picture support
Language Conventionality and Clarity	challenging vocabulary, unfamiliar meanings of words, dialogue, use of sound devices including rhyming song verses, onomatopoeia, and alliteration
Knowledge Demands	animals and their habitats, climate and location of Antarctica, print concepts

Part 2 Unlock the Writing

Part 2 of this handbook, titled Unlock the Writing, features two types of scaffolded writing lessons.

First, there are scaffolded lessons for each of the module-level Performance-Based Assessments in the core Teacher's Guide. Each lesson in the handbook walks students through the Performance-Based Assessment for that module, providing guidance with unlocking the task, breaking it apart, thinking through the process, and then evaluating their writing.

Next, there are scaffolded writing lessons that provide grade-appropriate support and guidelines for teaching each of the writing types required by the Common Core Learning Standards:

- Opinion Writing
- Informative/Explanatory Writing
- Narrative Writing

Each of these three lessons is divided into the tasks specific to the writing type. Instructional support is provided to help you introduce and model each task so that students will better understand the writing type and how to become proficient writers of each. There are ample opportunities for practice, including robust Deeper Practice activities.

As in Part 1, Unlock the Text lessons, the Unlock the Writing lessons provide specific scaffolded "notes" to support English language learners as well as both struggling and accelerated writers.

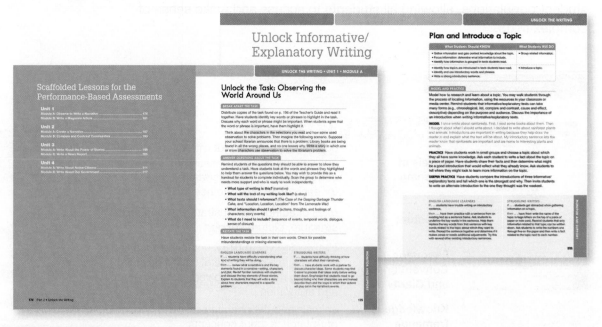

Part 3 Routines and Activities

Part 3 of the *Scaffolded Strategies Handbook* is a collection of routines and reproducible graphic organizers as well as engaging activities that you can use for support as you teach English Language Arts skills and address the Common Core Learning Standards. When appropriate, specific routines and activities are suggested and referred to in the lessons in Part 1 of this handbook.

You will find routines, many with accompanying graphic organizers, for teaching skills in

- Reading
- Writing
- Listening and Speaking
- Language, including Vocabulary and Conventions

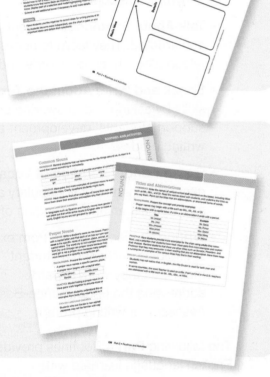

Part 3 also contains a variety of activities that provide extra scaffolded practice and instruction for language skills and vocabulary development, such as

- Noun and Pronoun Activities
- Verb Activities
- Adjective and Adverb Activities
- Sentence Activities
- Punctuation Activities
- Word Study Activities
- Vocabulary Activities and Games

In Kindergarten, there are also foundational skills activities in Part 3 that provide the practice and additional scaffolds kindergarteners need to be successful in reading and writing.

This section of the handbook will be useful at any time during your teaching day. As you become familiar with the routines, graphic organizers, and activities, feel free to use them whenever they fit the needs of your students. Think of this section as a toolbox of ideas and suggestions to use with your struggling readers and writers. Turn to it often.

Using the Scaffolded Strategies Handbook

Part 4 Unlock Language Learning

Part 4 of the *Scaffolded Strategies Handbook* provides additional instruction for each Anchor Text selection and for each Supporting Text selection in the ReadyGEN program. Use these lessons to help English language learners construct meaning in the selections and explore vocabulary in order to develop mastery of reading, writing, and speaking.

Part 4 scaffolded support includes:

- **Build Background** Students explore important information needed to comprehend and enjoy each selection. Student pages provide practice and stimulate conversation.

- **Talk About Sentences** Students discover how good sentences are constructed. They learn to access key ideas by understanding the relationships between words and phrases in sentences.

- **Speak and Write About the Text** Students build academic language skills by asking and answering critical questions. Writing frames support students' development as they express ideas in specific writing modes.

- **Expand Understanding of Vocabulary** Students discover the generative nature of vocabulary and develop a curiosity about language as they gain an understanding of how words function in sentences.

- **Writing** Students benefit from extra scaffolding, including a student model, as they work toward addressing the Performance-Based Assessment writing prompt.

The following **Part 4** Routines provide English language learners with additional scaffolded instruction in reading, speaking, and listening.

- Dig Deeper Vocabulary
- Sentence Talk
- Clarifying Key Details Routine
- Clarifying Information
- Reach an Routine
- Text-Based Writing Routine

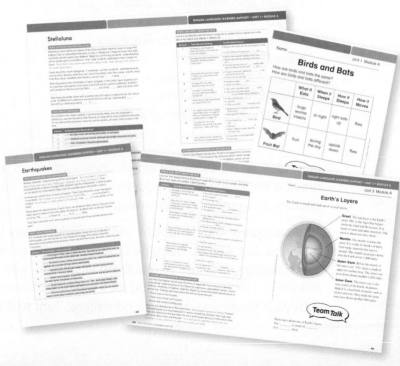

PART 1

Unlock the Text

Living Together: This Is Home

TEXT SET

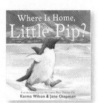

ANCHOR TEXT
Where Is Home, Little Pip?

SUPPORTING TEXT
A House for Hermit Crab

TEXT SET

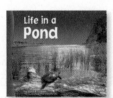

ANCHOR TEXT
Life in a Pond

SUPPORTING TEXT
A Bed for the Winter

Unlock the Text

QUALITATIVE MEASURES

Levels of Meaning	character-centered plot with theme of finding one's home, level of meaning extended to the concept of home as anywhere those who care for each other are together
Structure	roles of author and illustrator, chronological structure, picture support
Language Conventionality and Clarity	challenging vocabulary, unfamiliar meanings of words, dialogue, use of sound devices including rhyming song verses, onomatopoeia, and alliteration
Knowledge Demands	animals and their habitats, climate and location of Antarctica, print concepts

Prepare to Read

LEVELS OF MEANING

In *Where Is Home, Little Pip?,* the main storyline tells about Pip's search for her home after she becomes lost. The text supports the idea that homes may be different and home can be anywhere those who love each other are together.

STRUCTURE

PREVIEW Read the title of the book and the names of the author and the illustrator. Point out that the author, Karma Wilson, wrote the words for the story and the illustrator, Jane Chapman, drew the pictures.

ENGLISH LANGUAGE LEARNERS

Hold up the cover of the book showing a penguin, point to the picture of the penguin and have students say the word for *penguin* in their home language. Then say *penguin* several times, and have students repeat it. For some students, the words for *penguin* in their home language and in English will be cognates. For example, *pingüino* is the Spanish word for *penguin.*

STRUGGLING READERS

Take a picture walk through the book with students. Identify the animals pictured and have students discuss what the animals are doing.

Look at the title and illustrations with the class. Guide students to use information from the title and illustrations to respond to the following questions:

- Remember that the title of the book is *Where Is Home, Little Pip?* Who wrote the words of the title, the author or the illustrator?
- What kind of animal is this story about? How do you know?
- Who drew the pictures, the author or the illustrator?
- What do the pictures tell you about where the story takes place?
- What do the pictures tell you about the animals in the story?

LANGUAGE CONVENTIONALITY AND CLARITY

PREVIEW VOCABULARY Use the Learn New Words Routine in Part 3 to assess what students know about the following words: *baby, hatched, nest, cozy, waddled, creatures,* and *snuggled.*

CRITICAL VOCABULARY Preteach critical vocabulary words, such as *penguin, warned, home, oceans,* and *Antarctic.* Introduce critical vocabulary with age-appropriate terms. Display pictures or use actions when possible to reinforce and support meaning. Use the Vocabulary Activities in Part 3.

KNOWLEDGE DEMANDS

ACTIVATE BACKGROUND KNOWLEDGE Point to the cover illustration of Little Pip. Ask students to share what they know about penguins. Use pictures and/or words to record student responses on chart paper. Facilitate student input with guiding questions, such as: What kind of animal are penguins? What do penguins look like? Where do they live? How do they move? What do they eat? Review students' responses by asking students to follow along as you point to the pictures and words on the chart.

STRUGGLING READERS

The rich vocabulary with vivid verbs and adjectives may be challenging for students. Use pictures, realia, demonstrations, and synonyms to help students understand vocabulary such as *pebbles, minnows, plodded, pecking, craggy,* and *dreadful.* Also after reading a page, summarize the text in your own words.

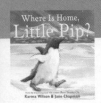

Interact with Text

As you read *Where Is Home, Little Pip?,* periodically stop to assess students' understanding of the characters in the story. Review with students that characters are the people or animals in a story. The main character is the most important character in the story.

Guide students to respond to the following questions: Who is the main character in this story? (Pip) What other characters have we met? (Mama, Papa, other penguins, whale, Kelp Gull, sled dogs, and person) What is Little Pip doing now? What are the other characters doing?

Point out specific examples in the text and illustrations that support student responses.

If . . . students have difficulty recalling the characters in the story,

then . . . revisit the illustrations. Point to and identify each character. Have students repeat the names after you.

STRUCTURE

Review with students that all stories have a beginning, a middle, and an end. Use Story Map A Routine with Graphic Organizer. Help students identify what happens at the beginning of the story. Draw a picture or use words to tell what happens in the beginning of the story—Little Pip is hatched and stays near home as she is told to do. Repeat the process for identifying what happens in the middle and at the end of the story. Then use the story map to retell the story.

If . . . students have difficulty identifying what happens in each part of the story,

then . . . reread several pages and ask questions to help students identify events.

MORE SUPPORT

ENGLISH LANGUAGE LEARNERS

Identify the animals Pip meets in her search for home. As you point to the picture of an animal in the text, say the name of the animal in English and in the student's home language. For example, for a student whose home language is Spanish, point to the pictures of whales on pp. 14 and 15 and say *whale* and *ballena*.

STRUGGLING READERS

Repeated readings make it easier for students to recall important passages and to process information. After you read aloud several pages and examine the illustrations with students, guide them to recount in their own words what happened.

LANGUAGE CONVENTIONALITY AND CLARITY

The author has used a variety of sound devices in the story including rhyming verses. Review with students that *rhyme* is the repetition of the ending sound in two or more words. Provide examples of rhyming words, such as *cat, bat,* and *hat.* Then read aloud Mama and Papa's song on p. 7. Ask students to listen for and identify the words that rhyme in the song. *(free, tree, sea, three)*

If . . . students have difficulty identifying the rhyming words,

then . . . then tell students to listen for specific rhyming words, such as *free* and *tree,* reread the verse lines ending with those words, and have students repeat them.

Continue reading the verses about homes on pp. 15, 18, 23, and 31 and helping students identify the words that rhyme.

KNOWLEDGE DEMANDS

Remind students that Pip and the other penguins live in Antarctica. Provide background information about Antarctica by using a globe or map to show its location and photographs to show its features and climate. Then use the text to identify features of Antarctica. For example, turn to pp. 4 and 5. Ask: What does this picture show about Antarctica? (Penguins live there; it has snow and mountains.) Then reread p. 26. Ask: What words help us understand what the weather is like in Antarctica? *(froze solid; cold)* Look at the picture on p. 26. What does it show about the weather in Antarctica? (It has heavy snowstorms.)

STRUGGLING READERS

Students may have difficulty hearing the rhymes in the animals' songs. Help them listen for and "see" the rhymes by pointing out that the last words in the lines of verse are the words that rhyme. Have students follow along as you read the first line of a verse, emphasizing the last word. Tell them to listen for words that rhyme with this word. Emphasize and point to each rhyming word as you read the rest of the verse.

Express and Extend

EXPRESS Discuss with students what the author wants them to know about homes. Help students review the songs that Mama and Papa, the blue whale, the Kelp Gull, and the sled dog sing. Read each song, summarize what it says, and then ask questions about the home. For example, after reading and summarizing Mama and Papa's song on p. 7, ask

- What is the penguin's nest made of? (pebbles)
- Where is the nest? (near the sea)
- Who lives in the home? (Mama, Papa, and Pip)

Continue asking similar questions about the other animals' homes. Then help students conclude that home is anywhere those who care for each other are together.

If . . . students have difficulty determining what the author wants them to know about homes,

then . . . reread and discuss Mama and Papa's song on p. 7.

EXTEND Read aloud Mama and Papa's song on p. 7. Discuss what the song says about Pip's home—no hills or mountains, no trees, pebbles for a nest. Have students draw a picture of the home based on the song.

STRUCTURE

EXPRESS Remind students that the author wrote the words of the story *Where Is Home, Little Pip?* and the illustrator drew the pictures. Tell students that the pictures help tell the story. Reread p. 2 and have students examine the picture on pp. 2 and 3. Discuss what the picture shows—Pip and Mama and Papa, other penguins, the pebbly nests, and the nearby sea.

EXTEND Have pairs of students examine one of the pictures in the text and describe what they see. Then have each student in the pair dictate or write a sentence telling about the picture.

MORE SUPPORT

ENGLISH LANGUAGE LEARNERS

Some students may be familiar with multiple-meaning words because multiple-meaning words are in their home language. For example, in Spanish, a word for *school* when referring to a school of fish is *banco*. However, the word *banco* also means "bench" or "bank."

STRUGGLING READERS

Have students work in small groups to retell the story events. Encourage them to use the pictures as visual prompts to story events. Guide the retellings with questions, such as "Is Pip staying where the other penguins are?" "What are Pip's Mama and Papa doing?"

LANGUAGE CONVENTIONALITY AND CLARITY

EXPRESS Talk about Sentences and Words

Display and read aloud the following sentence in verse form from *Where Is Home, Little Pip?*

> Home is under the oceans deep,
> by the coral beds where the minnows sleep,
> where fish are in schools and sea creatures creep,
> where my babies and I swim and leap.

Briefly discuss the sentence. Then underline the word *schools*. Say: You know this word. You come to school to learn. Do you think fish are in schools like our school? (no) The word *schools* has more than one meaning. It can mean "places where children learn," but it can also mean "groups of fish."

TEAM TALK Have pairs discuss the meaning of *schools* in the sentence and also identify clue words that helped them understand the meaning.

If . . . students have difficulty identifying clue words to the meaning,

then . . . reread the sentence and ask leading questions, such as Where is the home of whales? (the oceans) Who are in the schools? (fish)

EXTEND The sentence also includes an unfamiliar meaning for the word *beds*. Have small groups discuss what they know about the word *beds*. Then use pictures to show examples of coral beds and lead students to understand that in the text *beds* refers to the place where groups of coral live under the water.

KNOWLEDGE DEMANDS

EXPRESS Review with students that you always read a page from left to right and top to bottom. Choose a page and have students tell you where to begin reading and in which direction you should read.

If . . . students have difficulty identifying where to begin reading,

then . . . point to the first word on a page and ask if you should begin reading there.

EXTEND Provide another book to pairs of students. Monitor them as they take turns showing each other where to begin reading a page and in which direction to read.

ACCELERATED LEARNERS

Remind students that the story is about the meaning of *home*. Have them write or dictate sentences that tell what *home* means to the penguin family. Encourage students to illustrate their sentences.

MORE SUPPORT

Unlock the Text

QUALITATIVE MEASURES

Levels of Meaning	character-driven plot with unified theme of making a house a home; building relationships
Structure	roles of author and illustrator; chronological structure; pictures support text; setting
Language Conventionality and Clarity	dialogue; descriptive language
Knowledge Demands	ocean life, particularly hermit crabs; relationships

A House for Hermit Crab, pp. 5–32

Prepare to Read

LEVELS OF MEANING

In *A House for Hermit Crab,* there are two levels of meaning. One purpose of the text is to tell the main story of Hermit Crab making his house a home, and the other is to describe the relationships he develops along the way.

STRUCTURE

PREVIEW Display the cover and read the title to students, pointing to each word as you read it. Point out the author's name. Explain that the author who wrote the story is the same person as the illustrator, or the person who drew the pictures. Help students try to predict what each scene is about. Ask:

- Where does the story takes place? (on the ocean floor)
- What do you notice about Hermit Crab's shell in each picture? (He's adding more sea creatures to his shell as the story progresses.)
- What is the story about? (how a hermit crab finds a home)

ENGLISH LANGUAGE LEARNERS

Display a variety of pictures of the ocean. Have students say the word for *ocean* in their home language. Then say the word *ocean* in English, and have students repeat it.

STRUGGLING READERS

Many words in this story are compound words, such as *starfish, seaweed, lanternfish,* and *nighttime.* Explain that some words are made by putting two words together, and the meaning of those two words can help students understand the meaning of the compound word. Have students tell the two words in each compound word, and help them use the two words to tell its meaning.

LANGUAGE CONVENTIONALITY AND CLARITY

PREVIEW VOCABULARY Use the Learn New Words Routine in Part 3 to assess what students know about the following words: *plain, snug, decorate, protect,* and *gloomy.* Think aloud to provide further clarification of each word in relation to students' own experiences. For example, say: I remember when I moved into my house; my bedroom was very plain. It was all white with no pictures. I decorated it by painting it bright blue, adding pictures of dolphins, and hanging painted butterflies from the ceiling. Now my bedroom reflects the things I like. What are some things that you think are too plain and need to be decorated?

CRITICAL VOCABULARY Preteach critical vocabulary words, such as *hermit crab, sea anemones, starfish, coral, snails, sea urchins, seaweed,* and *lanternfish.* Use the Vocabulary Activities in Part 3 to support meaning.

KNOWLEDGE DEMANDS

ACTIVATE BACKGROUND KNOWLEDGE Ask students to share what they know about hermit crabs and other animals that live in the ocean. Create a class chart to record student responses. Ask: What is a hermit crab? What other animals live in shells? What are some other things you would find at the bottom of the ocean?

Before students get started, model an example of some things you know that live in the ocean. For example, say: Last summer I visited an aquarium. I saw crabs, starfish, coral, fish, seaweed, sea urchins, and many other living things that make their homes in the ocean.

ENGLISH LANGUAGE LEARNERS

Ask students to act out the words *wiggling, waggling,* and *swayed* as they repeat each word being acted out.

Interact with Text

LEVELS OF MEANING

As you read *A House for Hermit Crab,* periodically stop to assess students' level of understanding of the relationships Hermit Crab develops throughout the story.

Guide students to respond to the following questions: What has happened so far? Who has Hermit Crab met? How have they helped him? What do you think will happen next?

> **If . . .** students have difficulty keeping track of the characters Hermit Crab meets,
>
> **then . . .** together, have students act out different motions that will help them remember each animal and how it helps Hermit Crab.

For example, point out the illustration of the sea anemones. Read aloud the following sentences as you act out the motion of swaying: In March, Hermit Crab met some sea anemones. They swayed gently back and forth in the water.

Point out that the sea anemones help make Hermit Crab's house more beautiful. Guide students in understanding that decorating a house can make it feel more like a home or more comfortable. Continue with each animal and its movements, using words from the text to support understanding.

STRUCTURE

As students read, periodically stop to assess their understanding of the story's structure. Remind them that the story takes place over one year. Point out details from the text and illustrations to support understanding.

> **If . . .** students have difficulty understanding the concept of one year,
>
> **then . . .** show students a calendar, and say the months of the year in order as you page through the calendar. Point out that the calendar begins with the month of January and ends with the month of December, just like *A House for Hermit Crab.*

ENGLISH LANGUAGE LEARNERS

Encourage students to ask questions about any sea creatures that are unfamiliar to them. Make a list nd draw sketches of simple creatures, and refer to throughout the reading.

STRUGGLING READERS

This story chronicles Hermit Crab's activities in each month of the year. The names of the months may be unfamiliar or difficult for students. Help them by naming the months and connecting each to a holiday or event in that month. Use a calendar and have students repeat the names of the months after you.

LANGUAGE CONVENTIONALITY AND CLARITY

While the language of the story is direct and can be understood on a literal level, some of the text uses dialogue and descriptive language.

If . . . students have difficulty understanding and following dialogue,

then . . . demonstrate using examples from the text.

Point to and read aloud some lines of dialogue from the story. For example, "But it looks so—well, so *plain,*" thought Hermit Crab. "How beautiful you are!" said Hermit Crab. "Would one of you be willing to come live on my house?" "I'll come," whispered a small sea anemone. Explain to students that sometimes Hermit Crab is talking or thinking to himself. And at other times he is talking with other sea creatures. Point out the different dialogue tags, and explain how they help readers know which character is talking. Then reread the examples of dialogue, using a different voice for each character. Explain that using different voices when reading dialogue is another way readers can know which character is talking.

KNOWLEDGE DEMANDS

Revisit the previously completed chart about ocean life. Then, use the Web Routine and Graphic Organizer in Part 3 to brainstorm other sea animals that have shells. Show students pictures of various animals with different kinds of shells, such as clams, crabs, snails, mussels, scallops, and lobsters. Guide students to name the animals and add them to the chart.

If . . . students have difficulty understanding that hermit crabs live in borrowed shells,

then . . . revisit the text and reread examples that support the idea of borrowed homes, such as: The following January, Hermit Crab stepped out and the little crab moved in. Guide students to the understanding that hermit crabs use the shells other creatures have moved out of to make their homes.

ENGLISH LANGUAGE LEARNERS

Ask: How would you borrow something from a friend? What would you say? Record student responses and read them together. To facilitate understanding of the word *borrowing,* demonstrate how to borrow something from a student. Act out the difference between borrowing and giving or keeping.

Express and Extend

LEVELS OF MEANING

EXPRESS Revisit the illustrations. Ask: How does each creature help Hermit Crab? Use the Three-Column Chart Routine and Graphic Organizer in Part 3. Above the columns, write the headings *Decorate, Clean,* and *Protect.* Under the appropriate heading, help students list each sea creature that helps Hermit Crab.

> **If . . .** students have difficulty completing the three-column chart,
>
> **then . . .** revisit the text to provide additional support for understanding.

Reread specific words and phrases from the story to provide support for the help each animal gives to Hermit Crab.

EXTEND Ask: Why do you think each creature agrees to be part of Hermit Crab's house? How does Hermit Crab help each creature? Provide opportunities for students to share their responses orally. Encourage them to use examples from the story to support their responses.

STRUCTURE

EXPRESS Provide students with a picture of or a sign with the name of each of the following objects and characters: Hermit Crab's plain shell, sea anemone, starfish, coral, snails, sea urchins, seaweed, lanternfish, and pebbles. Reread the story. Guide students to line up the pictures or signs in the order in which each object and character appears in the story.

> **If . . .** students have difficulty identifying the order in which objects and characters are introduced,
>
> **then . . .** read each page and pause to guide each picture or sign to its correct place in line.

EXTEND Have students use the words *first, second, third, fourth,* and so on, to describe the order in which the objects and sea creatures are introduced.

MORE SUPPORT

ENGLISH LANGUAGE LEARNERS

Students may need help understanding that many English words can have similar meanings, such as *dark, dim, gloomy,* and *murky.* Ask students if there are such words in their native language and to give examples.

STRUGGLING READERS

Help students draw one small and one large outline of Hermit Crab's shell. Lead them in using the story illustrations and text to draw Hermit Crab leaving the shell he outgrew. Then, lead them in using the story illustrations and text to draw what they think Hermit Crab's new shell will look like, once he makes it a home.

LANGUAGE CONVENTIONALITY AND CLARITY

EXPRESS Talk about Sentences and Words

Display the following sentences from *A House for Hermit Crab,* and read them aloud.

"It's so dark here," thought Hermit Crab.

"How dim it is," murmured the sea anemone.

"How gloomy it is," whispered the starfish.

"How murky it is," complained the coral.

Say: Hermit Crab says it's dark in the seaweed forest. The sea anemone says it's dim. The starfish says it's gloomy. And the coral says it's murky. How do these characters feel about the seaweed forest? (They don't like the seaweed forest.) What do the words *dim, gloomy,* and *murky* mean? (They all mean "dark.")

TEAM TALK Have students look at the last page in the story. Have them turn to a partner and tell how they think each creature will describe Hermit Crab's new home. **Say:** Tell your partner how you think the sea anemone will describe Hermit Crab's new home. How will the starfish describe it?

If . . . students need more support with descriptive language,

then . . . display and read other examples from the text that use descriptive language to tell about the animals and objects.

EXTEND Guide students to predict what Hermit Crab will do to make his new home perfect. **Ask:** What do you think Hermit Crab will do first to decorate his new shell? What will he do to clean it? What will he do to make it safe?

KNOWLEDGE DEMANDS

EXPRESS Ask students to recall how the animals in the story help each other. Support student responses with evidence from the text and illustrations. **Ask:** What would happen if Hermit Crab did not have the sea urchins? The snails?

EXTEND Guide students in determining the physical features or personality traits of each animal or object that helped Hermit Crab make the "perfect" home. **Ask:** What do sea urchins look like? How do they act? How would this help Hermit Crab? (The sea urchins have sharp, prickly needles and they look fierce, so they can help protect Hermit Crab.)

ACCELERATED LEARNERS

To challenge students, ask: If you were Hermit Crab and you could choose only one creature or object to help you, which would you choose? Provide opportunities for students to talk about their choices and tell why they made their decision. Create a chart with the creatures and objects from the story. Have students write their name under the creature they chose. Together, tally the number of choices each creature received.

MORE SUPPORT

Unlock the Text

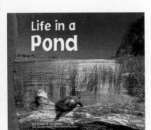

QUALITATIVE MEASURES

Levels of Meaning	explanation of ponds and pond life
Structure	informational facts and details with photographs to support text; book cover; table of contents; section headings; glossary
Language Conventionality and Clarity	short, simple sentences; some challenging vocabulary
Knowledge Demands	animal behavior; interdependence of plants and animals

Prepare to Read

LEVELS OF MEANING

In *Life in a Pond,* the main purpose of the text is to convey information about ponds and pond life and explain how plants and animals depend on ponds to live.

STRUCTURE

PREVIEW Display the cover of *Life in a Pond.* Read the title and author's name, tracking the print as you read. Say: The title of the book is *Life in a Pond.* The author, or person who wrote the book, is Carol K. Lindeen.

Take a picture walk with students to preview the photographs. Guide students in determining that the pictures in this book are photographs of real animals, plants, and places. Ask: What does that tell us about *Life in a Pond*? (It will be about real ponds. It is an informational book.) Next, read the table of contents, tracking the print as you read.

ENGLISH LANGUAGE LEARNERS

To help students better understand informational headings and what they tell us, frame a heading, read it aloud, and ask students to repeat it. For example, read the heading "Pond Animals" on p. 8. Have students repeat it and tell what they think the section will be about.

STRUGGLING READERS

Some students may have never seen a pond. To help students gain a better grasp of ponds and pond life, provide additional pictures or a video clip of pond life and the activities that occur in a pond.

Preview the headings on pp. 4, 8, 14, and 20 of the text. Ask: What might we learn about as we read this book? (ponds and what lives in ponds)

LANGUAGE CONVENTIONALITY AND CLARITY

PREVIEW VOCABULARY Use the Learn New Words Routine in Part 3 to assess what students know about the following words: *forests, farms, cities, insects, float, bloom, fuzzy, shallow.* Ask students questions related to their own experiences, such as: How would you describe a forest? What have you touched that is fuzzy? Encourage students to use the vocabulary words in their responses.

CRITICAL VOCABULARY Preteach domain-specific vocabulary words, such as *pond, gills, water lilies,* and *cattails*. Introduce critical vocabulary by revisiting the photos and pointing out the corresponding vocabulary term on each page. Then point to each picture, and ask students to repeat the word after you.

Use the Vocabulary Activities in Part 3 to support understanding.

KNOWLEDGE DEMANDS

ACTIVATE BACKGROUND KNOWLEDGE Ask students to share one thing they know about ponds. Record their responses on chart paper. Facilitate student input with guiding questions, such as: What is a pond? Where have you seen a pond? How is a pond different from a lake? What might you see at a pond?

To aid understanding of ponds, model an experience you have had with ponds. For example, say: When I was a child, I often visited my uncle's farm. There was a big pond in the middle of a field with lots of cattails. I saw ducks, geese, frogs, fish, and lily pads in and on the pond. It was a great place to watch plant and animal life.

STRUGGLING READERS

Some students may have difficulty responding to vocabulary questions that relate to their own experiences. Provide these students with photographs or pictures for them to describe. Guide students in using the vocabulary terms in their descriptions.

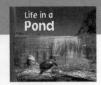
Life in a
Pond

Interact with Text

As you read *Life in a Pond,* periodically stop to assess students' level of understanding of what a pond is. Guide students to respond to the following questions. Ask: What does a pond look like? What animals live in ponds? What plants live in ponds?

Return to the text and photographs to support student responses.

If . . . students have difficulty recalling the information in each section,

then . . . reread each heading aloud and ask: What did we learn in this section? Which words tell you? What does the picture show?

For example, turn to pp. 8–9, and read the heading while tracking the print. Say: I see a fish in the picture. So this tells me that fish live in a pond. If I read the words on the page, I find out more about fish—they breathe through gills. Provide sentence frames to aid students in their responses, such as: ___ live in a pond. Fish ___.

STRUCTURE

As you read aloud the text, assess if students understand the selection's structure. Point out the section headings and the photographs on each spread. Remind students that the headings and photographs both give clues to what the words on the page will tell us.

If . . . students have difficulty understanding the informational structure,

then . . . revisit a heading and discuss how it relates to the photograph on the spread.

For example, point out the heading "Pond Plants." Then have students look at the photographs on pp. 15, 17, and 19. Stop on each spread and ask: What does this picture show? Let's read the words again. What do the words and pictures together tell us?

ENGLISH LANGUAGE LEARNERS

Use the Two-Column Chart Routine and Graphic Organizer in Part 3 with the headings *Animals* and *Plants* to help students keep track of the wildlife discussed in the selection. As you read about each animal or plant, have students suggest in which column to write the name. Have them repeat each name after you write it.

STRUGGLING READERS

When you ask questions, pause to provide ample wait time for students to process each question and formulate a thoughtful response.

LANGUAGE CONVENTIONALITY AND CLARITY

While most of this text is written in short, simple sentences, there is some challenging vocabulary.

If . . . students have difficulty understanding a vocabulary word,

then . . . reread the sentence and explain the word's meaning. This would be a good opportunity to explain the use of a glossary.

For example, read aloud the text on p. 4. Students may not understand the term *still.* Explain that *still* means "not moving." Then turn to the glossary and explain its purpose. Point out the word *still.* Read the definition, tracking the print as you read.

KNOWLEDGE DEMANDS

Students may be unfamiliar with behaviors of animals they have not encountered before. Guide them in identifying action words, or words that describe the animals' movements.

If . . . students have difficulty understanding the behaviors or actions of pond animals,

then . . . have students record the actions of two pond animals (such as a duck and a frog). Use the Two-Column Chart Routine and Graphic Organizer in Part 3 to record the action words that describe each animal.

For example, reread the text that describes each animal, such as "Frogs kick and swim in the water." Record the words *kick* and *swim* in the *Frog* column. As an additional aid, lead students in acting out each action. Say the word, and point to it on the chart. Repeat with text that describes ducks or a different animal mentioned in the text.

ENGLISH LANGUAGE LEARNERS

To further facilitate understanding of action words, use visuals, such as vocabulary cards or pictures of people engaging in these actions, to help students visualize each word. Then have students act out the words as they repeat them aloud.

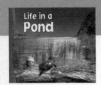
Express and Extend

EXPRESS Have students share one interesting piece of information they learned about ponds from *Life in a Pond.* Students should tell something they learned that they did not know before.

> **If . . .** students have difficulty stating a piece of information,
>
> **then . . .** reread sections of the text and review the photographs (animals: fish, ducks, frogs; plants: water lilies, cattails, plants at the bottom). Provide a sentence frame, such as: I learned that ___.

EXTEND In small groups, have students think about other animals or plants that might make their homes in a pond, based on what they have learned about life in ponds. If needed, provide some suggestions, such as turtles, snakes, beavers, dragonflies, and grasses. Have them draw a picture of a pond with this additional wildlife. Have groups share their pictures with the class and say one sentence that tells about the new wildlife they drew.

EXPRESS Review and discuss the informational text structure of *Life in a Pond.* Reread the title of the book and the headings inside. Ask: What is the big idea of this whole book? (Many different things live in a pond.) What are some details or examples of pond life that we read about? (Animals, such as fish, ducks, and frogs, live in ponds. Plants, such as water lilies and cattails, live in ponds. They all live together.)

EXTEND Guide students to closely examine one photograph in the text. Ask them to point out details using descriptive and action words. Have students suggest a caption to a partner that would tell about the photo, such as "This frog dives for food."

MORE SUPPORT

ENGLISH LANGUAGE LEARNERS

To help students better understand domain-specific vocabulary, have manipulatives, if possible, such as toy fish, ducks, frogs, turtles, and real or dried cattails. Pass around each as students repeat the object's name.

STRUGGLING READERS

If students have difficulty expressing or articulating their confusion, help them with asking questions by offering sentence frames, such as: What does ____ mean? I don't understand ____.

LANGUAGE CONVENTIONALITY AND CLARITY

EXPRESS Talk about Sentences and Words

Display and read aloud the following sentence from *Life in a Pond.*

Sunlight shines through shallow pond water.

Ask: What does the word *shallow* mean? ("not very deep from the top to the bottom") What other word in the sentence has the same beginning sound as *shallow*? (*shines*) Read the sentence again so that students can listen for the sounds. Encourage students to use the photograph as you ask: What does the word *shines* mean? ("sparkles" or "glows")

TEAM TALK Say: Turn to a partner and tell about a place where you might find shallow water.

If . . . students have difficulty understanding the meaning of *shallow,*

then . . . demonstrate by filling a shallow bowl or sink with a small amount of water. Lead students in using the word *shallow* in a sentence to describe what they see.

EXTEND Have students draw a picture to illustrate a new word they learned from reading *Life in a Pond.* Have them write or dictate the word or a caption for their illustration.

KNOWLEDGE DEMANDS

EXPRESS Discuss and review the various plants and animals that live in a pond. Ask: What do plants need to grow? (sunlight) What do insects eat? (plants) What do ducks and frogs eat? (insects)

If . . . students have difficulty answering the questions,

then . . . reread the text and point out clues in the photographs to help them understand what plants and animals in a pond each need to live.

EXTEND Draw four boxes in a horizontal line connected by arrows to make a simple food chain. Lead students in drawing or dictating answers to the Express questions in the boxes to complete the food chain: sunlight → plants → insects → ducks and frogs. Lead them to conclude that ducks and frogs need insects; insects need plants; and plants need sunlight to live.

ACCELERATED LEARNERS

Have student partners discuss the body parts of a pond animal that help that animal do the things it does. For example, frogs kick and swim because they have long legs. Ask: What helps ducks catch food underwater? (their beaks)

Unlock the Text

QUALITATIVE MEASURES

Levels of Meaning	one level of meaning; information is factual with a clearly stated purpose
Structure	repeated sentence; labels; picture word list
Language Conventionality and Clarity	simple sentences; literal language
Knowledge Demands	basic knowledge of meadow animals and habitats; winter season

ReadyGEN
Text Collection

A Bed for the Winter,
pp. 33–54

Prepare to Read

LEVELS OF MEANING

In *A Bed for the Winter,* the main storyline tells about a little dormouse's search for its winter home. The selection also explores how and where a variety of animals make their homes for the winter.

STRUCTURE

PREVIEW Read the title and author's name aloud, tracking the print as you read. Point out that in this book, the pictures are photographs that show real animals. Guide students to use information from the title and photographs to respond to questions. Ask:

- What is a dormouse? (A dormouse is a very small mouse.)
- What do the pictures tell you about the story? (A mouse sees where other animals live.)
- What do you think we will learn about?

MORE SUPPORT

ENGLISH LANGUAGE LEARNERS

To support word meaning, act out vocabulary words, such as *gathers, scurries, squeezed, trembles, huddle,* and *swoops.* Then say each word, and have students act it out. Have them demonstrate how scurrying is different from walking and running.

STRUGGLING READERS

Support vocabulary development by connecting words with images. Provide additional pictures of animal homes. To reinforce understanding, say the words together as you talk about the pictures.

PREVIEW VOCABULARY Use the Learn New Words Routine in Part 3 to assess what students know about the following words: *gathers, scurries, squeezed, trembles, huddle, underground, swoops, snug.*

Facilitate understanding with guiding questions that relate to students' lives, such as: When something feels *snug*, how does it fit? What is another word for *snug*? *(tight, cozy)* Encourage students to dictate a sentence of their own, using the word *snug*.

CRITICAL VOCABULARY Preteach domain-specific vocabulary words, such as *dormouse, meadow, nest, stump, toad, den, cave, burrow,* and *tree trunk*. Support meaning by pointing to and naming each object in the photographs.

Support understanding with Vocabulary Activities in Part 3.

KNOWLEDGE DEMANDS

ACTIVATE BACKGROUND KNOWLEDGE Ask students to share what they or their families do to get ready for winter. Record student responses on chart paper. Facilitate student input with guiding questions, such as: What kinds of clothing do you wear in winter? What kinds of activities do you do in winter? How is winter different from summer? Why might animals need to prepare for winter? Review responses by having students follow along as you read each word or phrase on the chart.

STRUGGLING READERS

Some students may not understand the concept of changing seasons or winter. Provide these students with photographs of the different seasons, including winter. Then describe winter weather in your area. Lead students to identify ways their lives are different in winter compared with the other seasons.

MORE SUPPORT

Interact with Text

LEVELS OF MEANING

As you read *A Bed for the Winter,* check that students understand the different events and animals the dormouse encounters. Guide students to respond to the following questions. Ask: What animals does the dormouse meet? Where are those animals making their beds for the winter? What problem does the dormouse have?

As students suggest animals the dormouse meets, reread that part of the text to confirm the response.

If . . . students have difficulty recalling the animals and their homes in the story,

then . . . revisit the text and photographs. Write the name of each animal on an index card, and draw a simple picture of its home on another. Display the cards next to each other on a chart or board. Review them as you reread the selection.

STRUCTURE

Discuss the text structure. Point out that the pictures give information to help readers understand where the animals make their homes. Also point out the small picture and label on many pages. Point to a small picture, and read its label. Ask students why this feature is helpful. (It shows a close-up picture of the animal's home and names the place.)

Next, display the Picture Word List on p. 54, and explain that the list shows all of the small pictures and labels that appear in the text. Point out that below each picture is the page number where the picture and label appear. Model using the Picture Word List to find a picture in the text. Point to the picture of the den and say: This is a picture of a den. Say the word with me, *den*. The text below this picture says, "page 42." This tells us that the picture of the den appears on page 42. Let's turn to page 42. Turn to p. 42 and point out that the same picture and label that were in the Picture Word List appear on this page. Explain to students that readers can use the Picture Word List to review the different types of animal homes and to find where in the text each home is described.

ENGLISH LANGUAGE LEARNERS

Encourage students to ask questions about any animal homes they are not familiar with. Provide sentence frames to help them formulate their questions, such as: I don't understand why ___. What is a ___?

STRUGGLING READERS

To facilitate discussion for students, guide them in thinking about why the dormouse would not be comfortable in each home. Use sentence frames, such as: A squirrel's nest is not good for the dormouse because ___.

MORE SUPPORT

LANGUAGE CONVENTIONALITY AND CLARITY

While the language in this text is clear and literal, students may be unfamiliar with some of the words.

If . . . students have difficulty with understanding a specific word, such as *meadow,*

then . . . have them refer to the Picture Word List on p. 54, and point out key identifying features of the unfamiliar word.

For example, read aloud the following sentence on p. 34: A fluffy-tailed dormouse stops by a meadow. Help students find the picture of the meadow in the Picture Word List. Point out that as readers can see in the picture, a meadow is an open field filled with tall grass and flowers.

Use the Learn New Words Routine in Part 3 to help students understand the meanings of other unfamiliar words, such as *stump, cave,* and *burrow.*

KNOWLEDGE DEMANDS

After reading, revisit the animal and home index cards you created. If you did not previously create index cards, do so by writing the name of each animal from the text on an index card and drawing a simple picture of its home on another. Scramble the cards and work together to match each animal with its home. Use guiding questions to explore why each animal home is good for that animal. For example, ask: Why is a nest in a tree not a good home for a dormouse? Where does a queen wasp sleep? Why is that a good home for a queen wasp but not for a dormouse?

If . . . students have difficulty discussing animal homes,

then . . . guide them in comparing and contrasting two different animal homes. For example, ask: How are a bat's cave and a bear's den similar? How are they different? Encourage students to use words and phrases from the text and point out details from the photographs to support their responses.

Express and Extend

LEVELS OF MEANING

EXPRESS Lead a discussion about homes. Say: People live in many kinds of homes. What are some homes that you have seen? Chart student responses. Then ask: Animals live in many kinds of homes too. What are some animal homes you are familiar with? Why do some animals have different homes for the winter?

> **If . . .** students have difficulty determining how each animal's home meets its needs,
>
> **then . . .** choose one example and point out specific features of the animal home in the text or photograph that support the animal's needs.

EXTEND In small groups, have students take turns revisiting the photographs and telling why each home is right for that animal. Provide a sentence frame, such as: The nest is right for the squirrel because ___.

STRUCTURE

EXPRESS Point out the repetitive sentence, "The dormouse . . ., then scurries by," throughout the text. Ask: Why do you think the author repeated this sentence? (It helps readers know that the dormouse is still looking for just the right bed for winter.) Next, reread *A Bed for the Winter,* tracking the print as you read. Each time you get to the repetitive phrase, pause slightly to give students time to join in by echoing your words.

Point out that the repeated phrase also reminds us to turn the page to find out what animal the dormouse will meet next. Allow students to take turns turning the page when it's time.

EXTEND Allow students who are able to read the entire sentence with the repetitive phrase to do so. Remind students that the dormouse does something different each time. Sometimes she looks in, sometimes she looks up, and so on. Have students act out the sentence after they read it.

MORE SUPPORT

ENGLISH LANGUAGE LEARNERS

To help students identify each animal in the text, draw or attach pictures of the animals onto the six sides of a square box to make an animal cube. Allow students to take turns rolling the cube and naming the animal picture that lands face-up. Have students share what they know or what they want to know about the animal.

STRUGGLING READERS

If students struggle to determine why animals choose certain homes, relate the activity back to their lives. Ask: Why do we live in homes with heat, water, and electricity? Then point out the features of each home that make it safe and comfortable for each animal.

LANGUAGE CONVENTIONALITY AND CLARITY

EXPRESS Talk about Sentences and Words

Read aloud the following sentences from *A Bed for the Winter.*

The dormouse runs through the meadow. Her heart pounds like a drum.

Say: The word *pounds* can have different meanings. What does *pounds* mean in this sentence? ("hits or beats again and again") What are other meanings for the word *pounds*? ("measures of weight," "places for lost animals") What word could we use in this sentence instead of *pounds*? Have students share their suggestions. Ask: Why do you think the author chose to say *pounds like a drum*? (It helps us hear the sound in our head.)

TEAM TALK Say: Turn to a partner, and use the word *pounds* in a sentence of your own.

If . . . students have difficulty applying meaning,

then . . . think aloud to provide students with additional support. For example, say: I know that when I run in a race, I run my fastest. At the finish line, I can sometimes feel my heart beating. It is almost like a drum. The beats are very rhythmical. Thinking about this helps me understand the phrase *pounds like a drum*.

EXTEND Have students think about and then tell why the dormouse's heart pounds like a drum. Use text evidence about what happened and photos to support understanding. Have students dramatize the scene in groups.

KNOWLEDGE DEMANDS

EXPRESS Have students refer back to the text and photographs to describe the differences in animal homes. Ask: Which two homes do you think are the most different? Why? Guide students to use text and photo details to support their responses.

EXTEND Have students play a game called "Where Do I Live?" Have students take turns choosing a picture from the Picture Word List and using a sentence frame, such as: I live in a ___. Who am I? Guide other students to find the animal that lives there and respond with the correct answer.

ACCELERATED LEARNERS

Have students think about animals that migrate, or leave the area, instead of staying and making their home for the winter. Have students draw an animal that leaves (for example, duck, goose, or butterfly). Ask them to tell why they think some animals leave instead of stay. (It's too cold here; there is no food here during the winter.)

MORE SUPPORT

Understanding Then and Now

TEXT SET

ANCHOR TEXT
The Little House

SUPPORTING TEXT
Four Seasons Make a Year

TEXT SET

ANCHOR TEXT
Farming Then and Now

SUPPORTING TEXT
The Old Things

Unlock the Text

QUALITATIVE MEASURES

Levels of Meaning	event-driven plot; effects of urbanization; family ties
Structure	changes related to setting; events occur in chronological order over many years; unconventional text placement; pictures
Language Conventionality and Clarity	some unfamiliar verbs; descriptive words; personification
Knowledge Demands	city life versus country life; one home's experience with urban sprawl; passage of time

ReadyGEN●●●
Text Collection

The Little House,
pp. 4–28

Prepare to Read

LEVELS OF MEANING

The Little House is the story of how the landscape around a house changes over time. On a deeper level, it addresses how encroaching urbanization affects life in the country and how the world changes over a long period of time.

STRUCTURE

PREVIEW Read aloud the title of the story, sweeping a finger under each word. Point out to students the picture of the house on the cover. Then preview the pictures with students. **Ask:** What is the same in every picture? (the house) What is different in the pictures? (the land around the house) What do you think this story will be about?

ENGLISH LANGUAGE LEARNERS

Show students a wide range of pictures from urban, suburban, and rural neighborhoods. Encourage students to point to things they do not recognize in the pictures. Provide students with the words that name the unknown objects.

STRUGGLING READERS

Some students may have difficulty describing the countryside and the city, based on the pictures from the book. Provide these students photos of a real countryside and a real city, and help them identify what is in each photo.

Next, point out the unconventional text placement throughout the story. Run a finger under the words from left to right, and demonstrate return sweep. Remind students that words are always read from left to right.

LANGUAGE CONVENTIONALITY AND CLARITY

PREVIEW VOCABULARY Use the Learn New Words Routine in Part 3 to preteach the following vocabulary: *great-great-grandchildren, countryside, carriages, busy, shabby, surveyors, robin, elevated train, subway, trolley cars, foundation, shade, steam shovel, steam roller.* Introduce critical vocabulary with age-appropriate terms. Include pictures or video clips, when possible, to reinforce and support meaning. You can use the Vocabulary Activities in Part 3.

KNOWLEDGE DEMANDS

ACTIVATE BACKGROUND KNOWLEDGE Explain to students that in this story, they will read about a house in the countryside and a house in the city. Display the picture on p. 6. Say: This picture shows the countryside. Then display the picture on p. 21. Say: This picture shows the city. Next, ask students what they know about the countryside and the city. Ask guiding questions, such as: Are the buildings in the countryside near each other or far away from each other? What about in the city? Where might you find more trees and plants, in the city or in the countryside? Refer back to the pictures on pp. 6 and 21 as needed. Encourage students to describe what they see in each picture.

Interact with Text

LEVELS OF MEANING

As the story develops, pause to assess students' understanding of the changes taking place.

> **If . . .** students have difficulty understanding the changes taking place in the story,
>
> **then . . .** ask students to describe the specific changes they see in the illustrations on pp. 8–19.

Encourage students to point out specific details from the illustrations, such as a steam shovel and steam roller building a road, many small houses, gasoline stations, electric lines, and so on.

After reading the text aloud to students, ask: What has happened around the Little House? (A city has been built around the Little House.) Next, reread the text on p. 20 and ask: How does the Little House feel about living in a city? How do you know? (She doesn't like it. I know because the text says so.) Guide students in understanding that although the Little House is surrounded by people and other buildings, she feels lonely. This is because the people in the city walk past her and don't notice her.

STRUCTURE

Point out to students that many events occur in this story, and they all take place in time order. Explain that at the beginning of the story, the changing of the seasons lets us know that the events occur in time order. Point out the following phrases for students: *In the Spring,* p. 8; *In the long Summer,* p. 9; *In the Fall,* p. 10; *In the Winter,* p. 11. Say: The author also uses other words to let us know when events take place. Some of these words include *one day, pretty soon, then,* and *now.*

> **If . . .** students have difficulty understanding that events in the story take place in time order,
>
> **then . . .** use the Story Map A Routine and Graphic Organizer in Part 3 to help students keep track of the events and changes in the story.

MORE SUPPORT

ENGLISH LANGUAGE LEARNERS

Some students might be unfamiliar with the seasons and how they change. Display and label photos of each season in order. Ask students to describe each photo. Then explain how the seasons always occur in the same order.

STRUGGLING READERS

Remind students that telling what happened in their own words will help them remember the important ideas. Use the sentence starter: On this page, ____.

Point out that in the story, the house is referred to as "she." For example, "She was a pretty Little House." Explain that the author gives the house human characteristics. Say: In this story, the Little House watches the land change around her, she wonders about life in the city, she thinks, and she has opinions. Are these things a real house can do? (no) Have students point out other ways in which the Little House is like a person. Then ask: Why do you think the author chose to give the Little House human abilities? Guide students in understanding that by giving the Little House human characteristics, the author helps readers gain insight into her thoughts and feelings.

KNOWLEDGE DEMANDS

The pictures in this story show many different settings surrounding the Little House. Students may have difficulty understanding that until the end of the story, the Little House does not move. Instead, the landscape around the Little House changes.

> **If . . .** students have difficulty understanding that the Little House does not move,
>
> **then . . .** review the pictures throughout the story with students, pointing out what things around the house stay the same and what things change in each picture.

For example, on p. 8, there are trees and other houses around the Little House. On pp. 9–12, those same trees and houses are around the house. However, on p. 13, some of the trees are gone and there are a lot more houses around the Little House. Help students understand that as the city is built around the house, the landscape changes.

Express and Extend

LEVELS OF MEANING

EXPRESS Remind students that the man who built the Little House wanted his family to always live there. Read aloud the following passage from p. 5.

> The man who built her so well said, "This Little House shall never be sold for gold or silver and she will live to see our great-great-grandchildren's great-great-grandchildren living in her."

Ask: Did the man's family live in the house? How do you know? (Yes. The Little House watched the children playing in the brook, swimming in the pool, and going back to school.) Then point out that at the end of the story, the man's great-great-granddaughter saves the Little House by moving it back out to the countryside. Ask: Why do you think the great-great-granddaughter saves the Little House? How does the Little House feel about being back in the countryside with her family? Help students answer these questions by going back into the text with them to find evidence when possible.

EXTEND Ask students: If you were the great-great-granddaughter, would you have saved the Little House? Why or why not? Have partners discuss this question and then share their responses with the class.

STRUCTURE

EXPRESS Remind students that the pictures in the story show the changing landscape. Have students pretend they are the Little House and choose which landscape they would like to live in. Ask them to tell why they chose that landscape and describe what they would see, smell, feel, or hear there.

Model completing the activity by thinking aloud. For example, say: I would choose to live in the landscape on page 19, because I think it would be fun to watch the buildings go up. I would hear the sounds of construction and feel the breeze from the passing cars.

If . . . students have difficulty identifying the senses,

then . . . provide examples of things in the classroom that students can see, smell, feel, and hear.

EXTEND Ask students to create their own illustrations of either a city scene or a country scene, and encourage them to include as many details as possible. Provide time for students to tell about their illustrations in a teacher-led small group or with the whole class.

ENGLISH LANGUAGE LEARNERS

Some students might have a hard time using descriptive language to tell about the trees. Provide these students with a list of descriptive words and phrases to use, such as *beautiful, huge, magnificent.*

STRUGGLING READERS

Students may struggle to understand that things, such as cars, telephones, and street lights, did not always exist. Show these students historical photos of towns and cities. Explain that throughout history, people invented things that changed the way we lived.

EXPRESS Talk about Sentences and Words

Display the following sentences from *The Little House*. Read them aloud with students and discuss the meaning. Clarify any misunderstandings.

"This must be living in the city," thought the Little House, and didn't know whether she liked it or not. She missed the field of daisies and the apple trees dancing in the moonlight.

Ask: Can apple trees really dance? (no) Do trees and flowers sometimes look like they are dancing? (yes) What might make them look that way? (the wind) Close your eyes and imagine a field of daisies and apple trees dancing in the moonlight.

TEAM TALK Have students work with a partner to find illustrations in the book that show apple trees. On each page where they find them, ask students to take turns describing the trees. Partners can pretend they are an apple tree and dance in the moonlight, sway in the breeze, shiver in the cold, or grow apples, for example.

EXTEND Remind students that the Little House missed living in the country. She missed the flowers and the apple trees. Ask: Have you ever missed a place? Describe that place to your partner and tell why you missed it.

KNOWLEDGE DEMANDS

EXPRESS Have small groups look at illustrations from the beginning, middle, and end of the story. Point out the changes, and talk about how much time might have passed. Guide students to look at specific parts of the pictures, such as the house itself, the people, the vehicles, and the buildings. Ask: Do you think these changes could happen over a short period of time, like five days, or a longer period of time, like five years?

EXTEND Ask students to imagine and create an illustration of how their neighborhood or home might change over time. Have students summarize orally the changes that might occur by the time they have grown up.

ACCELERATED LEARNERS

Encourage students to label their illustration with words or sentences. Provide opportunities for students to read their words and describe their illustrations to a partner.

Unlock the Text

QUALITATIVE MEASURES

Levels of Meaning	simple, character- and event-driven plot explaining the effects of seasonal changes
Structure	chronological order beginning with spring; first-person point of view; picture details
Language Conventionality and Clarity	familiar vocabulary with some unfamiliar and domain-specific words; action words; multiple-meaning words
Knowledge Demands	seasons cause changes in plant and animal life; life on a farm

ReadyGEN Text Collection

Four Seasons Make a Year, pp. 29–59

Prepare to Read

LEVELS OF MEANING

Four Seasons Make a Year is about the changing seasons, but it is also about how the changing seasons and weather affect plant and animal life, as well as life for one girl living on a farm.

STRUCTURE

PREVIEW Display and read aloud the title. Then display a yearly calendar. Point out and say the names of the spring months: March, April, May. Ask students to say them again as you point to each word. Point out the illustrations in the text that correspond to spring. Take some time to examine the details of the illustrations. Explain details with which students may not be familiar, such as the robins returning in the spring and the pear blossoms that form fruit. Follow the same procedure to introduce the names of the months associated with summer, fall, and winter.

MORE SUPPORT

ENGLISH LANGUAGE LEARNERS

This text is packed with critical vocabulary, including many unfamiliar plant names. Be sure to preview the vocabulary, using the pictures of the flowers and plants. Have students say each name after you.

STRUGGLING READERS

If students are having difficulty understanding the meaning of the descriptive vocabulary, have them pick a descriptive word from the vocabulary words, such as *droop, flutter, peck,* or *twirl,* and act it out.

PREVIEW VOCABULARY Use the Learn New Words Routine in Part 3 to assess what students know about the following words: *spring, droops, plow, bloom, blossom, sprout, bouquets, frantically, ripe, slippery, snowbank, crackle, flutter, peck, jacket, shrivel up, twirling.*

Model a think aloud to provide further clarification of each word. For example, say: This morning I woke up and went into my kitchen to get a glass of water. I took a step, and all of a sudden—WHOOSH! (Act out almost falling.) I almost fell on the floor! My dog had spilled his water bowl, and the floor was wet and slippery. What else can you think of that's slippery?

When possible, act out words, show pictures or video clips, or elicit students' own experiences to help them form connections with the words.

CRITICAL VOCABULARY Preteach domain-specific vocabulary, such as *squash, stalks, ears of corn, daffodils, crocuses, zinnias, sweet peas, lilies, black-eyed Susans, cosmos, evergreens, chickadees,* and *cardinals.* Use the Vocabulary Activities in Part 3 to provide support.

KNOWLEDGE DEMANDS

ACTIVATE BACKGROUND KNOWLEDGE Ask students to share what they know about the four seasons. Ask: How does the weather change each season? How do plants change? How do animals change? Chart students' responses using the Web Routine with Graphic Organizer in Part 3.

To provide support, model an example of what happens to a specific plant or animal as it changes with the seasons. For example, say: There is a cherry tree in the park. In the spring, it grows pretty pink blossoms. In the summer, fat, juicy cherries grow where the flowers were. In the fall, the leaves change colors and start to drop to the ground. In the winter, the tree is bare—it doesn't have any leaves, flowers, or cherries. Then, the next spring, the cycle starts all over again with the pretty pink blossoms.

Interact with Text

LEVELS OF MEANING

As you read *Four Seasons Make a Year,* assess students' level of understanding of seasonal changes through guided questioning. Ask: What season is it now? What is happening to the plants and animals on the farm? To further students' understanding of seasonal changes, display the names of the four seasons on a chart. After reading about a season, ask students to draw something associated with that season. For example, for winter, one student might draw a bare tree. Another might draw snow. Display students' drawings under the corresponding season.

If . . . students are unsure what to draw for the chart,

then . . . provide them with four tree outlines. Using the story illustrations and other seasonal photographs, have students color and draw leaves for each tree to represent each season. For example, they might draw pink blossoms on the spring tree and green leaves on the summer tree.

STRUCTURE

Explain to students that this story is told from the point of view of a young girl. Display a picture of the girl. Say: This girl is telling the story. We know she is telling the story because she uses words such as *I* and *my.* Help students understand that the girl is telling about how life on her farm changes as the seasons change. Then point out details in the illustrations that serve as evidence to the changing seasons, and ask students to do the same. Encourage students to notice the different clothing the main character wears in the illustrations to serve as clues to the seasons. For example, display the illustration on pp. 32–33. Say: The girl is wearing a rain jacket, because it often rains in the spring. What other clothing might someone wear in spring? Have students examine other illustrations to find clues that represent each season.

MORE SUPPORT

ENGLISH LANGUAGE LEARNERS

Encourage students to ask questions about plants and animals that are unfamiliar to them. Provide question stems to encourage interaction, such as: What is ___? I don't understand ___. How did ___ happen?

STRUGGLING READERS

Encourage students to make personal connections to the text. Ask them to think about what they like to do in each season. Correlate students' responses to an event in the text.

LANGUAGE CONVENTIONALITY AND CLARITY

This text includes many domain-specific words that might be confusing, especially the names of plants.

If . . . students have difficulty with the specific plant names,

then . . . make a classroom "garden" on chart paper to reinforce understanding of the plants and their names.

For example, on chart paper or the board, post pictures or drawings of some of the plants named in the text. On a repeated reading, ask students to raise their hands when they hear a plant name. Call on students to point to the picture of the plant on the page while you point to the chart and read the word aloud. Then have a volunteer come to the chart and dictate the name of the plant to include in the "garden."

KNOWLEDGE DEMANDS

Revisit the chart that you created earlier of what students know about the changing seasons. Ask: Do we know any new information? What can we add to our chart? Encourage students to share information they learned not only about the seasons but also how they affect people, plants, and animals.

If . . . students have difficulty determining information to add to the chart,

then . . . revisit the text and reread specific examples of plants and animals changing with the seasons. For example, in the spring, the girl plants the sunflower seed; in the summer, it sprouts and grows into a sunflower; in the fall, it develops seeds; and in the winter, it dries up.

Express and Extend

LEVELS OF MEANING

EXPRESS Have students work in small groups. Assign each group one season and one of the following categories: people, plants, animals. Display the chart with the names of the four seasons and students' drawings. Have groups discuss how their assigned season affects their assigned category. For example, groups that are assigned summer and plants should discuss how plants, such as sunflowers and pear trees, change in summer. Students can use evidence from the class chart and the illustrations from the text in their discussions. Have groups share with the class a sentence or two about their discussions.

> **If . . .** students have difficulty discussing how plants, animals, or people are affected by their assigned season,
>
> **then . . .** point to one specific plant or animal in the text, or the main character, and have students focus on how that one plant, animal, or character is affected by their assigned season.

EXTEND Have students discuss what season they think is most important and why. For example, some students might think that fall is the most important season because many vegetables are harvested in the fall. Have students share their responses with a partner.

STRUCTURE

EXPRESS Ask students to choose the sunflower, the pear tree, or the pumpkin. In small groups, have them tell how that particular plant changed as the seasons changed and find the illustrations that show the changes. To help students articulate their thoughts, provide the following sentence starters: In spring, the ___ looks like ___. In summer, the ___ looks like ___. In fall, the ___ looks like ___. In winter, the ___ looks like ___.

EXTEND Help students fold a drawing paper into quarters, and have them draw a picture in each box of how a tree might look in spring, summer, fall, and winter. Help students print the words for the seasons at the top of each box. Encourage students to tell you the correct order of the seasons as you write them.

MORE SUPPORT

ENGLISH LANGUAGE LEARNERS

Pair and group students thoughtfully and flexibly so that they have opportunities to work with people of varying abilities and personalities. For example, pairing outgoing students with more reserved students will often help the reserved students become more willing to take verbal risks and express themselves freely.

STRUGGLING READERS

Some students may struggle with multiple-meaning words, such as *blows, bloom, sprout,* and *plow.* Help these students use context clues to determine the correct meaning. You might also work with them to look up the words in a dictionary.

LANGUAGE CONVENTIONALITY AND CLARITY

EXPRESS Talk about Sentences and Words

Display the following sentences from *Four Seasons Make a Year* and read them aloud.

> Wind blows and birds sing. Daffodils and crocuses pop up through melting snow to bloom in the dark, wet earth. Leaves sprout on the trees. It's time to plow the field.

Say: Close your eyes and listen to the sentences. Reread the sentences. Ask: What season do you think it is? (spring) How do you know? (Daffodils come out in spring; the snow is melting; the leaves are sprouting; the field will be plowed.)

Point out the action words and phrases in the sentences. Then read aloud this sentence: Wind blows and birds sing. Ask: What does the wind do? (It blows.) Demonstrate the action of blowing by swaying your hands like the wind, and invite students to do the same as you repeat the phrase *wind blows, wind blows.*

TEAM TALK Help partners identify other action words and phrases in the passage, such as *sing, pop up, bloom, sprout,* and *plow,* and have them repeat the words to each other as they perform the actions.

EXTEND Whisper an action from the text to a volunteer. Have the student act out the action word without speaking. Invite other students to guess the action word. Repeat this activity with a different action and volunteer.

KNOWLEDGE DEMANDS

EXPRESS Ask students to review the text and illustrations of *Four Seasons Make a Year* to determine one thing they learned about plants, animals, the seasons, or life on a farm from the text. Use the sentence starter: I learned ___. Have students share their ideas with the whole class.

EXTEND Have students create a class booklet about the four seasons. Have each student contribute a page with a drawing of one season. Have students write or dictate a fact about their drawing to accompany their page.

ACCELERATED LEARNERS

Provide picture books, magazines, and appropriate websites, and ask students to find out more about one of the specific plants or animals in the story. Have them draw to show what they found out, or have them write or dictate some words or sentences.

MORE SUPPORT

Unlock the Text

QUALITATIVE MEASURES

Levels of Meaning	fictional time travelers used as means for examining actual past-and-present farming methods; theme of change developed through changes on the farm
Structure	past and present farming methods in then-and-now format for comparison; clear connection between past and present; information in text boxes, speech bubbles, and sidebars, photographs supporting written text
Language Conventionality and Clarity	challenging academic and domain-specific vocabulary, some in-context clues to meaning and a glossary, time-related words, comparison words, simple and complex sentences
Knowledge Demands	farming and farm work, farm crops, past and present

Prepare to Read

LEVELS OF MEANING

Farming Then and Now is a nonfiction informational text comparing farm work and methods one hundred years ago with those of today. The text introduces an element of fiction by using an old pocket watch that two children use to go back and forth in time. The text explores past and present ways of milking cows, feeding animals in winter, harvesting crops, and shearing sheep. It includes Did You Know sidebars with interesting farm facts.

ENGLISH LANGUAGE LEARNERS

The terms *Then* and *Now* in the text's title may be unfamiliar to some students. Guide them to understand that both terms are time related and *then* refers to the past and *now* refers to today. Contrast examples of previous-day classroom activities with those of today to reinforce the concepts of *then* and *now*. If possible, introduce the equivalent terms in students' home languages.

STRUGGLING READERS

When previewing pictures, some students may not recognize that some pictures are in full color and some are sepia or black and white. Tell students that pictures without full color show farming in the past and pictures with full color depict farming today.

PREVIEW Read the title of the book and the names of the author and the illustrator. Point out that the author, Charles Smith Jr., wrote the words for the story and the illustrator, Jessika von Innerebner, drew the time-traveling guides and helped choose photographs for the text.

Read the text's title and look at its pictures with students. Guide them to use information from the title and pictures to respond to the following questions:

- Remember the title of the book is *Farming Then and Now.* Who wrote the words of the title, the author or the illustrator?

- Think about the title of this book. What do you think this book is about?

- The book tells about farming long ago and farming today. Look at the pictures. What do the pictures help you understand about farming?

LANGUAGE CONVENTIONALITY AND CLARITY

PREVIEW VOCABULARY Use a variety of strategies to assess what students know about the following words: *farm, chores, work, cows, machines, sheep, crops, corn, change.* Use pictures, pantomime, examples, synonyms, and glossary definitions to help students understand the vocabulary.

KNOWLEDGE DEMANDS

ACTIVATE BACKGROUND KNOWLEDGE Students are likely to be familiar with farms and farm structures. Display pictures of farms including pictures with farm buildings, equipment, animals, and fields. Ask students to share what they know about farms by identifying features in the pictures. Facilitate student input with guiding questions, such as: Is this building the farmhouse or the barn? A silo is a tall round building. Which building is a silo? What animal is this? Where do farmers plant seeds?

Interact with Text

Remind students that the selection *Farming Then and Now* tells about farming. As you read each set of two pages, discuss what the pages say about farming. Guide students to understand that the author is telling us about farming chores in the past and farming today.

Guide students to analyze what the author says about milking cows, feeding animals, harvesting crops, and shearing sheep. Focus the discussion by asking the following questions: What are some chores that farmers do now that they did one hundred years ago? (milk cows, feed animals, shear sheep, harvest crops) Have the ways they do these chores stayed the same or changed? (changed) What does the author want you to know about farming? (The ways farmers do things have changed, but they still do the same things.)

Point out specific examples in the text and illustrations that support student responses.

> If . . . students have difficulty identifying ways faming chores have changed,
>
> then . . . revisit the illustrations to point out differences.

STRUCTURE

Remind students that the author wrote the words of the selection *Farming Then and Now* and used different features to present his words. Point to features on pp. 8–9 as you explain that the headings tell what the pages are about, the main text describes farming in the past and in the present, the Did You Know? sidebars give interesting farm facts, and the speech bubbles are the words the characters say. Also discuss how the photographs and illustrations support the author's words. Reread pp. 10–11. Ask questions about the features, such as: Where will I look to find out how workers harvested wheat a long time ago? (main text on p. 10) What feature tells about ways of celebrating harvests? (Did You Know? on p. 11)

ENGLISH LANGUAGE LEARNERS

English customary units of liquid measurement may be unfamiliar to students. To help students conceptualize one pint (p. 6, *Did You Know?*), measure two cups of water into a clear container. You might also display six empty gallon bottles and draw a line dividing one bottle in half.

STRUGGLING READERS

Because the text does not have a straightforward top-to-bottom, consistent text layout, preview the print design features with students. Open the text to pp. 6–7, and identify the section head, main text, speech bubble, and Did You Know? sidebar.

MORE SUPPORT

LANGUAGE CONVENTIONALITY AND CLARITY

The author uses several comparative words. Provide the examples from the text, *faster* and *easier* on p. 7 and *bigger* on p. 10. Write each comparative and its base word next to it. Explain that the *-er* ending on the words *faster, easier,* and *bigger* means "more," so, for example, *bigger* means "more big."

> **If . . .** students have difficulty understanding the meaning of the comparative words,
>
> **then . . .** use pictures and/or demonstrations to illustrate the meanings of the base word and the comparative word.

KNOWLEDGE DEMANDS

Page 8 names turnips, potatoes, beets, and alfalfa as food for animals. Display pictures of beets, potatoes, and turnips. Discuss what children know about these vegetables by asking questions, such as Have you eaten potatoes? beets? turnips? How were they fixed? Then reread p. 8 and discuss what the text says about these vegetables. Ask: What does page 8 say about potatoes, turnips, and beets? (Farmers fed them to their animals in winter.) Where do you think the farmers got these vegetables? (Farmers grew them.) Point to the picture of alfalfa on p. 8. Ask: What do we learn about alfalfa? (It is healthful animal food and has been used to feed animals for longer than other plants.)

ENGLISH LANGUAGE LEARNERS

In English, the comparative is formed in different ways. To make shorter words comparative, we add the ending *-er*, as in *bigger*. To make longer words comparative, we add the word *more*, as in *more beautiful*. A few words have irregular comparative forms. For example, the comparative form of *good* is *better*. Students' home language may form the comparative differently. For example, in Spanish, the word *más* is added to form the comparative, so *más grande* in Spanish has the same meaning as *bigger* in English.

Express and Extend

LEVELS OF MEANING

EXPRESS Remind students that this selection is a nonfictional informational text. Point out that it does use fictional characters to guide readers back and forth from past to present. Turn to p. 5, identify the characters, and read the speech bubbles. Help students recognize that the watch and characters are make-believe, but they are used to present facts. Ask:

- What do the boy and girl use to travel back in time? (a pocket watch)
- Can a watch really take people back to the past? Explain what a watch does. (No, an old watch just shows the time.)
- Why do you think the author decided to use the watch and characters? (The characters are fun guides to information about how farming has changed over time. The watch helps set the time frames.)

Guide students to conclude that the characters and time travel are make-believe, but they help guide readers from the past to the present and back again.

If . . . students have difficulty determining that the characters are make-believe,

then . . . point out how illustrations show the characters, but photographs show actual farm scenes.

EXTEND Read aloud the Did You Know? sidebar on p. 11. Discuss what the characters might say about the harvest parade. Have students draw a picture of one of the characters and write or dictate a speech bubble comment about the parade.

STRUCTURE

EXPRESS Review with students that the main part of the text is organized to tell first how farmers did a chore long ago and next how they do the same chore today. Use the Venn diagram with Graphic Organizer Routine in Part 3 to help students identify how farming tasks have remained the same and have changed over time.

If . . . students have difficulty identifying how the chores are the same,

then . . . ask questions about whether a farmer did a chore in the past, such as milk cows, and still does it today.

EXTEND Have pairs of students use a Venn diagram and the text pages to explain how one farming chore has changed and remained the same over time.

MORE SUPPORT

ENGLISH LANGUAGE LEARNERS

Grouping challenging or unfamiliar words by categories may help students better understand them. For example, group *scythe* and *sickle* in the category tools for cutting crops; and group *cows* and *sheep* in the category farm animals.

STRUGGLING READERS

To help students focus on the topic of changes in farming, read only the main text several times. Tell students that the main text presents the selection's most important ideas. Use guiding questions to help students identify the important ideas on each page.

LANGUAGE CONVENTIONALITY AND CLARITY

EXPRESS Talk about Sentences and Words

Display and read aloud the following sentences from *Farming Then and Now.*

> Today, animals such as cows and sheep eat silage in the winter. This is a type of food made from grass crops such as corn.

Briefly discuss the sentences, pointing out that each tells a complete idea. Then underline the word *silage*. Say: This is the word *silage*. This sentence says that animals eat silage. I do not know what silage is. I can figure out that it must be a food because animals eat it. But what kind of food is it? The first sentence does not tell me, so I will read the next sentence. It says that silage is *food made from grass crops such as corn*. Now I know what kind of food silage is. Point out that often readers can find clues to the meanings of words in sentences around the words.

TEAM TALK Have students turn to p. 11. Read aloud this sentence:

> Today, a combine harvester can cut twenty acres of wheat in one hour.

Have pairs discuss what a combine harvester is. Ask partners to look for clues to the meaning of *combine harvester* in the sentence.

> **If . . .** students have difficulty noting that *cut* provides a clue to the meaning of *combine harvester,*
>
> **then . . .** have them use the picture to identify other clues such as a combine harvester is a machine.

EXTEND Have partners work together to tell what a combine harvester is. Encourage them to use this sentence starter: A combine harvester is ___.

KNOWLEDGE DEMANDS

EXPRESS Ask questions about the text to elicit details from students about what they have learned about farming, such as: What is a job people do on a farm? How did people do this job in the past? How do they do the job today? Is ___ easier today than it was in the past? Why?

> **If . . .** students have difficulty recalling key details about farming in the past and in the present,
>
> **then . . .** have them use the photographs as visual prompts to the text information.

EXTEND Have partners page through the selection and take turns telling facts about farming in the past and today.

ACCELERATED LEARNERS

Have students choose another book to explore farm life in the past or present. Then invite them to tell the class about how the ideas in the book they selected were either the same as or different from those in *Farming Then and Now.*

MORE SUPPORT

Unlock the Text

QUALITATIVE MEASURES

Levels of Meaning	old and new communication devices used for the same purpose; reason for giving away things; change
Structure	nonfiction narrative, front cover and title page with title and author's name; text organized by kind of communication tool in old and new versions; text presented as a series of initial e-mails and replies, traditional letter format
Language Conventionality and Clarity	mostly familiar vocabulary, multiple-meaning words, mostly short simple sentences, some repetition, prepositional phrases
Knowledge Demands	letter format, communication tools, e-mail, mail, strong picture support

Prepare to Read

LEVELS OF MEANING

The Old Things is a nonfiction narrative between a grandmother and her grandson. Communicating by e-mail, Gran offers to give her grandson her old communication tools. In response, Tom identifies newer communication tools that serve the same purpose. Through this exchange, opportunities are provided to compare old and new tools for playing music, taking pictures, typing letters, communicating by phone, and writing.

MORE SUPPORT

ENGLISH LANGUAGE LEARNERS

To reinforce the meaning of the noun *Things* in the title *The Old Things* and to distinguish it from the specific names of items, discuss the use of *things* as a generic term. One by one, hold up an item, identify it, and place it on a table.

STRUGGLING READERS

A few sentences in the selection are more than one line long. Turn to p. 7. Review with students that sentences begin with capital letters and end with end punctuation. Help them find the beginning and end of each sentence.

STRUCTURE

PREVIEW Hold up the front cover of the selection. Read the title of the book *The Old Things*, and the name of the author, Diana Noonan. Point out that the author wrote the words of the selection. Turn to the title page and ask students to point to the title of the book and the name of the author.

Read the text's title and look at its photographs with students. Guide them to use information from the title and pictures to respond to the following questions:

- Remember, the title of this book is *The Old Things.* Think about the title. What do you think this book is about?

- Look at the photograph on the cover. Have you ever seen a machine like this? What do you think it does? Do you think this is an old thing?

- Now let's look at the pictures in the book. What old things do you see? What new things do you see?

LANGUAGE CONVENTIONALITY AND CLARITY

PREVIEW VOCABULARY Use the Learn New Words Routine in Part 3 to assess what students know about the following words: *moving, e-mail, record player, MP3 player, records, camera, film, photo, typewriter, laptop, phone.*

KNOWLEDGE DEMANDS

ACTIVATE BACKGROUND KNOWLEDGE Students are likely to be familiar with present-day communication devices. Display pictures of the present-day devices or the devices themselves. Ask students to share what they know about each one. Facilitate student input with guiding questions, such as: What is this? What do we use it for? How do we use this tool? When do we use it?

STRUGGLING READERS

The reading selection is written as a series of e-mails between Gran and Tom. Some readers may have difficulty tracking the e-mails. Point out features that can help students identify the sender of each e-mail. Open the book to pp. 4–5. Point to the headers on the e-mails, noting that the word *To* tells who is receiving the e-mail and the word *From* tells who is sending the e-mail. Also point out that the background colors of the e-mails differ. Gran's e-mails have purple backgrounds and Tom's e-mails have green backgrounds.

Interact with Text

LEVELS OF MEANING

Remind students that for every old thing, there is a new thing that can be used to do the same thing. Discuss what each old thing does and help students note which new thing takes the place of the old thing. Record the information on a three-column chart with the first column labeled Old Thing, the second column labeled Use, and the third column labeled New Thing. As you discuss the items, complete the chart. For example, under Old Thing, write *record player*; under Use, write *listen to music*; and under New Thing, write *MP3 player.* Use the chart to focus on how the old and new things are alike.

If . . . students have difficulty identifying how the new things and old things are alike,

then . . . review the photographs and reread Tom's responses to Gran's e-mails.

STRUCTURE

The selection uses a traditional paragraph format on pp. 2 and 3 and a letter format for the remainder of the text. Display p. 4 and discuss the letter format of the e-mail. Identify the greeting, the body of the letter, the closing, and the signature. Discuss the purpose of each part of the format: the greeting, to say hello; the body, to tell the message; the closing, to say goodbye; and the signature, to show who wrote the letter. Display p. 5 and ask students to identify parts of the letter format. For example, point to the greeting, read it, and say: This part of the letter says *Dear Gran.* What is this part of the letter for? (to say hello)

If . . . students have difficulty identifying parts of a letter and their purpose,

then . . . prepare a chart in letter format and label the parts of the letter.

MORE SUPPORT

ENGLISH LANGUAGE LEARNERS

Students may not be familiar with the word Gran as an affectionate name for *grandmother*. Help students relate the name Gran to the word for *grandmother* in both English and their home language—for example, the word for *grandmother* is *abuela* in Spanish.

STRUGGLING READERS

Gran's and Tom's e-mails include repetitive phrases and sentences. Point out these phrases and sentences as you read. Encourage students to read them along with you.

LANGUAGE CONVENTIONALITY AND CLARITY

The text uses a number of words that have more than one meaning. These include the words *moving, play, like, record, film, type,* and *still*. Make sure students understand the meaning of each word as it is used in the text. For example, discuss the word *moving* on p. 2. Jumping and walking are ways of moving. *Moving* can also mean "changing where you live." The text says "Gran was moving to a small house." The words *small house* help me understand that *moving* in the text means that Gran is changing where she lives.

If . . . students have difficulty understanding the meaning of multiple-meaning words in the selection,

then . . . discuss the meanings of the word and help students choose the correct one for the selection.

KNOWLEDGE DEMANDS

In *The Old Things*, Gran is moving and cannot take all of her things with her. The text does not explicitly state why Gran cannot take everything she has. Help students infer that Gran will not have enough space in her new home for all of her old things. Use questions to guide inferences: Is Gran moving to a large house or a small house? (small house) Could you put more things in a large house or a small house? Why? (a large house because it has more space) Why can't Gran take all of her things to the new house? (The house is small and does not have enough space.)

Express and Extend

EXPRESS Remind students that Gran offered to give Tom many of her old things. Tom wanted some of the things but not others. Use a two-column chart, labeling one column Things Wanted and the other Things Not Wanted. Guide students to identify each object Gran offered Tom and tell whether he wanted it or not. Have them tell you in which column of the chart to put each old thing. Guide the discussion with questions about each item such as: This is a ___. Does Tom want it? Why does/doesn't he want it? In which column of our chart should I put the ___? Have students use the chart to note that Tom wanted all of the old things except the camera and the telephone.

If . . . students have difficulty determining whether Tom wanted an item,

then . . . read aloud his e-mail reply to Gran about the item.

EXTEND Have each student draw a picture of one of the old things. Then have students put their pictures in a pile labeled Things Tom Wanted or Things Tom Did Not Want.

STRUCTURE

EXPRESS The photographs in the text provide strong support for the written text by showing the old and new communication devices. For each set of e-mails exchanged by Gran and Tom, the photographs show one of Gran's old things and the new thing that Tom uses for the same purpose. Guide students to understand that the thing named in Gran's e-mail is shown in the photograph next to her e-mail and the thing Tom uses is shown next to his e-mail. Have students identify the item depicted in a photograph and tell whether it is an old thing or a new thing. Then refer students to the chart on p. 16 and have them identify which old things and new things go together.

If . . . students have difficulty identifying what is shown in a photograph,

then . . . read the sentence in the e-mail that names the thing.

EXTEND Have students in small groups take turns describing one of the communication tools in the selection. The group should then identify the photograph that depicts the item. For example, a description might be "This is an old thing that was used to play music." Group members would show the photograph of the record player and name it.

ENGLISH LANGUAGE LEARNERS

Students are likely to be familiar with the use of prepositions and prepositional phrases because they are also used in their home language. Prepositions in the student's home language serve the same purpose as they do in English.

STRUGGLING READERS

If students have difficulty reading the chart on p. 16, discuss its features. Identify the meanings of the heads Back Then and Today. Note that old things and new things used for the same purpose are across from each other.

MORE SUPPORT

LANGUAGE CONVENTIONALITY AND CLARITY

EXPRESS Talk about Sentences and Words

Display and read aloud the following sentence from *The Old Things*.

> I will put the old things in a box.

Circle the word *in*. The word *in* is a preposition. Remind students that a preposition is a word that tells more about a naming word. Point to the word *in* as you reread the sentence. In this sentence, the word *in* tells more about the naming word *box*. It tells us where the old things will be put. The old things will be put *in the box*. The word *in* connects the word *box* to the rest of the sentence.

TEAM TALK Write and read aloud the following sentence frame: I will put ___ in the ___. For example, say: I will put paper in the notebook. Have pairs of students complete the frame by naming objects and a container they can place the objects in.

> **If . . .** students have difficulty completing the frame,
>
> **then . . .** display a number of items and a container and have them choose an item to put in the container. They can use the names of the item and the container to complete the frame.

EXTEND Have each student draw a picture of something in a container. Ask the student to write or dictate the completed sentence frame to describe his or her picture. Have the student circle the preposition in the sentence and then share the picture and sentence with the group.

KNOWLEDGE DEMANDS

EXPRESS Tom and Gran communicate mostly by e-mail, but Gran sends the old things to Tom by mail. What does Gran say about the mail? (There was mail when she was a girl and there still is mail. That has not changed.) Have children discuss how Tom lets Gran know he received her package in the mail. (He uses pen and ink to write Gran a letter.) Ask how he gets his letter to Gran.

> **If . . .** students cannot identify that Tom sends a letter rather than e-mail,
>
> **then . . .** point out how the letter differs from the e-mail message.

EXTEND Have partners discuss how sending the e-mails and sending the letter by mail are alike and different. Encourage them to draw a picture of Tom sending an e-mail and another picture of Tom mailing a letter.

ACCELERATED LEARNERS

Have students think about the old things Gran sent Tom in *The Old Things*. Ask them to draw a picture of the one old thing they would most like to have. Ask each student to show his or her drawing and to tell why he or she wants the object.

Predicting Change

MODULE A

TEXT SET

ANCHOR TEXT
Come On, Rain!

SUPPORTING TEXT
The Snowy Day

MODULE B

TEXT SET

ANCHOR TEXT
What Will the Weather Be?

SUPPORTING TEXT
Weather Words and What
They Mean

Unlock the Text

Come On, Rain! pp. 5–30

QUALITATIVE MEASURES

Levels of Meaning	predicting weather; anticipation; feeling refreshed after an event finally occurs
Structure	chronological events; narrative prose; illustrations; ellipses
Language Conventionality and Clarity	descriptive and figurative language; dialogue
Knowledge Demands	weather patterns; city life; events can bring people together to feel refreshed; compare environments

Prepare to Read

LEVELS OF MEANING

There are two levels of meaning in *Come On, Rain!* One is the main storyline of Tessie's anticipation for a rainstorm on a sweltering summer day in the city. The second, deeper purpose is to show how an anticipated event can bring people together and leave them feeling refreshed.

STRUCTURE

PREVIEW Ask students to look at the cover. Introduce the title, *Come On, Rain!,* the author, and the illustrator. Remind students that the author writes the words, and the illustrator draws the pictures. Ask students to examine the cover with a partner and share what they think this story might be about. In small groups, have students take a picture walk through the text. Ask: Where does the story take place? (in a city) Looking at picture clues, can you determine in which season the story takes place? (in the summer)

MORE SUPPORT

ENGLISH LANGUAGE LEARNERS

To help students understand the meanings of new action words and phrases, such as *come on,* demonstrate the definition with a hand gesture. Ask students to infer what you are gesturing for them to do. (hurry up)

STRUGGLING READERS

Have students create a synonym picture book to help organize their vocabulary. For example, the author describes the children "squealing" and "whooping" in the rain. Group *squealing* and *whooping* as having similar meanings. ("making a loud noise")

Based on the illustrations in the book, who is most likely the main character in this story? (the young girl in the white dress)

LANGUAGE CONVENTIONALITY AND CLARITY

PREVIEW VOCABULARY Use the Learn New Words Routine in Part 3 to assess what students know about the following words: *parched, sizzling, broiling, drooping, bulging, rumbles, sparkles, swollen, glistening, racket.* Give an example of each word, and use it in a question to students. Have students use the word in their response. For example, say: If someone or something is parched, it is very, very dry. If a plant were parched, what could you do to help it? (If a plant were parched, I could give it some water.) You can also use the Vocabulary Activities in Part 3 to preteach critical vocabulary words.

KNOWLEDGE DEMANDS

ACTIVATE BACKGROUND KNOWLEDGE Ask students to share what they know about rainstorms. Record student responses on chart paper. To assist with student discussion, ask guiding questions, such as: Why do we need rain? What does rain do for people, plants, and animals? What happens if there is no rain for a long time? How can you tell if a rainstorm is going to happen soon? Review responses by having students follow along as you read each word or phrase on the chart.

Interact with Text

The author builds anticipation for the rainstorm by describing the events of the sweltering summer day. While reading, assess students' understanding of the events of the story through guided questioning. Ask: What clues does the author give to tell you that Tessie is hopeful for rain? (Tessie continues to say, "Come on, rain!" and is determined to put on her swimsuit.) What clues does the author give to tell that Mamma is waiting for rain? (Mamma sighs over her wilting plants, saying, "Three weeks and not a drop." Later Mamma says, "It's about time.") Why was everyone so excited to jump and dance in the rain? (Everyone was hot from the heat of the sun, so the rain was refreshing.)

STRUCTURE

As you read the story, pause periodically to assess students' understanding of the story's structure. Point to an example of ellipses in the text. Then explain that the author uses ellipses at various points in the story to indicate when the reader should pause before continuing to read. Discuss the importance of pausing at the proper points when reading, such as for commas, ellipses, and periods.

If . . . students have difficulty understanding the use of ellipses,

then . . . model reading an excerpt for students to show proper fluency.

For example, display and read aloud the following passage from p. 18: All the insects have gone still. Trees sway under a swollen sky, the wind grows bold and bolder, . . . and just like that, rain comes. Explain that just as you pause your reading for a comma and stop at each period, you take a break when you see an ellipsis, or three dots in a row, in a sentence. Point out the ellipsis on p. 18. Reread the sentence without taking breaks for commas, periods, or the ellipsis, so students can hear the difference. Then have students echo read the same passage, pausing at the appropriate places.

ENGLISH LANGUAGE LEARNERS

Help students associate word meanings within groups of words. Use the Web Routine and Graphic Organizer in Part 3 to create a word map of related words. For example, write *rain* in the center, and then help students come up with words that relate to rain, such as *storm, thunder,* and *lightning.*

STRUGGLING READERS

Help students group words with similar meanings into pairs. For example, *sagging/drooping, sizzling/broiling, bulging/swollen, glistening/sparkles,* and *racket/rumbles.* If necessary, associate pairs of words with a simpler term (*leaning, hot, big, shiny,* and *loud*).

LANGUAGE CONVENTIONALITY AND CLARITY

This story uses many examples of figurative language to paint a picture in various parts of the story. Explain to students that authors often describe something as a comparison to help readers create a picture in their mind.

For example, read aloud the following sentence from p. 12: Her long legs, like two brown string beans, sprout from her shorts. Explain that *sprout* means "to grow." Ask: What do string beans look like? (long and skinny) Does Jackie-Joyce have string beans growing where her legs should be? (no) Why does the author say that her legs are like two brown string beans? (The author is comparing her legs to string beans because both string beans and her legs are long and skinny.)

If . . . students have difficulty understanding similes,

then . . . review more familiar similes, such as "I am sizzling like a hot potato" from p. 8, having students share what they know about a just-baked potato and how hot Tessie must feel.

KNOWLEDGE DEMANDS

The text and illustrations provide clues that it has not rained for a while. Have students look through the illustrations. Then use the Venn Diagram Routine and Graphic Organizer in Part 3 to compare the environment (plants, colors of the sky, scenery) at the beginning of the story with the environment at the end of the story.

If . . . students have difficulty describing the illustrations,

then . . . model how to reread sections of the text to remember the author's words and review vocabulary.

For example, if students are looking at the text on p. 30 to describe the environment at the end of the story, reread the text aloud. Have students repeat phrases that describe the environment to practice using the author's vocabulary.

Express and Extend

LEVELS OF MEANING

EXPRESS A deeper level of meaning within the story is how an anticipated event can leave one feeling refreshed. Explain that when someone feels refreshed, it means that he or she feels happy and has new energy. Ask: What are the mammas all doing at the beginning of the story? (gardening) Why aren't any kids playing outside? (It is too hot to play outside.) What happens to the kids and mammas when it rains? (They all go outside and dance together.) Why do you think the author says, "The rain has made us new"? (Everyone feels better now that they have cooled off in the rain.)

EXTEND Have students draw a picture of something they like to do that makes them feel brand new or refreshed. Ask them to dictate or write a caption for their picture. Have students use a word from this lesson's vocabulary, as appropriate, in their caption. Provide time for students to share their drawings in small groups.

STRUCTURE

EXPRESS Have students use a piece of paper folded into four sections to create a sequence chart. Have students break down the story into four events. Students should draw a picture in each box and dictate or write a sentence describing the event.

> If . . . students have difficulty understanding the sequence of events in the story,
>
> then . . . model breaking down the story into smaller events.

For example, break down the story into smaller events, such as Tessie watching Mamma working outside in the heat, Tessie getting ready for the rain to start, Tessie playing in the rain with friends, and the mothers joining to dance in the rain.

EXTEND Have students look at the illustration on p. 30. Have them work with a partner or in small groups and draw a picture of what they think Tessie and her mamma did after they finished dancing in the rain. Have students talk about and compare their illustrations with partners.

MORE SUPPORT

ENGLISH LANGUAGE LEARNERS

To help students gain a deeper understanding of the words *rain, thunder,* and *lightning,* show photographs, video clips, and/or play sound effects for the words. Provide correct pronunciation of these words as you show the photographs and listen to the sounds.

STRUGGLING READERS

Since this story is written in prose with many precise verbs, take the opportunity to allow students to act out the interesting actions, such as *twirl, sway, tromping, skid, squealing,* and *whooping.* Provide students with word meanings as needed.

LANGUAGE CONVENTIONALITY AND CLARITY

EXPRESS Talk about Sentences and Words

Display the following sentences from *Come On, Rain!* and read them aloud with students.

"Is there lightning?" Mamma asks.

"No lightning," Jackie-Joyce says.

Explain that authors use quotation marks to help readers know the exact words a character speaks. Point out that clue words, such as *she says, he asks,* and *I say* help readers know who said the words. Ask: Which characters are speaking? (Mamma and Jackie-Joyce) How do you know? (There are quotation marks and clue words.) What does Mamma say? ("Is there lightning?") How are the words *Jackie-Joyce says* helpful to the reader? (They tell who is speaking.)

TEAM TALK Have partners find another example of quotation marks in the story and determine who is speaking and what the character says.

EXTEND Have students search through other books in the classroom for quotation marks and clue words that tell who is speaking. Record these examples on a bulletin board to use as a reference.

KNOWLEDGE DEMANDS

EXPRESS Have small groups discuss what they learned about weather from reading *Come On, Rain!*

If . . . students have difficulty sharing new concepts they learned about weather,

then . . . have them discuss a particular scene that impacted them.

EXTEND Have students choose a favorite descriptive passage about the weather from *Come On, Rain!* and draw a picture to go along with it. Remind students that they may refer to the illustrations in the story for inspiration. Have students present their completed drawings to the class.

ACCELERATED LEARNERS

Provide students the opportunity to enrich their vocabulary by examining precise descriptive words from the text, such as *listless* and *sagging.* Have students create word maps of related words.

MORE SUPPORT

Unlock the Text

Ready GEN
Text Collection

The Snowy Day, pp. 31–59

QUALITATIVE MEASURES

Levels of Meaning	adventures on a snowy day; finding wonder in simple pleasures; setting, character, plot
Structure	chronological events; third-person narrative; pictures
Language Conventionality and Clarity	straightforward sentences; descriptive words; onomatopoeia
Knowledge Demands	winter weather; properties of snow

Prepare to Read

LEVELS OF MEANING

In *The Snowy Day,* the clear theme is the sequence of events of a young boy enjoying a snowy day full of adventures. A deeper meaning of the story is the boy's ability to find wonder in the simple pleasure of playing alone outside.

STRUCTURE

PREVIEW Have students look at the cover and track print while you read aloud the title and the author. Remind students that the author writes the words, and the illustrator makes the pictures. Point out that in this case, Ezra Jack Keats did both. Ask students to examine the cover with a partner and share what they think this story might be about. Then have students look at the illustrations. Ask: What is the boy doing? (playing in the snow) During which season does this story take place? (winter)

ENGLISH LANGUAGE LEARNERS

For some students, snow may be an unfamiliar concept. Provide pictures or videos of snow and activities people do in the snow. Provide photos of specific vocabulary, such as *snowsuit, snowman, snowball, mittens,* and *boots,* to support meaning.

STRUGGLING READERS

If students have difficulty generating sentences to describe their pictures, provide them with sentence frames. For example: I like to ___ in the snow. When it snows, I want to ___.

LANGUAGE CONVENTIONALITY AND CLARITY

PREVIEW VOCABULARY Use the Learn New Words Routine in Part 3 to assess what students know about the following words: *path, crunch, dragged, smacking, heaping, firm, adventures, melted.* Use each word in a sentence related to students' own experiences. You can also use the Vocabulary Activities and Games in Part 3 to preteach critical vocabulary words.

KNOWLEDGE DEMANDS

ACTIVATE BACKGROUND KNOWLEDGE Ask students to share what they know about snow. Ask: What do you like about snow? What don't you like about snow? How do you dress to go out in the snow? What are some activities you like to do in the snow?

Before students get started, model sharing what you know about snow. For example, say: I know that it snows in winter when the weather is cold. I like to play in the snow. I have to wear boots, mittens, a hat, and warm clothes when I play in the snow. Sometimes my family and I go sledding in the snow.

Have students draw a picture of themselves on a snowy day. Students can dictate or write a sentence to describe their picture.

Interact with Text

LEVELS OF MEANING

As the story develops, pause to assess students' understanding of key events in the story. Ask: What clues tell you the setting of the story? (tall buildings in the background; traffic light; snow piled by the street; probably in a city, perhaps near a park) What clues tell you how Peter feels about the snow? (excited; ran outside after breakfast; did various activities, including making a smiling snowman) Why doesn't Peter join the snowball fight? (He isn't old enough to play with the big kids.)

STRUCTURE

As students read, periodically stop to assess their understanding of the story's structure, detailing chronological events. Have students use index cards to create their own sequence picture cards.

If . . . students have difficulty understanding the sequence of events in the story,

then . . . model creating a list of events, and help students choose the most important ones or group similar events into one.

Brainstorm with students a list of events in the story, starting from the beginning and progressing forward. Guide students to see that some events, such as making a snowman and making snow angels, could be grouped into the event playing in the snow. Model the importance of the first event, waking up to see snow, by pointing out that if Peter hadn't noticed the snow, he may not have run outside immediately after breakfast.

ENGLISH LANGUAGE LEARNERS

Write and draw compound word parts, such as *snow, man, suit,* and *ball,* on index cards. Have students practice putting the parts together and saying the compound words. For example, *snow + man = snowman.*

STRUGGLING READERS

Assign each student a section of the story to illustrate, such as: Peter walks in the snow; Peter makes a snowman and snow angels; Peter puts a snowball in his coat pocket; Peter checks his pocket to find the snowball has melted. After students describe their pictures, have them work together to put them in chronological order.

LANGUAGE CONVENTIONALITY AND CLARITY

The author uses onomatopoeia as a way to bring the story to life. Help students understand this concept by explaining that the author uses words that imitate the sounds associated with the objects or actions they refer to. For example, the author uses the word *crunch* when describing how Peter's feet sounded sinking into the snow. Reread p. 36, emphasizing the noise Peter's feet make. Have students act out walking in snow and making crunching sounds with their feet. Ask: What other things make a crunching sound? (chips, crackers, dry leaves) Point out that another example of onomatopoeia is when the author describes how the snow fell. Reread p. 42 and ask: What sound did the snow make when it fell on Peter's head? (plop!) What are some other things that plop? (raindrops, a stone dropping into water)

If . . . students do not understand how words can imitate sounds or actions

then . . . provide additional examples, such as *buzz, hiss, whiz, chug, fizz,* and so on.

KNOWLEDGE DEMANDS

Students should understand the concept of a snowy day as well as winter weather. Encourage students to share their experiences with winter weather. Ask guiding questions, such as: How do you feel after being outside for a long time in winter weather? Why were Peter's socks wet when he got home? What happened to the snowball that Peter placed in his pocket? Have students revisit the text to locate the picture of Peter checking his pocket for the snowball. Have groups of students determine what clue the illustration gives as to what happened to the snowball.

Express and Extend

LEVELS OF MEANING

EXPRESS The implicit theme of the story is the pleasure Peter is able to find in the simplicity of playing alone when outside in the snow. Peter does not have expensive toys yet finds pleasure in exploring his surroundings. Ask: What did Peter find in the snow to play with? (a stick) What was Peter's reaction to seeing a big mountain of snow? (pretended to be a mountain climber, slid down) How does Peter's action of making a snowball to keep for tomorrow tell you he had a great day? (He wants to play with the snowball again tomorrow.) Create a class list of fun things to do both inside and outside using one's imagination instead of toys.

EXTEND Have students draw a picture of what they would do if they saw a big mountain of snow. Ask them to dictate or write a caption for their picture. Have students use a word from this lesson's vocabulary, as appropriate, in their caption. Provide time for students to share their drawings in small groups.

STRUCTURE

EXPRESS Use the Story Map A Routine and Graphic Organizer in Part 3 to identify what happens during the beginning, middle, and end of *The Snowy Day.* Remind students to think about the most important events that took place on Peter's snowy day.

> **If . . .** students have difficulty telling events in order,
>
> **then . . .** use the words *beginning, middle,* and *end* as you lead students on a picture walk through the story.

EXTEND Have students draw pictures on the graphic organizer of what they think Peter will do in the snow with his friend the next day. Help students dictate or write a sentence describing each picture.

ENGLISH LANGUAGE LEARNERS

Allow students to listen to a recording of *The Snowy Day* while following along in the text. Pause when you hear key words or phrases and point them out to students.

STRUGGLING READERS

Help students better understand the sequence of the story by using the previously made sequence cards with pictures of the major story events. Mix up the cards, and have students re-create the sequence of events. Guide students to tell about each event using the sentence frames: First, ___. Then, ___. Next, ___. Finally, ___.

LANGUAGE CONVENTIONALITY AND CLARITY

EXPRESS Talk about Sentences and Words

Display the following sentence and accompanying illustration on p. 38 from *The Snowy Day.* Read it aloud with students.

> Then he dragged his feet s-l-o-w-l-y to make tracks.

Discuss the meaning of this sentence. Ask: Why do you think the word *slowly* is written this way? (So it will be read slowly.) What are tracks? (marks left in the snow) Look at the tracks. How are the tracks from dragging his feet different from when he walked with pointed toes? (There is a long line instead of single footprints.)

> If . . . students have trouble understanding the meanings of *drag* and *slowly,*
> then . . . lead them in dragging their feet slowly while saying, "I drag my feet s-l-o-w-l-y."

TEAM TALK Have students practice saying the sentence to a partner, pronouncing the word *s-l-o-w-l-y* the way it is written.

EXTEND Write the following words on the board: *ran, crunch, dragged, plop.* Remind students how the word *slowly* was written *(s-l-o-w-l-y)* to emphasize meaning. Ask students to say the words in a way that emphasizes their meaning. For example, they might say *ran* very quickly, they might enunciate each separate sound in *crunch,* they might stretch the /a/ sound in *dragged*, and they might emphasize the /p/ sounds in *plop*.

KNOWLEDGE DEMANDS

EXPRESS Have small groups discuss what they learned about what it's like to go on a personal adventure from reading *The Snowy Day.*

> If . . . students have difficulty sharing new things they learned,
> then . . . provide the opportunity for them to draw a picture of and tell about a particular scene that impacted them.

EXTEND Lead students in dictating or writing a sentence about an adventure they went on, and have them draw a picture to go along with it. Remind students that they may refer to the illustrations in the story for inspiration. Encourage students to present their completed drawings to the class.

ACCELERATED LEARNERS

Have students create a mini book that retells the story in their own words, using *first, then, next,* and *last* in their sentences. Encourage students to include new vocabulary words as well as onomatopoeia, just as the author did.

Unlock the Text

QUALITATIVE MEASURES

Levels of Meaning	explains how weather is predicted; cause and effect; wide range of weather
Structure	explicit informational text; cause and effect; illustrations that serve to clarify the text
Language Conventionality and Clarity	domain-specific vocabulary, mostly defined in context; labels and speech boxes provide clarity within illustrations
Knowledge Demands	instruments used to measure and predict weather; warm and cold fronts; air pressure

Prepare to Read

LEVELS OF MEANING

What Will the Weather Be? introduces readers to the world of weather forecasting, a science that enables meteorologists to make educated guesses about when to expect rain, snow, storms, wind, or clear and sunny skies.

STRUCTURE

PREVIEW The predominating structure in this selection is cause and effect. Introduce students to these terms, explaining that a cause is what makes something happen and an effect is what happens as a direct result of the cause. Discuss simple examples of cause and effect from students' own lives. (For example, **Cause:** I stand in the rain; **Effect:** I get wet. **Cause:** I go out in the snow without a coat; **Effect:** I get cold.)

ENGLISH LANGUAGE LEARNERS

Use the cover of *What Will the Weather Be?* to introduce weather vocabulary. Have students mime using an umbrella as they say, "I use an umbrella when it rains" and putting on a scarf as they say, "I wear a scarf when it is cold outside."

STRUGGLING READERS

Help students internalize the domain-specific terms by categorizing them on different word walls. For example, create word walls called Weather Words and Weather Instruments. When posting a word, add a picture to help students associate the word with the definition.

LANGUAGE CONVENTIONALITY AND CLARITY

PREVIEW VOCABULARY Use the Learn New Words Routine in Part 3 to assess what students know about the following words: *wispy, drizzle, liquid, gas, vapor, collapses, puffy, prepare, howl, expect, warn.*

CRITICAL VOCABULARY Preteach domain-specific vocabulary words, such as *weather, temperature, front, meteorologist, forecast, measure, humid, weight,* and *pressure.* Use the Vocabulary Activities and Games in Part 3 to support meaning.

KNOWLEDGE DEMANDS

ACTIVATE BACKGROUND KNOWLEDGE Write *weather* on the board and read it aloud. Invite students to look outside, or display a local weather report from the newspaper or an online source. Ask: What is the weather like today? What else do you know about weather? Then ask: What are some different kinds of weather? Why does the weather change? Can we predict what the weather will be tomorrow? Why or why not? Use the Web Routine and Graphic Organizer in Part 3, and write *weather* in the center and weather-related words in the surrounding circles. Review responses with students, reading aloud for students to repeat.

If students have a limited vocabulary of weather words, provide them with a list of weather words and pictures. For example, you might include *sunny, windy, rainy, cold, warm, wet, dry,* and *cloudy* on the list. Encourage students to share additional weather words they are familiar with.

Interact with Text

As you read *What Will the Weather Be?* periodically stop to assess students' level of understanding of how weather is predicted.

If . . . students are having difficulty understanding how meteorologists predict weather,

then . . . explain that meteorologists use cause-and-effect relationships to predict weather.

Explain how people use what they know to help them make predictions, or guesses, about what will happen next. Reread the text, and point out that the author tells us the effect of cold and warm fronts. Explain that meteorologists locate cold and warm fronts (the causes) so they can tell people what weather to expect (the effects). Guide students to examine facts that lead to a prediction. Ask: What does the text tell us about cold fronts? (A cold front is cold air pushing against warm air. A cold front moves fast and causes sudden storms.) What can you predict will happen when a cold front moves in? (It will cause a quick rain or snowstorm.)

STRUCTURE

As you read, periodically stop to assess students' understanding of how the pictures help explain the explicit information in the text.

If . . . students are having difficulty understanding the explicit information provided in the text,

then . . . model how to relate the text to the picture on the page.

For example, have students turn to pp. 12–13 and look at the illustration while you read aloud the text. Then reread the text aloud a second time, modeling how you can trace the illustration with your finger. Point out that the illustration explains the text you are reading. Read aloud the first sentence on p. 12: Where cold air pushes against warm air, we say there is a cold front. As you read, trace the blue arrow that is labeled *cold air* to the point of the label for *cold front.* Continue for the remainder of the page, pointing out how the illustration helps better explain the text.

ENGLISH LANGUAGE LEARNERS

Use gestures, along with text illustrations, to aid students' understanding of unfamiliar words and processes. For example, as you read aloud *Where cold air pushes,* push your hands forward and have students mime and say "push."

STRUGGLING READERS

To help students maintain newly learned vocabulary, have them create a glossary of domain-specific terms they learned from the text. Give students a piece of paper with blank squares drawn on it. Have them draw a picture of a term and write a word, if they are able to, inside each square.

LANGUAGE CONVENTIONALITY AND CLARITY

Students may need additional support with understanding domain-specific vocabulary in this selection. Guide students to use the text to help define new words.

If . . . students have difficulty understanding new vocabulary,

then . . . reread context clues in the text.

For example, after reading p. 12, say: We learned the meanings of some new words on this page. One word is *vapor.* Let's read the sentences that tell about vapor: "The rising air carries water. The water is not a liquid. It is a gas called water vapor." What are some things we learned about vapor? Encourage students to respond using the word *vapor.* For example: Vapor is made of water. Vapor is not a liquid. Vapor is a gas.

KNOWLEDGE DEMANDS

As you read, stop periodically to assess whether students are grasping the new and challenging ideas about instruments, air pressure, and fronts in *What Will the Weather Be?*

If . . . students are struggling to understand scientific concepts related to weather and the study of weather,

then . . . have students carefully analyze the weather illustrations to support understanding.

For example, show how the illustration on p. 13 helps explain what happens when a cold front meets warm air. Point to each part of the illustration, and tell what it depicts. Say: Everything colored pink is air. The shape colored blue is the cold front. The puffy shapes are clouds. The blue arrow inside the cold-front shape shows that the cold front is pushing toward the air. The pink arrow shows the air is going up and around the cold front. See how clouds are forming above the cold front? What are these clouds made of? (drops of water) Have a volunteer point to the water drops in the illustration.

Express and Extend

EXPRESS Remind students that *What Will the Weather Be?* is about how people predict the weather. Review the various instruments detailed in the text, focusing on their uses. Create a list of ways meteorologists predict the weather.

EXTEND Have students choose a weather instrument from the text and draw a picture explaining how the instrument helps predict weather.

STRUCTURE

EXPRESS Guide small groups to discuss examples of causes and effects from *What Will the Weather Be?*

If . . . students have difficulty understanding how temperature, air pressure, humidity, and wind speed affect weather,

then . . . use the Cause and Effect Routine and Graphic Organizer in Part 3 to examine relationships. For example, in the Cause box write *weather data.* Ask: What happens after meteorologists study weather data? (They can predict the weather.) Record students' responses in the Effect box.

EXTEND Have students create a weather journal in which they can record their own weather observations throughout the unit. Have students compare their observations with information learned in the text. Work with them to determine cause-and-effect relationships within their observations. For example, if they observed a warm breeze and wispy clouds followed by a light rain and warm weather, help them relate that a warm front caused the light shower and warm weather. Help students label or write captions for the various drawings in their journals.

ENGLISH LANGUAGE LEARNERS

To practice weather words, such as *cold, warm, shower, drizzle, wind, humid, rain, snow,* and *sunny,* print them on index cards. Have partners take turns choosing a card and acting out or describing the word for the other to guess.

STRUGGLING READERS

As students discuss causes and effects of weather and weather-related instruments, remind them to refer to the word walls started at the beginning of the lesson for support, as needed.

MORE SUPPORT

EXPRESS Talk about Sentences and Words

Display the following sentence from *What Will the Weather Be?* and read it aloud to students.

Weather forecasts tell us what kind of weather is coming.

Discuss the meaning of this sentence. Say: One of the words in this sentence means almost the same thing as *predictions.* What word is it? *(forecasts)* What do weather forecasts predict? (the kind of weather that is coming)

TEAM TALK Remind students that predictions are guesses based on things we know. Discuss how weather forecasts are similar to predictions. Encourage students to use related words such as *meteorologist, weather, forecast,* and *prediction* in their responses. Then have students turn to a partner and make a prediction about tomorrow's weather using *forecast* in their response.

EXTEND Have partners look at the weather forecast today and compare it with today's weather. Then have them illustrate their prediction about the weather forecast for tomorrow. Have them write a sentence that explains their illustration. Provide them with the following sentence frame: The forecast for tomorrow is ___. Follow up by comparing their forecasts with tomorrow's actual weather to see if their predictions were correct.

KNOWLEDGE DEMANDS

EXPRESS Ask students to describe a time during this lesson when they used pictures from *What Will the Weather Be?* to help them understand something explained in the text.

If . . . students have difficulty recalling a specific illustration,

then . . . revisit the explanation of a hygrometer on p. 21. Guide students to describe what the illustration shows and tell what the illustration helps explain.

EXTEND Have students draw a picture that helps explain a weather-related idea from *What Will the Weather Be?* Encourage students to present their illustrations to the class.

ACCELERATED LEARNERS

Help students use a news source to find out what the weather will be over the coming week. Then invite them to explain any weather changes that are predicted, using facts they learned from *What Will the Weather Be?*

MORE SUPPORT

Unlock the Text

QUALITATIVE MEASURES

Levels of Meaning	facts and details explain weather vocabulary and basic weather-related concepts; wide range of weather topics covered
Structure	definitions and examples; sequence; cause and effect (explaining formation of rain, snow, clouds)
Language Conventionality and Clarity	many domain-specific (content-area) words, most of which are directly defined
Knowledge Demands	factors that affect temperature and weather

Prepare to Read

LEVELS OF MEANING

The main purpose of *Weather Words and What They Mean* is to define weather-related terms while also explaining the science behind weather forecasting.

STRUCTURE

PREVIEW Have students preview the illustrations for *Weather Words and What They Mean.* **Ask:** What kinds of weather are shown in the illustrations? Encourage students to use weather words they know. Then point out the speech bubbles in the illustrations. Tell students that when text appears in these shapes, it indicates that someone is speaking. The person speaking may be a character shown in the illustration or it may be a character not shown in the illustration. Using the first page of the

ENGLISH LANGUAGE LEARNERS

Have students Think-Pair-Share their ideas with a partner before asking them to respond to questions during whole-class discussions.

STRUGGLING READERS

If you created word walls during *What Will the Weather Be?*, consider keeping them posted during the reading of *Weather Words and What They Mean.* Encourage students to refer to the previous word walls, as needed, and add to them as new terms are introduced during reading and discussion.

selection, show how *It's beginning to SNOW* in the speech bubble points toward the character who is speaking. Have students point to additional examples of speech bubbles in the text.

LANGUAGE CONVENTIONALITY AND CLARITY

PREVIEW VOCABULARY Use the Learn New Words Routine in Part 3 to assess what students know about words such as the following: *fair, changes, causes, oceans, motion, rises, cool, mild, chilly, forms, freezes, surface, develops, damage.*

CRITICAL VOCABULARY Preteach domain-specific vocabulary words, such as *temperature, weather, forecast, air pressure, moisture, seasons, wind, storm,* and *earth.* Introduce critical vocabulary using visual aids, such as pictures, photographs, and video clips.

Use the Vocabulary Activities and Games in Part 3 to support understanding.

KNOWLEDGE DEMANDS

ACTIVATE BACKGROUND KNOWLEDGE Ask students to share one thing they know about weather. Ask: Have you ever heard someone talk about a weather forecast? How would you describe what the weather is like today?

To support understanding of different weather-related words, model describing an experience you had with unusual weather. For example, say: I visited the desert last year. Before I went to the desert, I thought it would be hot all the time. I was wrong! During the day, it is hot, but there is no humidity, so the air feels dry. You don't sweat much. Then at night, the sun goes down, and it gets freezing cold. Sometimes it even snows! Deserts have some very interesting weather.

STRUGGLING READERS

Some students may find it confusing that an informational text includes speech bubbles. With students, review the key features of informational texts. Then explain that although this text includes illustrations and speech bubbles, its primary purpose is to teach readers about weather-related words and ideas.

Interact with Text

Students may be challenged to understand all the weather-related terms and concepts. Help students analyze the text for explanations and information to provide meaning.

Remind students that when a text explains something, it includes reasons, facts, and examples that help readers understand how that something happens. Then reread the section of text that explains air pressure, and ask questions, such as: When does high air pressure happen? (It happens when air particles are close together.) What is an example of what happens when there is high air pressure? (It brings fair weather.) What is a reason fair weather happens when there is high air pressure? (The air is usually cool and dry.)

STRUCTURE

As students read, periodically stop to assess their ability to use the text's structure to help them understand concepts explained in the text. Remind students to listen for reasons, facts, and examples during the reading. Explain that they can listen for clue words, such as *when, is called,* and *if.* These words often indicate that a fact or explanation will follow.

If . . . students are having difficulty with the definition-and-examples format,

then . . . encourage them to use the illustrations to follow the text and comprehend new ideas.

For example, using the third page in the "Moisture" section, read the paragraph, and then discuss how the illustration on this page supports, or helps explain, the information in the paragraph. Point to each part of the illustration, and read aloud its captions. Then ask questions, such as: What do the arrows show? (They show that the warm air goes up into the clouds.) What does the warm air take with it? (moisture or vapor)

MORE SUPPORT

ENGLISH LANGUAGE LEARNERS

Whenever possible, use realia, models, and pantomime to reinforce the meanings of new words. For example, to help students understand what the words *spiral-shaped* and *funnel-shaped* mean, allow them to see and hold objects with these shapes, such as funnel and spiral pastas or a small kitchen funnel and a spring.

STRUGGLING READERS

Some students may get lost with the number of concepts introduced on a page. Concentrate on one familiar concept at a time, such as snow, and use the text to stimulate discussion of students' experiences.

LANGUAGE CONVENTIONALITY AND CLARITY

If students are having difficulty understanding new weather terms, help them define the terms in their own words, using context clues from the text and illustrations. For example, after reading about rain, ask students to tell about different kinds of rain in their own words. Ask students to listen carefully as you reread the page. Following the second reading, ask: What size are the raindrops in a drizzle? (very small) Which is longer: a shower or rain? (rain) What can happen if it rains for a long time? (There can be a flood.) Which kind of rain do you think is the most dangerous? Why? (Possible responses: a rainstorm because there are strong winds with the rain; a thunderstorm because there is thunder and lightning)

KNOWLEDGE DEMANDS

Students may need additional support to understand factors that affect temperature. Use the Web Routine and Graphic Organizer in Part 3, and have students contribute their ideas about temperature to clarify meaning.

Display the graphic organizer. Write *temperature* in the middle circle, and draw a thermometer beside it to help students remember the word's meaning. Then, as factors affecting temperature are encountered in the text, prompt students to retell the new information. Record their responses in the web, using both words and drawings to help represent them. For example, when reading about how temperature rises and falls, you might note *sun up = temperature up* along with a quick sketch of a sun coming up over the horizon. Draw an "up" arrow beside the sun to clarify which direction the sun is moving. Then draw a thermometer beside the sun. Show that the thermometer is registering a higher temperature by shading it almost to the top and drawing another "up" arrow beside it.

If . . . students have a hard time understanding how a thermometer measures temperature,

then . . . provide a thermometer and lead students in observing how it changes when placed in ice water and then placed in the sun or another warm spot.

STRUGGLING READERS

Help students internalize the meanings of words by categorizing them. For example, Temperature: *warm, hot, chilly, cold;* Rain: *drizzle, shower, rainstorm, flood, thunderstorm, thunder, lightning, rainbow;* Snow: *snowflakes, flurries, sleet, snowstorm, blizzard;* Wind: *gusty, breezy, windy, gale, hurricane, tornado.*

Express and Extend

EXPRESS Ask: What are some new things you learned about why the weather changes? If students are not able to respond effectively, write on chart paper the following sentence starter: *I learned that one reason weather changes is ___.* Reread parts of the book and ask students to identify reasons, facts, or examples in each part that help explain why the weather changes. Record students' responses and draw pictorial representations, as appropriate.

EXTEND Have students discuss the current day's weather. Ask them to describe the weather right now. Then have them predict how the weather will change in the evening. Tell students to provide one fact, reason, or example that helps explain their prediction.

STRUCTURE

EXPRESS Show students the illustrations on the pages about rain, and remind them that the illustrations help explain the meanings of the terms *drizzle, shower, rain,* and *rainstorm.* Define each term in random order, using the text from the page. Then have volunteers point to the picture that represents the term. Ask students to explain how they know the picture matches the definition.

> **If . . .** students have difficulty matching pictures to definitions,
>
> **then . . .** ask guiding questions about the illustrations, such as: How does the shower illustration show that a shower is brief? (The sun is already peeking out from around the rain cloud.)

EXTEND Ask students to draw a picture that shows one of the weather-related terms they read about, such as *tornadoes* or *lightning*. Tell them to include as much detail as possible. Then have pairs exchange pictures and explain what the pictures show. Have students refer to the text to find supporting evidence.

MORE SUPPORT

ENGLISH LANGUAGE LEARNERS

To help students describe the weather, provide sentence frames, such as: ___ is wet (Rain). ___ is cold (Snow). As needed, guide students in choosing the word to complete each sentence. Then have them draw pictures showing what the sentences mean.

STRUGGLING READERS

Provide sentence starters to help students use correct grammar when forming responses, such as: The weather will become ___ tonight (colder). This is what happens when the sun goes ___ (down).

LANGUAGE CONVENTIONALITY AND CLARITY

EXPRESS Talk about Sentences and Words

Display the following sentences from *Weather Words and What They Mean.* Read it aloud to students.

> Snow falls to the earth in different ways. Flurries are when it snows lightly. A snowstorm is when a lot of snow falls. It can be windy.

Discuss the meaning of this passage. Ask: Which has more snowflakes, flurries or a snowstorm? (a snowstorm) When might it be windy, during flurries or during a snowstorm? (during a snowstorm)

TEAM TALK Have partners share experiences they have had with snow. Ask students to describe what they remember about the temperature and wind during the snowfall they are describing.

If . . . students have trouble recalling snowfall or have little experience with this type of weather,

then . . . display photographs or play videos of snow falling, snowstorms, and flurries for students to describe.

EXTEND Reread the pages on temperature and discuss with students what the temperature is like when it snows. Ask: What causes snow to melt? (the sun; a warm temperature) What must the temperature be like in order for it to snow? (It must be cold.)

KNOWLEDGE DEMANDS

EXPRESS Have students tell some things they have learned from *Weather Words and What They Mean* about why the temperature changes. Read aloud p. 8, and ask students to restate the cause-and-effect relationship. Ask: What makes the temperature go up? (The sun heats the air.) What happens to make the temperature go down? (The sun sets, and the air cools off.) Provide time for students to practice what they will say to a partner, using the following sentence frames: I learned that temperature goes up when ___. I learned that temperature goes down when ___.

EXTEND Tell students to think about what they learned about why the temperature changes. Then ask them to think about something they still want to know about how weather changes are predicted. Ask students to dictate a question that asks for the information they want to know.

ACCELERATED LEARNERS

Help students use the Internet and other resources to find answers to questions generated during discussions about weather changes. Ask them to present their findings to the group.

Learning About Each Other and the World

TEXT SET

ANCHOR TEXT
I Love Saturdays y
domingos

SUPPORTING TEXT
Apple Pie 4th of July

TEXT SET

ANCHOR TEXT
Making Music

SUPPORTING TEXT
Clothes in Many Cultures

Unlock the Text

QUALITATIVE MEASURES

Levels of Meaning	different cultures; implicit meaning that multiple cultures can come together; importance of family
Structure	first-person narrative; predictable, parallel text; multiple methods of telling about events
Language Conventionality and Clarity	use of both English and Spanish languages; some unfamiliar Spanish words defined in context and through illustrations
Knowledge Demands	relationships with grandparents; being bilingual; English, Spanish, and Native American cultures

Prepare to Read

LEVELS OF MEANING

I Love Saturdays y domingos is a first-person narrative told by a young girl. The story describes the parallel events that take place on Saturdays with her paternal grandparents and on Sundays, or *domingos* (the Spanish word for *Sundays*), with her maternal grandparents. The story explores life in a multicultural family and how people across cultures share similarities, such as how they love and celebrate their families.

STRUCTURE

PREVIEW Preview the text structure with students, pointing out similarities and differences between the left side and the right side of facing pages. Explain that *I Love Saturdays y domingos* tells about a girl's weekend adventures with her grandparents. Explain that on the left side of the page they will read about Saturdays and on the right side about *domingos.*

ENGLISH LANGUAGE LEARNERS

Write *Saturday/Saturdays* and *Sunday/Sundays* on the board. Point to and pronounce each word. Explain that sometimes when -*s* is added to a word to form the plural, it sounds like /z/. Share other examples of plural words with the -*s* ending that sounds like /z/, such as *days, eggs, owls,* and *balloons.*

STRUGGLING READERS

If students have difficulty thinking of activities they enjoy doing with their grandparents or other family members, remind them to use the illustrations in the book as a guide. Lead students on a picture walk to help spark ideas for their responses.

The events on Saturdays and *domingos* are very similar. One text difference is the author's use of Spanish words set in italics on the pages about *domingos* with *Abuelito* and *Abuelita*.

LANGUAGE CONVENTIONALITY AND CLARITY

PREVIEW VOCABULARY Use the Learn New Words Routine in Part 3 to assess what students know about the following words: *serves, spongy, collection, hatched, aquarium, pressed, pier, nibbling, bouquet, soars, delivered, traditional, serenade.*

DOMAIN-SPECIFIC VOCABULARY Use the Vocabulary Activities and Games in Part 3 to assist students in better understanding domain-specific vocabulary, such as *Saturday, Sunday, domingo, grandma, grandpa, abuelita, abuelito, piñata.*

KNOWLEDGE DEMANDS

ACTIVATE BACKGROUND KNOWLEDGE Discuss with students the concept of spending time with grandparents and other family members, and have students share activities they enjoy doing with their grandparents or other family members. Make a list of their responses. Ask: What are some special activities that you like to do with your grandparents or other family members? Do you have a favorite place to visit with your grandpa or grandma? Do you have special days that you get to spend with your grandparents? What other family members do you spend time with?

Before students get started, model describing your relationship with your grandparents. Say: When I was younger, I would spend weekends at my grandparents' house. My grandma and I would bake cookies and then frost them. Sometimes we made cookies that looked like people in our family. My grandpa and I loved taking walks to see how many birds we could find. While we were walking, I enjoyed listening to my grandpa's stories about when he was a young boy.

ENGLISH LANGUAGE LEARNERS

Collect photographs of different families. If students have difficulty keeping track of the family members in the story, display a picture of a family with parents and two sets of grandparents. Draw a simple family tree identifying the family members: *mother, father, grandma, grandpa.* If students need more help, repeat this exercise with other pictures of families.

MORE SUPPORT

Interact with Text

As you read *I Love Saturdays y domingos,* periodically stop to assess students' level of understanding of the meaning of the story and its key details. Have students cite text evidence or picture evidence to support their statements.

> **If . . .** students are having difficulty understanding the meaning of the story,
>
> **then . . .** help them relate sections of the text to the main idea stated on the first page.

For example, after reading about how the narrator visits Grandma and Grandpa on Saturdays and Abuelita and Abuelito on Sundays, ask: Why is Saturday special to the narrator? (She visits Grandma and Grandpa.) Why is Sunday special to the narrator? (She visits Abuelita and Abuelito.)

STRUCTURE

Point out the parallel story events to show how the time the narrator spends with Grandma and Grandpa is both similar to and different from the time she spends with Abuelita and Abuelito.

Use the Venn Diagram Routine and Graphic Organizer in Part 3 to help students organize the similarities and differences in the text. Begin by focusing on one event from the story—for example, breakfast. Label one circle *Grandpa and Grandma* and the other circle *Abuelito and Abuelita.* Label the center section *Both.* Work with students to record details about the event on the Venn diagram. Help students repeat this activity with partners or in small groups for another event in the story.

ENGLISH LANGUAGE LEARNERS

Display facing pages that contain common elements, such as the pages that tell about the circus movie and the trip to the real circus. Have students point to two things that are alike on the pages, such as the mother elephant and the baby elephant. For each pair, say the English and Spanish name of the object for students to repeat.

STRUGGLING READERS

Help students follow the back-and-forth structure of the story by writing *Saturday* and *domingo* on the board. Place an arrow pointing to the day you are reading about. Switch the arrow when the day in the story switches.

LANGUAGE CONVENTIONALITY AND CLARITY

Students may struggle with the presence of both English and Spanish within this text.

If . . . students have difficulty understanding the Spanish text,

then . . . point out times when the Spanish words and phrases mirror the English words and phrases.

For example, after reading about the animals Grandma and Abuelita like, point out that the narrator likes to count both Grandma's owls and Abuelita's chicks. Say: The narrator counts twelve owls. How do we count to twelve in English? Write each numeral on the board as you say each number aloud: One, two, three, four, five, six, seven, eight, nine, ten, eleven, twelve. The narrator also counts at Abuelita's house. What does she count? (chicks) When the narrator counts chicks, she also counts to twelve, but she counts in Spanish: *uno, dos, tres, quatro, cinco, seis, siete, ocho, nueve, diez, once, doce.* As you count aloud in Spanish, point to the numeral that corresponds with each word. For example: *uno* (1), *dos* (2), *tres* (3).

If some students speak Spanish, encourage them to share their knowledge of the language with non-Spanish-speaking students. Consider pairing Spanish-speaking students with non-Spanish-speaking students during activities.

KNOWLEDGE DEMANDS

Explain that culture is the way in which a group of people do certain things. Discuss different ways people are divided into groups: by where they are from, by the languages they speak, or by the traditions they practice. Ask students to refer to the text for answers to the following questions. Say: The narrator's grandparents come from different cultures. What language do Grandma and Grandpa speak? (English) What language do Abuelita and Abuelito speak? (Spanish) Then say: In some ways, the narrator's grandparents are different, but they are also alike in many ways. How are Abuelita and Grandma alike? (Sample response: They both like birds.) How are Abuelito and Grandpa alike? (Sample response: They both like fish.)

Express and Extend

EXPRESS Explain that the most important ideas in *I Love Saturdays y domingos* have to do with how families from different cultures share characteristics and life experiences. Ask: How do we know that Grandma and Grandpa are similar to Abuelita and Abuelito? (All of them love their families and have similar interests.)

If . . . students are not able to name ways that Grandma and Grandpa are similar to Abuelita and Abuelito,

then . . . ask guiding questions to help students recall similarities between the two sets of grandparents. For example, say: Who likes to tell stories? (both Grandpa and Abuelito) Both Abuelito and Grandpa came from places outside of the United States. Where does the text say that Abuelito came from? (Mexico) Where does Grandpa come from? (Europe)

EXTEND Use the Two-Column Chart Routine and Graphic Organizer in Part 3 to create a list of ways in which both sets of grandparents show they care for their granddaughter. List the actions of Grandma and Grandpa on the left and the actions of Abuelita and Abuelito on the right.

STRUCTURE

EXPRESS Explain that the story's structure changes at the end of the story. Help students recognize that up until the narrator's birthday, Grandma and Grandpa are always on the left page, and Abuelita and Abuelito are always on the right page. Ask: How is the last event different for the little girl from the other events in the story? (Both sets of grandparents come to her house for her birthday.) How is her birthday party an example of the way her family celebrates both cultures? (They have unique elements of each culture, such as the birthday song and the *piñata*.)

If . . . students are unable to tell how the birthday party differs from the previous events in the story,

then . . . have students recall the activities the girl did separately with each set of grandparents. Ask them to give examples of ways in which the party is different from the previous events. Have students use words from the text in their responses.

EXTEND Have students draw a picture that shows how characters from *I Love Saturdays y domingos* are the same or different. After they are finished, help them label their drawings *same* or *different*. Provide time for students to discuss their drawings with partners.

MORE SUPPORT

ENGLISH LANGUAGE LEARNERS

To help students discuss what the narrator does at each house, provide sentence frames, such as: At Grandma and Grandpa's house she likes to ___. At Abuelita and Abuelito's house she likes to ___.

STRUGGLING READERS

Remind students that context clues can help them determine the definition of unfamiliar words. Pause at challenging words and model rereading surrounding sentences to locate contextual clues. Have students use the context clues found to give definitions in their own words.

LANGUAGE CONVENTIONALITY AND CLARITY

EXPRESS Talk about Sentences and Words

Display the following sentences from *I Love Saturdays y domingos* and have students follow in their books as you read the sentences aloud:

> We gather together to break the *piñata* that my Mom has filled with candy and gifts. *Abuelito* is holding the rope to make the piñata go up and down.

Circle the word *piñata* and ask: What clues in the text tell us what a piñata is? (It is filled with candy and gifts, and they have gathered to break it. Abuelito is holding a rope to move it up and down.) After they have defined the word, ask students to find an item in the illustration they think represents the piñata.

TEAM TALK Have partners answer the following question: What clues in the picture help us know what a piñata is? (The girl is holding a bat to the piñata in order to break it, and Abuelito is holding a rope tied to the piñata. These clues help us know that a piñata is something people play with at parties.)

EXTEND Have students use context clues and illustrations to figure out the meanings of other words in the text.

KNOWLEDGE DEMANDS

EXPRESS Revisit the list of activities from the Activate Background Knowledge section on p. 85 of this handbook. Use the Venn Diagram Routine and Graphic Organizer in Part 3 to compare the activities from the classroom list with the activities in the story. Discuss the many types of activities one can do with special family members.

EXTEND Have students write or dictate a letter to their grandparents or another special family member telling them about an activity they would like to do with them on their next visit. Have students include a drawing of themselves doing the activity with their grandparents or family member.

ACCELERATED LEARNERS

Have students create picture flashcards for some of the Spanish words in the story. Help students use context clues and illustrations to determine the Spanish words' definitions. Provide a children's Spanish dictionary as an additional reference. Examples of words to use include: *abuelito, abuelita, piñata, rancho, el circo, elefanta*.

Unlock the Text

QUALITATIVE MEASURES

Levels of Meaning	learning to balance two cultures
Structure	first-person narrative; chronological order; explicit connections among events
Language Conventionality and Clarity	clear, common language; some unfamiliar vocabulary defined in context and through illustrations; domain-specific vocabulary related to time and numbers
Knowledge Demands	concept of time; Fourth of July; multicultural families

ReadyGEN●●●
Text Collection

Apple Pie 4th of July,
pp. 5–32

Prepare to Read

LEVELS OF MEANING

Apple Pie 4th of July is a first-person narrative told by a young Chinese-American girl. By describing a day at work with her parents on the Fourth of July, the story chronicles the girl's changing feelings about her family's Chinese heritage and about embracing American traditions.

STRUCTURE

PREVIEW Explain that *Apple Pie 4th of July* is a story told by a young girl in chronological order, or time order. Discuss how the girl helps readers understand when the events of the story happen by using time-order words such as *yesterday, now, noon,* and *two o'clock.* As an example, read aloud these sentences from p. 6: "Even on Thanksgiving we open the store. Even on New Year's Day. Even today, the Fourth of July."

ENGLISH LANGUAGE LEARNERS

Show students pictures of fireworks displays and Fourth of July parades. Explain that July 4 is a holiday celebrating the birthday of the United States. Encourage students to discuss similar holidays to make connections to the text.

STRUGGLING READERS

Although the author doesn't directly use words to portray the feelings of the young girl, the illustrations help to express her feelings throughout the day. Have students describe the feelings of the young girl, using the illustrations as a reference. (p. 17, bored; p. 18, sad; p. 32, happy)

Then ask: When does this story take place? What word or words from the text tell you? (The story takes place on the Fourth of July. The words *today* and *the Fourth of July* tell me when the story takes place.) Start a word wall of time-order words and add *today* to it. As students read, help them add to the word wall other time-order words from the text. Use these words as a reference to help students follow the chronology of the story.

LANGUAGE CONVENTIONALITY AND CLARITY

PREVIEW VOCABULARY Use the Learn New Words Routine in Part 3 to assess what students know about the following words: *Thanksgiving, Christmas, New Year's Day, Fourth of July, parade, customers, straighten, hungry, swinging, expect, rooftop, beyond, crowd, fireworks, Chinese, American.*

DOMAIN-SPECIFIC VOCABULARY Use the Vocabulary Activities and Games in Part 3 to assist students in better understanding domain-specific vocabulary, such as ___ *o'clock, fifty-two, hundred, noon, today, days, week,* and *year.*

KNOWLEDGE DEMANDS

ACTIVATE BACKGROUND KNOWLEDGE Discuss with students what they know about the Fourth of July. Ask: Why do Americans celebrate the Fourth of July? What are some things that happen during a Fourth of July celebration? Create a web of students' responses.

Before students get started, model describing something you know about the Fourth of July: The Fourth of July is an important day in American history because it was the day the United States declared its independence. This happened on July 4, 1776, more than 200 years ago. Since then, Americans have celebrated Independence Day every year on the same day. Americans celebrate the Fourth of July to remember the importance of freedom and independence. This holiday also gives Americans a time to have fun together while showing pride in their country. Some ways Americans have fun on the Fourth of July include marching in parades, having picnics, and watching fireworks displays.

Interact with Text

LEVELS OF MEANING

As you read *Apple Pie 4th of July,* explain to students that the young girl is convinced that she knows more about American culture than her parents do. As you read p. 19, point out to students the following passage: "My parents do not understand all American things. They were not born here." Explain that the girl's parents are immigrants, which means they were born in another country and then permanently moved to America. Then ask: Based on what you know from the text, where were the girl's parents born? (China) Display a world map or globe and point out China and how far it is from the United States.

STRUCTURE

Explain to students that they can better understand the sequence of events in a story by identifying time-order words used in the text, which show how time passes. In this story, the author orders events with the construction ___ o'clock. Read aloud these sentences: "One o'clock, and they buy ice cream. Two o'clock. The egg rolls are getting hard. Three o'clock. Ice and matches. Four o'clock, and the noodles feel like shoelaces."

Explain that *o'clock* means "of the clock" or "according to the clock." Provide students with a simple copy or drawing of an analog clock face. Point out that the numbers are arranged in numeric order. Point to each number on the clock and say the time aloud. For example: One o'clock, two o'clock, three o'clock. Then ask students to identify examples from the text of events that happen in the story, based on time-order words. For example, ask: What happens at one o'clock in the afternoon? (The store customers buy ice cream.) What happens at two o'clock? (The egg rolls are getting hard from being left out.) How do you know that time is moving forward? (It goes in order: first one o'clock, then two o'clock.)

MORE SUPPORT

ENGLISH LANGUAGE LEARNERS

Display an analog clock in the front of the room, and adjust the hour shown as the story progresses. Have students take turns repeating the times in the story and adjusting the clock to show understanding.

STRUGGLING READERS

If students continue to struggle with the concept of traditions, point out that it is a tradition for many Americans to celebrate the holidays mentioned in *Apple Pie 4th of July.* Connect the idea of traditions to students' lives by asking them to tell how their families celebrate holidays each year.

LANGUAGE CONVENTIONALITY AND CLARITY

Students may struggle with some unfamiliar words in this text. Remind them to use context clues and illustrations to understand the words. For example, students may be unfamiliar with the term *chow mein*. Think aloud to remind them how to use context clues to understand the meaning of *chow mein*. Read aloud these sentences: "I smell apple pie in Laura's oven upstairs and—chow mein in our kitchen. Chow mein! Chinese food on the Fourth of July?" Then say: I know from reading the first sentence that chow mein is something the narrator can smell in the kitchen. The narrator's third sentence tells me that chow mein is a type of Chinese food. Model reading the second and third sentences fluently to accentuate the exclamation and the question. Explain that the third sentence defines the second sentence. Chow mein is one of the Chinese foods that the narrator doesn't believe Americans will want to eat on the Fourth of July. Point to the illustration on pp. 10–11 to show how noodles and vegetables for the chow mein are being prepared. Have students use context clues and illustrations to define other unfamiliar words as they encounter them.

KNOWLEDGE DEMANDS

The young narrator in *Apple Pie 4th of July* is struggling to balance her family's Chinese culture with the American culture in which she is growing up.

If . . . students struggle to understand the narrator's viewpoint about the differences between Chinese and American cultures,

then . . . show students how categorizing information will help them understand how it is related, or goes together. Use the Two-Column Chart Routine and Graphic Organizer in Part 3 to compare American culture with Chinese culture.

For example, ask: What are some examples of the foods the narrator views as not American? (chow mein, sweet-and-sour pork, egg rolls, noodles) What are some examples she views as American? (apple pie, soda, potato chips, ice cream) Record students' responses on the chart using words or pictures. Also, discuss differences between how the narrator's family observes holidays commonly celebrated in the United States and how the narrator sees other Americans observe these holidays.

Express and Extend

EXPRESS The most important idea in *Apple Pie 4th of July* is that American culture is a mixture of many cultures. Explain that all families have traditions that stem from their cultural backgrounds. Lead a discussion about family traditions, and make a class list of the students' favorites. Provide an example for students, such as: I enjoy celebrating St. Patrick's Day with my family. My grandmother came to America from Ireland. On St. Patrick's Day, she makes traditional Irish soda bread.

Help students make a list of Chinese and American traditions the narrator mentions in the text. Use the Venn Diagram Routine and Graphic Organizer in Part 3 to show similarities and differences in the traditions of each culture, referring to the text for support.

EXTEND Have students draw a picture of themselves and their family celebrating their favorite tradition. Then have students write or dictate a sentence describing their drawing.

STRUCTURE

EXPRESS Remind students that using a graphic organizer will help them understand the order of events in a story. Use the Story Map A Routine and Graphic Organizer in Part 3 to illustrate the main events from the beginning, middle, and end of the story for students. Then use the Talk to a Friend Routine in Part 3 to give students practice explaining the sequence of events in a story to a partner.

EXTEND Have students draw a picture of an event of their choice from the story. Then help them appropriately label the event *Beginning, Middle,* or *End* to show when in the story the event happened.

ENGLISH LANGUAGE LEARNERS

Guide students to use examples from their own lives to better understand new words such as *tradition*. Provide a definition and a sentence starter: My family's tradition is ___. Model an example from your own life, such as: My family's tradition is to go ice fishing every Saturday in the winter.

STRUGGLING READERS

To reinforce the concept of tradition, have students list the events in the story that are part of the Fourth of July celebration. Connect the idea of traditions to students' lives by asking them to share how their families celebrate different holidays. Provide the sentence frame: My family's tradition is ___.

EXPRESS Talk about Sentences and Words

Display the following sentence from *Apple Pie 4ᵗʰ of July* and read it aloud:

So, I straighten the milk and the videos and sample a few new candy bars until five o'clock.

Discuss the meaning of the sentence. Ask: What is the girl doing? (She is straightening up the store.) Why do you think she is doing this? (She is keeping busy because there are only a few customers.) How many are a few? (not many; two)

Discuss the meaning of the word *sample* in the sentence. Ask: What did the girl do when she sampled a few new candy bars? (She ate them.) What are some other words you could use for *sample*? (*try out, taste, nibble, test, eat*) Use each synonym in the sentence to determine which ones make the most sense or have the most precise meaning.

TEAM TALK Have students replace *sample* with another word that does not change the meaning of the sentence and say it with a partner, using the sentence frame: I ___ a few new candy bars.

EXTEND Ask students to write or dictate a sentence about something they would like to sample. Use the sentence frame: I would like to sample ___. Have students illustrate and share their sentences with a partner.

KNOWLEDGE DEMANDS

EXPRESS Introduce the concept of a time line by drawing a large analog clock on chart paper. From each hour on the clock, beginning at noon, extend a line to write the event that happens at that hour. Model finding the event for noon from the text. On the line extending from 12, write *customers buy soda and chips*. Have students work with a partner to find answers for the remaining hours.

EXTEND Have students create a similar time line that illustrates the events in their own school day. Have students begin the time line when school starts in the morning and end it when school is dismissed.

ACCELERATED LEARNERS

Have students make up a story about how the narrator's Fourth of July would have been different if her parents had closed the store that day. What would the family have done? Have them write their story and include a drawing. Then have students share their stories with the class.

Unlock the Text

QUALITATIVE MEASURES

Levels of Meaning	informational text; music; musical instruments, cultures
Structure	clear main idea with supporting details; table of contents; headings, illustrations, and labels supporting text; step-by-step directions
Language Conventionality and Clarity	many simple sentences and some complex sentences; domain-specific vocabulary; glossary definitions
Knowledge Demands	familiar topic of music, musical instruments, cultures

Prepare to Read

LEVELS OF MEANING

Making Music is an informational text that introduces students to music and musical instruments. The text includes subtopics, such as *Instruments Around the World* and *Ways to Play*, that explore different aspects of music. The text identifies different kinds of musical instruments, ways of playing music, the benefits of music, and directions for making an instrument.

STRUCTURE

PREVIEW Remind students that an informational text provides facts and details about a topic. Read the title of the text. Ask: Think about the title. What do you think this text is about? (music) Yes, this book is about music. It is divided into chapters. Each chapter tells something about

ENGLISH LANGUAGE LEARNERS

Reinforce the word *music* by playing a piece of music or humming a tune. Explain that students have just listened to music. Repeat the word several times. For some students, the words for *music* in their home languages and in English are cognates, so they will understand the English word.

STRUGGLING READERS

To help students understand the purpose of the table of contents, model how to find a specific chapter in the text. Point to the second entry. The title of this chapter is "Musical Instruments." It begins on page 4. Have students turn to p. 4.

music. We can look at the table of contents to find out the name of each chapter and the page that it begins on. **Display the table of contents. Read the first entry including the page number.** The first chapter is named "A Part of Our Lives." It begins on page 2. **Turn to p. 2.** The name of the chapter is in large orange letters on the page. Read the title as you point to the words. Remember that this book is about music. Think about the title of the chapter—"A Part of Our Lives." What do you think this chapter is about? (Music is a part of our lives.)

LANGUAGE CONVENTIONALITY AND CLARITY

PREVIEW VOCABULARY Use the Learn New Words Routine in Part 3 to assess what students know about the following words: *music, culture, voice, important, instrument, world, bells, note, memory, stomp, hum.* Use pictures where appropriate to support meaning.

Use the Vocabulary Activities and Games in Part 3 to provide practice with the vocabulary words in meaningful contexts.

KNOWLEDGE DEMANDS

ACTIVATE BACKGROUND KNOWLEDGE Display the cover of the book. The cover shows a boy playing a drum. A drum is a musical instrument. Ask students to name other musical instruments. Record their responses in pictures or words on chart paper. Encourage students to page through the book and identify instruments shown in the pictures. Guide students to understand that each kind of instrument has its own sounds and the instruments can be played alone or with other kinds of instruments to make music. Save the chart for later use.

Interact with Text

LEVELS OF MEANING

The text notes that music is an important part of people's lives. Emphasize that people everywhere enjoy music, although the form and the sound of the music may differ from place to place and age to age. Remind students that they have opportunities to enjoy music at home and in school. Discuss the kinds of music you enjoy in class, such as traditional nursery songs and seasonal songs. If possible, play a variety of music, including classical pieces, music from other cultures, and familiar tunes. Talk about how all of the music is alike and different.

STRUCTURE

Lead a discussion about how the photographs—some with labels—support the written text. Begin the conversation by discussing the labeled photographs on pp. 4 and 5 and their connection to the written text: The text says that most music is made with musical instruments, and there are many kinds of musical instruments. What do the pictures show? (children playing a piano, a guitar, a recorder, and a violin) How do the pictures help us understand the words? (The text says there are many kinds of instruments, and the pictures show some of them.) Read the picture labels. What do the labels tell readers? (the names of the instruments shown)

Turn to p. 9 and point to the photograph of the girl playing the panpipes as you read the text. The text tells us about playing the panpipes. How does the photograph support the words? (It shows panpipes, so a reader knows what they are. It also shows what the words say about playing the panpipes.)

ENGLISH LANGUAGE LEARNERS

Students may be familiar with the term *note* as it relates to a written message but not as it relates to music. Point to the word *note* on p. 13 and give its glossary definition. Discuss the notes in the illustration, explaining that they are symbols for musical sounds to play or sing.

STRUGGLING READERS

As students encounter unfamiliar words, use the pictures as clues to the meanings of unfamiliar words as well. For example, p. 8 says that some children play ankle bells. If students are unfamiliar with the word *ankle*, point to the picture. Look at where the bells are. They are around the boy's ankles. The ankle connects the leg to the foot. Show me your ankle.

LANGUAGE CONVENTIONALITY AND CLARITY

Understanding the meanings of words is critical to understanding a text. *Making Music* includes a glossary that defines several words in the text. Explain what a glossary is. You may not know the meanings of all the words in this book, so this book has a section called a glossary. A glossary lists words and their meanings. When we read this book, we will see some words in dark type. These words are the words that are in the glossary. Turn to p. 13 and read aloud the first sentence as you point to the words. Then run your finger under the word *note* and repeat the word. Look at this word. It is in dark type. That means we will find its meaning in the glossary. Turn to the glossary and read the meaning—*note, a musical sound*. Return to p. 13 and reread the second sentence. The word *note* has many meanings. What does the word *note* mean in this book? Yes, *note* is a musical sound. Look at the picture. The picture shows a sheet of musical notes. They stand for the sounds a player would play on an instrument. Knowing the meaning of the word *note* helps us understand the text.

If . . . students have difficulty identifying words that are in the glossary,

then . . . point to the words as you read them and turn to the glossary and read the definition.

KNOWLEDGE DEMANDS

Define *cultures* and discuss how music is related to cultures. Explain that a culture is the way of life of a group of people. A people's way of life includes how they live, what they wear, what they eat, their customs, and their arts such as music, dance, and painting. The text explains that all cultures enjoy music, but people in different cultures may make music in different ways and use different instruments. Turn to the chapter "Instruments Around the World" beginning on p. 8. Explain that this chapter tells about instruments people from different cultures use. As you read the information on each page, have children examine the picture showing an instrument being played.

Express and Extend

EXPRESS Ask students what the book is all about. (music) Remind them that each chapter tells a big idea and details about music. Review the chapters with children to help them identify what they learn about music. Do this by rereading each chapter, using the chapter title as its big idea, and helping students identify details in the chapter. You may want to create an idea web for each chapter by writing its big idea in the center circle and then listing details in the outer circles.

If . . . students have difficulty providing key details for a chapter's big idea,

then . . . guide them to use the photographs as clues to details.

EXTEND Assign partners a chapter from the book. Have the partners ask and answer questions about what their assigned chapter says about music. Partners should take turns asking each other a question and answering it. Encourage them to use the photographs in the chapter as prompts for generating questions.

STRUCTURE

EXPRESS Discuss the structure of the last chapter in the book. Tell students that this chapter tells how to make a drum. Turn to the list of materials on pp. 20–21. These pages show pictures of the materials needed to make a drum. The label with each picture tells what it is. Point to the numbered directions. Look at the numbered steps on these pages. The steps tell us what to do first, next, and last to make a drum. How many numbered steps are there?

EXTEND The pictures on pp. 22 and 23 depict a child following some of the steps. Tell students that they can draw their own pictures to go with each step. Then assign a step to each child in a group of five. Have the students draw pictures of their assigned steps and dictate or write simple directions to go with their pictures. Then bind the drawings of group members together to make a booklet.

MORE SUPPORT

ENGLISH LANGUAGE LEARNERS

The word *step* is a multiple-meaning word. As you discuss making a drum, explain that the directions are written in numbered steps. Each numbered step tells something you do to make the drum.

STRUGGLING READERS

Use a reread-and-question strategy to help students identify details related to a chapter's big idea. For example, reread the second paragraph on p. 8. Then ask: What do some children use to play music? (ankle bells) How do they play the ankle bells? (by moving their feet)

EXPRESS Talk about Sentences and Words

Display and read aloud the following sentence from *Making Music:*

Some children play the ankle bells.

Review with students that a complete sentence tells who or what does something (subject of the sentence) and what the person or thing does (predicate of the sentence). Read the sentence and ask: Who is doing something? (some children) What are the children doing? (playing ankle bells) Reread the sentence. Did I just read a complete sentence? How do you know? (Yes. It tells who does something and what they do.)

TEAM TALK Display and read the sentence: *Some children play the panpipes.* Ask partners to discuss whether the sentence is a complete sentence. Encourage them to answer these questions: *Who is doing something? What are they doing?* From their responses, they should conclude that the sentence is complete.

> **If . . .** students have difficulty identifying complete sentences,
>
> **then . . .** provide short example sentences and draw a line between the subject and predicate.

EXTEND Write the subject *Some children.* Ask students to tell whether you have written a complete sentence. Then guide them to complete the sentence by adding what the children do. If necessary, provide examples, such as *Some children take music lessons.*

EXPRESS Display the chart identifying musical instruments. Read the list and remind students that they saw pictures of children playing many of the instruments by hitting them, plucking strings, pressing keys, or blowing into them. Work with students to organize the instruments on the chart by the way they are played.

EXTEND Assign each small group a way of playing an instrument, such as hitting it. Write a heading, such as *Instruments Played by Hitting,* on a large sheet of paper. Then have students in the group draw or find pictures of instruments played that way. Have them display their pictures on the sheet of paper.

ACCELERATED LEARNERS

Have students choose one of the following instruments: ankle bells, clapsticks, panpipes, tribal drums, chapchas. Then supervise students in an Internet search to find out where the instrument is played. Help them locate and label that place on a map. Have students share their findings with the class.

Unlock the Text

QUALITATIVE MEASURES

Levels of Meaning	informational text; explicit purpose is to convey factual information about clothes
Structure	clear organizational text; maps and photographs directly support and help interpret words on the page
Language Conventionality and Clarity	mainly simple sentences and simple language style; vocabulary mostly defined in context and supported by photographs
Knowledge Demands	idea that clothes represent cultures

ReadyGEN
Text Collection

Clothes in Many Cultures, pp. 33–51

Prepare to Read

LEVELS OF MEANING

Clothes in Many Cultures is a straightforward informational text telling when and why certain clothing is worn, while also reflecting the culture of the wearer.

STRUCTURE

PREVIEW Have students preview the text. Then display pp. 36–37. Ask: What do you see on this spread? (a sentence, a map, a photo of people) Let's look at pages 38 and 39. What do you see on this spread? (a sentence, a map, a photo of people) How is this spread like the last one? (They are set up the same—a sentence, a map, a photo of people.) Lead students to see that the format of each spread is the same.

MORE SUPPORT

ENGLISH LANGUAGE LEARNERS

Using your clothing, students' clothing, and any classroom dress-ups, help students identify common types of clothing, such as boots, sweaters, and shorts. Point to an article of clothing and say its name. Then have students say and repeat the name.

STRUGGLING READERS

Remind students that *tradition* is a word they have encountered while reading other texts for this unit. Ask them to describe in their own words what a tradition is. (a way of doing things that has been passed down within a group of people)

LANGUAGE CONVENTIONALITY AND CLARITY

PREVIEW VOCABULARY Use the Learn New Words Routine in Part 3 to assess what students know about the following words: *culture, parkas, sarongs, office, business suits, rancher, sturdy, traditional, fancy, powwows, kilts, ceremonies, different.*

KNOWLEDGE DEMANDS

ACTIVATE BACKGROUND KNOWLEDGE Have students share what they know about the different purposes of clothes and ask: What kinds of clothes do you wear when you play? What kinds of clothes do you wear to school? What kinds of clothes do you wear on special occasions, such as weddings or holidays? Do you wear certain types of clothing in different seasons?

Before students get started, model describing something you know about how clothes reflect different activities: I wear special clothes to go to the beach. For example, I wear a bathing suit that dries quickly when I am not in the water. I wear plastic sandals that won't get ruined by the sand. I also wear a tunic over my bathing suit to keep the sun off my shoulders when I am sitting on the beach. The tunic is a long shirt made of light cotton fabric that helps me stay cool in the sun.

STRUGGLING READERS

Display pictures of several types of unusual clothes. Ask students in what culture or climate they think the type of clothing might be worn, and have them explain why they think that.

MORE SUPPORT

Interact with Text

LEVELS OF MEANING

Remind students that nonfiction texts provide information. While you are reading, ask questions to gauge students' understanding of the purposes of clothing. Lead students in a discussion about how weather and circumstance affect clothing choices. For example, ask: Why do people in Kenya wear sarongs on hot days? (Sarongs help to keep them cool.) When do Scottish men wear kilts? (They wear kilts at parades and in ceremonies.)

STRUCTURE

As you read, pause to discuss the photographs and maps within the text structure. Guide students to see how the photographs support the text and that without them, the text would be less clear. For example, look at pp. 36–37 and ask: What does the photograph on page 37 show? (It shows three people wearing heavy coats in the winter.) Read aloud the text on p. 36 and then ask: What is a parka? (It is a heavy coat to wear on cold winter days.)

Guide students to understand that the photographs and maps clarify the text. Ask: Without looking at the photograph, would you know what a parka looks like? (No, I could only guess that it is something heavy like a coat that keeps people warm.) Without looking at the map, would you know where people typically wear parkas? (No, I could only guess that people wear parkas in places that are cold.)

If . . . students have trouble connecting the photographs, maps, and text,

then . . . repeat the discussion activity using the text, maps, and photographs on pp. 38–39 (sarongs), pp. 40–41 (business suits), and pp. 42–43 (jeans).

MORE SUPPORT

ENGLISH LANGUAGE LEARNERS

Remind students to ask clarifying questions when they do not understand something. Provide question frames, such as: What does ___ mean? Can you repeat that please? Why do the people wear ___?

STRUGGLING READERS

To internalize meaning, have students use their own words to tell how clothing is related to culture. Remind students to think about where people live and the purposes for each type of clothing.

LANGUAGE CONVENTIONALITY AND CLARITY

Guide students to use contextual clues and photographs to help clarify word meanings.

For example, display the following sentence on the board and read it aloud: "Sarongs keep people cool on hot days." Circle the word *sarongs*. Ask: What does the text tell you about sarongs? (They keep people cool on hot days.) Underline the words *keep people cool on hot days*. Ask: What does the photograph show you about sarongs? (They look like a piece of cloth that you wrap around your body.) Point to the map and explain that Kenya has many warm days because of intense heat from the sun. Ask: How might a sarong keep someone cool? (It protects a person's skin from the sun.)

If . . . students have difficulty identifying a sarong,

then . . . provide additional pictures of sarongs. You may wish to provide a 36-inch long piece of cloth for students to wear like a sarong. Instructions for wrapping and tying a sarong can be found on the Internet.

KNOWLEDGE DEMANDS

As you read *Clothes in Many Cultures,* periodically stop to assess students' understanding of how clothing relates to culture.

If . . . students are having difficulty relating these two ideas,

then . . . help them understand how clothing reflects the place in which it is worn and the activities for which it is worn.

For example, when reading the "Traditional Clothes" section on pp. 44–49, point out the differences between the various traditional clothing. Remind students that if something is traditional, it is handed down from previous generations. Explain that the photographs show special clothing that is worn for special occasions. Discuss similarities and differences between the clothing in the photographs and the clothing students wear to weddings, ceremonies, and parades.

ENGLISH LANGUAGE LEARNERS

Encourage students to draw a type of clothing they might wear on a special occasion, and ask volunteers to share their drawings in small groups. Display the pictures on the wall and create a clothing collage.

MORE SUPPORT

Express and Extend

EXPRESS Use the Speak in a Group Routine in Part 3 to have small groups answer questions about which types of clothing people wear in different situations. For example: Would someone in Kenya wear a parka? Why or why not? (No, it is too hot in Kenya for a parka.) Would a Scottish man wear a kilt to work? (No, Scottish men wear kilts on special occasions.)

If . . . all the students in a group are not getting a chance to speak,

then . . . provide a decorated "talking stick" for students to pass around. Explain that only the student holding the stick may speak.

EXTEND Have students choose their favorite type of clothing discussed in the text and write or dictate a sentence telling when they would wear that type of clothing. For example, I would like to wear a kilt during a parade.

STRUCTURE

EXPRESS Show students a two-page spread from *Clothes in Many Cultures.* Have them name the text features shown on the spread and tell how each feature helps them understand what the text describes. For example, display pp. 44–45. Read the text aloud. Point to the map and ask: What does this map tell us about the bride and groom? (They live in India.) Then point to the photograph and ask: How does this photograph help you understand the text? (It shows the fancy clothes a bride and groom in India wear.)

EXTEND Give students a blank piece of paper, folded in half to resemble a book. On the left side, have students write or dictate a sentence telling what clothes they wear to school. Students can draw or trace a map underneath their sentence to show where they live. Then have students draw a picture of themselves in their school clothes on the right side.

MORE SUPPORT

ENGLISH LANGUAGE LEARNERS

Support students as they discuss text features by providing sentence starters, such as: This is a ___. It shows ___.

STRUGGLING READERS

Reinforce students' understanding of text structures by pointing to the heading "Work Clothes" on p. 40. Remind students that headings organize the information in the text. Point out work-related words on pp. 40 and 42. Create a word wall with students that displays words grouped according to each of the headings as a reference.

LANGUAGE CONVENTIONALITY AND CLARITY

EXPRESS Talk about Sentences and Words

Display and read aloud the following sentence from *Clothes in Many Cultures.*

Ranchers wear sturdy jeans when they work outside.

Circle the word *sturdy* and underline *when they work outside.* Discuss the types of clothes students wear when they play outside. Compare those clothes with clothes they wear for special occasions. Ask: Would you be allowed to wear fancy clothes to play outside at the park? Why or why not? (No, they would get messy or torn.) The rancher is putting a horseshoe on a horse. He needs to wear clothes that are sturdy. When might you wear sturdy clothes? (when going to the park or playing outside) Remind students that context clues can be used to help understand new words. Sturdy clothes are tough, strong clothes that can be worn outside, where they can get dirty and won't wear out easily. *Sturdy* means "strong."

TEAM TALK Have students turn to a partner and say the sentence, using a word that means the same as *sturdy.*

EXTEND Have students use context clues and background knowledge to determine the definition of *fancy* on p. 44. Then have them create a list of words that can replace *fancy* in the sentence.

KNOWLEDGE DEMANDS

EXPRESS Ask students to tell how *Clothes in Many Cultures* shows the similarities among people of different cultures. (Sample response: It shows how people in all cultures dress for their work, play, and special occasions.) Use the Two-Column Chart Graphic Organizer in Part 3 to create a list that compares the clothing in the text with the clothing that students wear. Label one column *Other Cultures* and the other column *Our Class.* Students should compare the clothing in the text with clothing they would wear. For example, when thinking of hot days, students might say: "In Kenya people wear sarongs. I wear shorts and a T-shirt."

EXTEND Have students use the two-column chart as a guide to complete a Venn diagram. Have them label one circle *Other Cultures* and the other circle *My Family.* Have them label the center *Both.* The Venn diagram will give students the opportunity to think about the similarities and differences between the clothing worn in other cultures and the clothing their families wear, not just what their classmates wear.

ACCELERATED LEARNERS

Provide additional texts about different cultures for students to read. After reading, have students report to the class about how the text was similar to or different from *Clothes in Many Cultures.*

Knowing About
Patterns and Structures

TEXT SET

ANCHOR TEXT
The Tiny Seed

SUPPORTING TEXT
Jack's Garden

TEXT SET

ANCHOR TEXT
Plant Patterns

SUPPORTING TEXT
Swirl by Swirl

Unlock the Text

QUALITATIVE MEASURES

Levels of Meaning	explicit: how a seed travels in the wind, lands in soil, and becomes a plant; implicit: perseverance and basic needs of plants
Structure	illustrations to support the text; chronological order
Language Conventionality and Clarity	simple and compound sentences; domain-specific vocabulary; conjunction words *and, but*
Knowledge Demands	basic needs for plant growth; plants and their life cycle; seasons

Prepare to Read

LEVELS OF MEANING

The Tiny Seed follows the events in the life of a seed blown by autumn winds toward its fate of becoming a flower. The tiny seed shares its journey with other seeds, some of which are bigger, faster, and stronger. But not all seeds will realize their purpose—to become full-grown plants and make more seeds. While learning about the life cycle of a plant and the basic needs of seeds, readers are also gently introduced to the theme of perseverance.

STRUCTURE

PREVIEW Have students preview the cover, title, and illustrations to make a prediction about the text. Ask: What clues do the title and illustrations provide to help you predict what this book will be about? What do you think will happen to the tiny seed? (It will become a flower.)

ENGLISH LANGUAGE LEARNERS

To help students activate background knowledge about seeds and plants, provide pictures, diagrams, or real seeds and plants for students to examine prior to reading. If possible, plant seeds in the classroom at the beginning of this unit and monitor their progress in a journal.

STRUGGLING READERS

Write *seed* on the board, read it aloud, and help students segment the phonemes. Point out that when two *e*'s are together in a word, they usually have the long *e* sound. Brainstorm other words with the long *e* sound spelled *ee*, such as *need, peek, deep,* and *bees.* Have students keep a list of these words and add to it as they read.

LANGUAGE CONVENTIONALITY AND CLARITY

PREVIEW VOCABULARY Use the Learn New Words Routine in Part 3 to assess what students know about the following words: *Autumn*, *Winter*, *Summer*, *Spring*, *seed*, *tiny*, *burn*, *sail*, *melt*, *drown*, *desert*, *dry*, *burst*, *break*, *leaves*, *bud*, *giant*, *sway*, *bend*, *seed pod*, *petals*, *shake*.

Use the Vocabulary Activities and Games in Part 3 to provide practice with the vocabulary words in meaningful contexts.

KNOWLEDGE DEMANDS

ACTIVATE BACKGROUND KNOWLEDGE Activate background knowledge by asking students what they know about a plant's life cycle. Ask: Where do plants come from? Where do plants grow? What do plants need to grow? Write student responses on chart paper. Post this list in the classroom and refer to the list as necessary while reading the selection.

Interact with Text

LEVELS OF MEANING

As you read, check students' understanding of the meaning and purpose of the text by asking guided questions. For example, ask: What is this story about? (a tiny seed that is trying to grow) What happens to some of the seeds? (Some of the seeds are not able to grow.) Guide students in understanding why some of the seeds are not able to grow (some float too close to the sun; some fall in the water; some are eaten). Knowing what happens to some of the other seeds, what words, aside from *tiny,* could you use to describe the seed? (*strong, lucky, brave*)

If . . . students do not know the meaning of *tiny,*

then . . . display two familiar objects, such as a large ball and a marble. Lead students in describing the marble in relation to the ball, using words such as *little, small, dinky.*

STRUCTURE

The illustrations offer a vivid representation of the main text. Encourage independence by having students look at each new illustration to predict the text prior to reading aloud. Be sure to have students first look to find the tiny seed and then assess the rest of the illustration to predict what will happen. Give students time to observe the illustration and think of their response. Then allow partners to take turns sharing their predictions with each other. Have partner A give a prediction first; then on the next page, allow partner B to give a prediction first.

If . . . students have difficulty expressing their predictions,

then . . . provide sentence frames, such as: I think the tiny seed will ___. I think another seed will ___.

ENGLISH LANGUAGE LEARNERS

Support students' understanding of seasons by providing photographs clearly depicting each season and comparing them with the illustrations in the book. Help students understand the differences in temperature and the varying effects on plants in each season.

STRUGGLING READERS

To help students understand and use the conjunctions *and* and *but* properly, have students describe an object as having a color *and* shape. Then have students describe the same object as having a certain color *but* not another color. Help students see that *and* joins items and *but* tells how they are different.

LANGUAGE CONVENTIONALITY AND CLARITY

Students may struggle to understand how the ideas presented in some of the longer, more complicated sentences are connected. Display these sentences from the text and read them aloud.

> One seed drifts down onto the desert. It is hot and dry, and the seed cannot grow. Now the tiny seed is flying very low, but the wind pushes it on with the others.

Underline or point to the words *and* and *but*. Then discuss how these words help connect ideas in the sentences. For example, the word *and* links these two ideas: *the desert is hot and dry; the seed cannot grow.* When these ideas are linked, it is clear that the seed cannot grow *because* the desert is hot and dry. The word *but* links these two ideas: *the tiny seed is flying low; the wind pushes the seed on with the others.* When these ideas are linked, it is clear that the seed is not low enough to drop from the air; it is still high enough to be carried by the wind.

KNOWLEDGE DEMANDS

As you read *The Tiny Seed,* use a four-column chart to help students observe how the seed develops during each season. Use each season name as a heading in the chart. As you read, pause after a season in the life of the seed to make notes about what happened to the seed during that season. Have students summarize what they have learned in their own words so that you can write it in the chart.

At the end of the selection, help students understand how the life cycle begins again with new seeds. Ask: What does the wind cause the flower to do at the end of the story? (open its seed pod to release its seeds into the wind) What do you think will happen to these seeds? (They will be carried in the wind until they land on the ground to become flowers.) Knowing where these seeds come from, where do you think the tiny seed came from in the beginning of the story? (the seed pod of a full-grown flower)

If . . . students have difficulty predicting the origin of the tiny seed,

then . . . reread the last page and then the first page, and discuss how the seeds come out of the seed pod (last page) and blow in the wind (first page), emphasizing how the story flows like a circle.

Express and Extend

EXPRESS One of the implicit themes from *The Tiny Seed* involves survival. Lead a discussion about how the tiny seed was able to survive all the dangers to seeds and plants when many of the other seeds were not able to survive. Ask: Does the tiny seed fly the highest of all the seeds? (No.) What happens to the seed that flies highest? (The sun burns it.) What happens to the largest seed? (The bird eats it.) Does the tiny seed grow the fastest of all the seeds? (No.) What happens to the seeds that grow fastest? (They get stepped on or picked.) Why might it be surprising to readers to find out that the tiny seed not only survives but also becomes the largest of all the flowers? (The seed is the smallest and takes the longest to grow.)

EXTEND Remind students that some stories help the reader learn a lesson. Lead students to connect the events in the story to infer a lesson that people can learn from reading *The Tiny Seed.* (Possible response: Even the smallest things can become great in time.)

STRUCTURE

EXPRESS Read the following excerpt and discuss the chronological order of events:

> But what is happening? First there are footsteps. Then a shadow looms over them. Then a hand reaches down and breaks off the flower.

Have students tell what happens first, next, and last, and explain how they know.

If . . . students have difficulty understanding the sequence of the passage,
then . . . help students decipher clue words for sequencing in the passage, such as *first* and *then*.

EXTEND Have students summarize the story using sentences with the sequencing words *first*, *next*, *then*, and *last*. For example: First, the tiny seed blew in the wind. Next, the tiny seed landed on the ground. Then, the tiny seed grew into a giant flower. Last, new seeds blew in the wind.

ENGLISH LANGUAGE LEARNERS

Draw a quick sketch of each event from the Structure excerpt (feet/footprints; shadow on the ground; hand reaching down). Have students order the pictures chronologically and tell about each event using the sentence frames: First, ___. Next, ___. Last, ___.

STRUGGLING READERS

To help students understand how to use a thesaurus, provide them with a definition of *synonym*. Then work together to make lists of similar words that might be interchangeable. Explain that when we write, we want to give our writing interest, and synonyms help us do that without using the same word over and over.

LANGUAGE CONVENTIONALITY AND CLARITY

EXPRESS Talk about Sentences and Words

Display this passage from *The Tiny Seed,* and read it aloud with students:

But the tiny seed sails on with the others.

Discuss the meaning of the sentence. Ask: What does the word *sails* mean? ("flies") Why do you think the author used the word *sails* instead of *flies?* (to make it sound more interesting and precise) Use a thesaurus to find additional words with the same meaning as *sails,* such as *flies, drifts, glides, floats, tumbles,* and so on. Use each word in the sentence above, and have students echo read each new sentence.

TEAM TALK Have partners discuss which word they would use instead of *sails.* Have students restate the sentence to a partner using the word of their choice.

EXTEND Repeat the activity with the word *giant* and words with the same meaning, such as *big, large, huge.* Have students substitute *giant* in the following sentence from the text: "It is a giant flower."

KNOWLEDGE DEMANDS

EXPRESS Using the text as a reference, create a list of needs for a plant to grow. Prompt students to review reasons other seeds were unable to grow and draw conclusions about what a plant needs in order to grow successfully. For example, ask: Why was the seed unable to grow in the desert? (It was too hot and dry.) What does that tell you about what seeds need to grow? (less sun and more water) Were there any other seeds that did not have the right amount of sun or water? (Yes, one plant was hidden from the sun and rain by a weed, and it could not grow.) As students prove the needs of plants with evidence from the text, record the needs on chart paper.

EXTEND Ask students to write or dictate a sentence telling their opinion about why the flower grew to be so big. Have them begin by using this sentence starter: I think the seed was able to grow into a giant flower because ___. Have students use text evidence to support their opinion.

ACCELERATED LEARNERS

Have students draw a prediction of what will happen to the seeds that blew out of the giant flower's seed pod at the end of the story. Then have students write a word, phrase, or sentence describing their prediction. Allow students to use the text and pictures to help make their predictions.

MORE SUPPORT

Unlock the Text

QUALITATIVE MEASURES

Levels of Meaning	explicit: the growth of a young boy's garden; implicit: in-depth gardening and animal vocabulary provided by illustrations and labels
Structure	cumulative, repeating verse; in-set illustrations contribute to understanding of text; labeled outer drawings are not referenced in the main text
Language Conventionality and Clarity	lengthy sentence to be read in rhythmic fashion; repetitive verse; use of *that* as repetition in text
Knowledge Demands	general knowledge of gardening; things that live in and around the soil and plants in a garden

Jack's Garden, pp. 5–26

Prepare to Read

LEVELS OF MEANING

Jack's Garden is written as a cumulative, repeating verse that explains the various stages of growth in a garden and the animals that interact with the garden. The labeled illustrations provide additional vocabulary words related to gardening.

STRUCTURE

PREVIEW Have students preview the text and illustrations. Ask: What clues about the subject of this text do the illustrations show? (The illustrations show a garden with lots of plants, insects, and birds. So the subject of this story is probably gardens.) Discuss with students the smaller illustrations in the margins. Point out the labels with the names of

ENGLISH LANGUAGE LEARNERS

The extensive vocabulary displayed on each page may seem overwhelming. Remind students that the author includes pictures with labels to provide additional information. Read the labels for students as they point to the pictures to help them associate the word to the picture.

STRUGGLING READERS

Help students who do not have firsthand experience with gardening build background knowledge. Review information discussed earlier in the unit, provide pictures of gardens, and allow students who have experience with gardening to share their knowledge.

gardening tools and supplies as well as the insects and birds commonly found in gardens. Ask: Do you see anything special about the words in the text? (The word *that* is used on almost every line.) Explain to students that some of the words in the text will repeat often.

LANGUAGE CONVENTIONALITY AND CLARITY

PREVIEW VOCABULARY Use the Learn New Words Routine in Part 3 to assess what students know about the following words: *garden, planted, soil, seeds, seedlings, sprouted, plants, grew, buds, formed, flowers, blossomed, insects, sipped, nectar, chased.*

Use the Vocabulary Activities and Games in Part 3 to provide practice with the vocabulary words in meaningful contexts.

KNOWLEDGE DEMANDS

ACTIVATE BACKGROUND KNOWLEDGE Ask students to share what they know about gardening. Ask: What is a garden? What are some examples of things you might find in a garden? What do plants in a garden need to grow?

Before students get started, model describing something you know about gardening: My grandma had a big garden when I was little. She grew vegetables, including tomatoes, zucchini, and beans. She also grew flowers like zinnias and marigolds. She used a long hose to spray water on her plants to help them grow. And she built a low fence around her garden to help keep away rabbits that liked to eat her plants. Once her vegetables were fully grown, she picked them from the garden and used them to make food that she shared with the whole family.

Interact with Text

LEVELS OF MEANING

As you read *Jack's Garden,* periodically stop to assess students' understanding of the steps Jack takes to grow his garden. As you introduce each step, take a moment to discuss the illustrations and how they contribute to the understanding of the step. For example, after reading aloud p. 8, pause to discuss the illustration on pp. 8–9. Say: The text says this is the soil. What do you see in the picture that helps you better understand what soil is? (dirt and rocks) What animals are living in the soil? (insects, worms, and other animals that live underground)

STRUCTURE

Students may find it difficult to connect the labeled illustrations with the main text on the page. Explain to students that even though the main text doesn't always say something specific about the illustrations, the illustrations are still providing additional information.

Help students make the connection between the information provided by the main text and the information provided by the illustrations. Read aloud the following sentence from p. 6: "This is the garden that Jack planted." Ask: What illustrations do you see in the margins of pages 6 and 7? (gardening tools: rake, hose, trowel, garden claw, pruning shears, watering can, and hoe) Ask: How are these tools related to the garden that Jack planted? (They are the tools he used to plant his garden.) Say: The labeled illustrations are similar to a picture dictionary of things related to gardening.

If . . . students struggle to understand how the main text is connected to the labeled illustrations,

then . . . repeat the activity above on a different spread of text. Help students understand that the labeled illustrations on each spread relate to the text on that spread.

ENGLISH LANGUAGE LEARNERS

Remind students to refer to the interior frame of the illustrations to help them with unfamiliar words in the text. For example, on pp. 14–15 help students understand that seedlings are the young plants that are just beginning to grow, which are shown in the illustration.

STRUGGLING READERS

The repetitive and predictable text will help struggling readers. As you read aloud the story, guide students to recognize the text pattern by asking them to choral read the repeating phrases of the text. Explain that the only new text on each spread is in the first few lines.

LANGUAGE CONVENTIONALITY AND CLARITY

Each page in the story contains a single sentence that the author builds upon as the story continues. A new subject is added to the beginning of the sentence on each new page, causing the sentence to grow longer. As you read, point out for students that the author has written this lengthy sentence in the form of a verse and that the reader should take a tiny pause at the end of each line. Model for students as you read first, and then have students mimic the proper rhythmic way of reading.

If . . . students have difficulty understanding the rhythmic verse,

then . . . have students join you in a back-and-forth rhythm of reading the selection. For example, as you read aloud, have the students say the portion of the text in parentheses: This is the (rain) that wet the (seeds) that fell on the (soil) that made up the (garden) that (Jack planted).

KNOWLEDGE DEMANDS

Students may not be aware of the insects and animals that live in and around a garden. Guide students to recognize that the illustrations show the types of things that live in soil and are attracted to the plants in a garden. As you read, point out features in the illustrations that help demonstrate the relationships between the living things. For example, point out the robin eating the earthworm on p. 15. Ask: Why is the robin in the garden? (to eat a worm) Then point out the butterflies sipping nectar from the flowers on pp. 22–23 and ask: Why are the butterflies in the garden? (to drink the nectar) Why do the butterflies and the robin come to the garden? (for food)

Express and Extend

EXPRESS The illustrations and labels elaborate on the information provided by the main text, identifying vocabulary words related to gardening. Have students help sort the words into categories, such as *Insects*, *Birds*, and *Plants*. For example, reread pp. 18–19 and discuss the types of plants and insects shown on the spread. Have students distinguish between the plant and insect pictures and labels to sort the words into two separate lists. Create the lists on chart paper for the class as students determine the category for each pictured item. Help students with pronunciation as needed.

> **If . . .** students have trouble categorizing the living things,
>
> **then . . .** explain that an insect is a very small animal with six legs and that a plant grows out of the ground and may have leaves or flowers. Point out that both insects and plants are living things.

EXTEND Have students add to the lists any additional vocabulary that was not in the text or labels. Perhaps students know of a type of plant, insect, or bird that was not pictured. Have students determine which list the vocabulary word should be added to and provide a description or photo of the plant or animal to help the class understand what it looks like.

STRUCTURE

EXPRESS Discuss the structure of the text, specifically how the text grows on each new page and repeats some text from the previous pages. Then review the text structure of *The Tiny Seed* from earlier in the unit. Discuss how the text is written as a story, following the tiny seed along its journey. Use the Venn Diagram Routine and Graphic Organizer in Part 3 to compare the structure of *Jack's Garden* with the structure of *The Tiny Seed*.

> **If . . .** students have difficulty understanding the differences in text structures,
>
> **then . . .** hold both texts side-by-side and point out the differences visually and verbally.

EXTEND Have students write or dictate a sentence telling which of the texts they preferred. Have students base their answer on the structure of the text and provide a reason for their opinion. Provide the sentence frame: I like ___. It has ___ in it.

ENGLISH LANGUAGE LEARNERS

When sorting the vocabulary into categories, remind students to refer directly to the illustrations in the text. Draw a simple example picture next to the title of each list so students may compare it with the illustrations. Model how to point to an illustration and then compare it with the example pictures on the list.

STRUGGLING READERS

To help students who are overwhelmed by the length of the text, have them copy a repeating phrase such as *made up the garden*. Then have students find the phrase in the text. Repeat the activity with other phrases to show students how to break text into manageable chunks.

LANGUAGE CONVENTIONALITY AND CLARITY

EXPRESS Talk about Sentences and Words

Display the following sentence from pp. 14–15 of *Jack's Garden* and read it aloud with students:

> These are the seedlings / that sprouted with the rain / that wet the seeds / that fell on the soil / that made up the garden / that Jack planted.

Discuss the repetition of the text. Point out that the word *that* is repeated in the text. Reread the first line, running your finger under each word as you say it. Ask: What is this sentence about? (seedlings) Circle *seedlings* and explain that what the sentence is about is the subject of the sentence. Reread the first and second lines together. Ask: What action did the seedlings do? (sprouted) Underline the word *sprouted.* Say: What did the seedlings do? The seedlings sprouted.

TEAM TALK Draw a box around the phrase *the rain that wet the seeds*. Have small groups answer the following questions: What is the subject? (rain) What does the rain do? (The rain wets the seeds.)

EXTEND Write simple sentences on the board that describe pictures in the text, such as *Jack digs* and *Bumblebees fly*. Have students identify the subject and action in each.

KNOWLEDGE DEMANDS

EXPRESS Discuss with students the items they need to grow their own garden. Brainstorm a list of the items as a class, and then decide on the necessary steps to begin a new garden. For example: 1. Rake the soil. 2. Plant the seeds. 3. Water the soil. 4. Watch and wait for your plants to grow!

EXTEND Have students draw a picture of their garden and write or dictate sentences telling what they would grow. Provide students with the following sentence frame: I would grow ___ in my garden.

ACCELERATED LEARNERS

Have students draw five boxes on a piece of drawing paper. Ask them to draw the five steps, one in each box, that show the sequence in which a flower in Jack's garden grows. Have them use evidence from this text and previous texts to determine the steps. Have students add captions and labels to each drawing. Encourage students to share their sequence with a partner.

Unlock the Text

QUALITATIVE MEASURES

Levels of Meaning	informational text; explicit purpose to provide awareness of patterns in nature
Structure	headings; table of contents; glossary; index
Language Conventionality and Clarity	simple and compound sentences with some complex sentence constructions; domain-specific vocabulary
Knowledge Demands	general patterns; specific details about patterns; plants and nature

Prepare to Read

LEVELS OF MEANING

Plant Patterns is an informational text that explores color and shape patterns, as well as patterns of growth, in both familiar and exotic plants. The author provides examples of both natural and human-made patterns.

STRUCTURE

PREVIEW After students have had a chance to preview the photographs, ask: What will this text be about? (plants) Will the text be real or make-believe? (real) How do you know? (It has photographs of real plants.) Point out that *Plant Patterns* is organized into sections, and each section has a heading and a main idea. Remind students that a main idea is what the text is mostly about. Preview the headings in the table of contents with students and discuss how these headings provide clues to the main ideas in the book.

ENGLISH LANGUAGE LEARNERS

Support students' understanding of the terms *stripes*, *spots*, *colors*, and *shapes*. Provide a variety of pictures that represent each term. Create a picture word wall to display examples of the terms. Have students describe and classify each picture and name the category in which it belongs.

STRUGGLING READERS

Help students understand the importance of paying attention to headings as they read. Remind them that headings tell the main idea for that section of the text. Review additional features of headings in comparison with the running text, such as the size and color, to help students differentiate between the two types of text.

PREVIEW VOCABULARY Use the Learn New Words Routine in Part 3 to assess what students know about the following words: *pattern*, *repeat*, *shade*, *stripes*, *prickly*, *spines*, *rows*, *spiral*, *scatter*, *burst*, *swirl*, *stalk*, *fern*, *blossom*, *kernel*, *sprout*.

Use the Vocabulary Activities and Games in Part 3 to provide practice with the vocabulary words in meaningful contexts.

ACTIVATE BACKGROUND KNOWLEDGE Ask students to share what they know about patterns. Ask: What are some examples of patterns? What are some things in our classroom that have patterns on them? Create a class list of patterns found in the classroom to display on the wall. Tell students to use vocabulary words when possible.

Before students get started, model describing something you know about patterns: One of my favorite patterns is a polka dot. Polka dots are solid colored circles that repeat over and over again. Each circle has the same amount of space around it, and each circle is the same size. Show students some examples of polka dots.

STRUGGLING READERS

During the preview, ask students to describe the photographs using adjectives. Remind students to describe the colors, textures, and shapes, such as pink flowers, prickly spines, or round tree rings. Discuss how adjectives help readers gain more information about nouns, or naming words, in the text.

Interact with Text

LEVELS OF MEANING

Have students explain the characteristics of informational texts and tell why *Plant Patterns* is a good example of an informational text. (Informational texts have facts and real information; *Plant Patterns* has photos and facts about real plants.) Record student responses in a visible place. Then ask: Why do people read informational texts? (to learn about something new; to get more information about a topic they are interested in)

If . . . students have difficulty describing the characteristics of informational texts,

then . . . review the features of informational texts and have partners discuss whether those features are present in *Plant Patterns.*

Ask: What are facts? (true statements; information) Where in the book can we find facts? (in the text and photographs) Then ask students to tell you some facts they learned about plant patterns. For example, "The heliconia is red and pointy" is a fact that can be observed by looking at the photograph of the plant.

STRUCTURE

Remind students that the main idea of a section of text is what the section is mostly about. Ask: What text features in this book tell us about a section's main idea? (the headings) Explain that details are pieces of information that support the main idea. As you read aloud the first heading, "What Is a Pattern?," point out that the main idea is in the first sentence. Say: The question in the heading is answered in the first sentence: "A pattern is made by a repeated shape or color." This is the main idea. Use the Main Idea and Details Routine and Graphic Organizer in Part 3, and have students listen for details that help explain patterns. (Items in a pattern must look the same. A group of similar items, such as different animals, is not a pattern.) Have partners summarize the details they learned about patterns after you have finished reading the section. Then write the main idea and details in the graphic organizer. As you progress through the selection, allow partners to determine both the main idea and details of each section.

ENGLISH LANGUAGE LEARNERS

If students have difficulty differentiating between the main idea and details of a section, use the Web Routine and Graphic Organizer in Part 3. Write the heading in the center circle. Then, as you read, point out specific details or words to write in the arms of the web. Explain that the arms are the smaller pieces that support the large circle.

STRUGGLING READERS

Remind students that creating a picture dictionary of unfamiliar words can help them remember the new vocabulary. Have students add the domain-specific vocabulary to their dictionary, and remind them to use it as a reference while reading the text.

LANGUAGE CONVENTIONALITY AND CLARITY

A heavy amount of domain-specific vocabulary is defined through the photographs accompanying the text. Students may struggle to understand plant names, such as *heliconia*, *tulip*, or *bamboo,* or plant parts, such as *spine*, *tassel*, or *stalk*. As you read, point out the domain-specific vocabulary shown in the photographs to help students associate an image with a new word. For example, as you read p. 24, say: The text tells me that a heliconia's leaves have a pointy, red pattern. Point to the heliconia on the page. This is the heliconia flower.

If . . . students have difficulty understanding the domain-specific vocabulary,

then . . . use the Vocabulary Activities and Games in Part 3 to aid students in understanding and remembering the domain-specific words.

KNOWLEDGE DEMANDS

Use the Three-Column Chart Routine and Graphic Organizer in Part 3 to track the kinds of patterns discussed in these sections: Color Patterns, Row and Ring Patterns, and Wildly Wonderful Patterns. After reading each section, ask students to identify details and add them in the appropriate column on the graphic organizer. Ask guiding questions as necessary, such as: What are some examples of (color/row and ring/wildly wonderful) patterns? What kinds of plants have these patterns? What does the pattern look like on this plant?

If . . . students have difficulty categorizing patterns,

then . . . have students wearing similar shirt colors stand together. Point out the color pattern formed. Have students stand and hold hands in groups of four to form ring patterns. Line students in a spiral to form a wildly wonderful pattern. To follow up, provide large-square graph paper and lead students in coloring patterns to fit each category.

Express and Extend

EXPRESS Ask: Why did the author write the text *Plant Patterns?* (to tell readers facts about plant patterns) What do you think the author wants you to notice around you after reading the text? (patterns in nature) What kinds of patterns will you look for? (color patterns, row and ring patterns, wildly wonderful patterns)

EXTEND Have students write or dictate a sentence sharing their opinion about which pattern they found most interesting. For example, I think spiral patterns are interesting because they almost look like they can bounce. Then have students draw a picture of their favorite pattern to represent their sentence.

STRUCTURE

EXPRESS Display the glossary and read the entries aloud. Ask: What is the purpose of a glossary? What is it used for? (It tells what some important words from the text mean. Readers use it to look up unfamiliar words in the text.) How is it organized? (in alphabetical order) What information is included in a glossary entry? (pronunciation; definition)

> **If . . .** students do not understand the purpose of a glossary,
>
> **then . . .** provide them with a picture dictionary and show them how to look up a word and use the picture to understand a word's meaning.

EXTEND Assign groups to a word listed in the index. Help them use the index to find the word in the text. Then have students write a sentence telling a fact about their word and draw a picture to represent their sentence.

ENGLISH LANGUAGE LEARNERS

Use the photographs in the text to teach students colors, shapes, and plant names. Say the word, have students point to an example in the book, and say the sentence: I see ___.

STRUGGLING READERS

Explain to students how color patterns, row and ring patterns, and wildly wonderful patterns are details that help tell more about the book's main idea: plant patterns. Have students draw each type of pattern. Discuss how these patterns help readers understand the varieties of patterns we see in nature.

EXPRESS **Talk about Sentences and Words**

Students may struggle to connect ideas within the longer, more complicated sentences in this text. Write this sentence on the board, and read it aloud:

> Plants trimmed into green, leafy animal shapes look fun, but they do not form a pattern.

Remind students that long, challenging sentences can often be broken into smaller parts or sentences. Model how to break the sentence into two sentences: Plants trimmed into green, leafy animal shapes look fun. They do not form a pattern. Then explain that the subject of a sentence is what the sentence is about. Ask: What is the subject of the first sentence? (plants) The subject of the second sentence is *they*. What is *they* talking about? (plants) What is the second sentence telling us about the plants? (They are not a pattern.) What is easier to understand, the one long sentence or the two shorter sentences? Which do you think is more interesting?

TEAM TALK Provide small groups with the following sentence from the text: "Bamboo can grow as tall as a tree, but it is really a grass." Help students break the sentence into two smaller parts. (Bamboo can grow as tall as a tree. It is really a grass.) Have students discuss what the sentences mean.

EXTEND Have students identify the two ideas in the sentence on p. 25 and discuss what the ideas mean.

EXPRESS Show students the illustration of bamboo from *Plant Patterns* and ask: Does bamboo show only one kind of pattern, or does it show more than one kind of pattern? (more than one) What patterns does it show? (color [green]; rings)

> **If . . .** students have difficulty understanding that more than one pattern can occur at a time,
>
> **then . . .** discuss how, although each plant in this book was used to illustrate one type of pattern, some plants are examples of many types of patterns.

EXTEND Have students create a drawing depicting a pattern of flowers. Students should create their own pattern of flowers, perhaps even creating a new flower, using examples in the text as a starting point.

ACCELERATED LEARNERS

Have students create a pattern book using examples from the text. On each page of the book, have students draw and label an example of each of the following patterns: stripes, spots, colors, and shapes.

Unlock the Text

QUALITATIVE MEASURES

Levels of Meaning	explicit: examples of spirals in nature; implicit: the strength of spirals
Structure	labels embedded in illustrations; illustrations convey meaning of the main text; ellipses; free-form design in main text
Language Conventionality and Clarity	vocabulary acquisition; figurative language
Knowledge Demands	general knowledge of shapes found in nature; understanding of the spiral shape

Swirl by Swirl, pp. 27–55

Prepare to Read

LEVELS OF MEANING

Swirl by Swirl is an informational narrative that presents examples and purposes of the interesting pattern of spirals found in nature. An implicit meaning of the text is that the shape of the spiral gives it strength.

STRUCTURE

PREVIEW Have students preview the text and illustrations in *Swirl by Swirl*. Say: Look at the illustrations in this selection. Do you notice anything in the illustrations that looks similar to another selection we recently read? (There are labels in the pictures, similar to *Jack's Garden*.) What do the labels tell us? (They tell us what is in the picture.) Display an illustration from *Jack's Garden* to show how the labels teach us about the objects in the picture.

ENGLISH LANGUAGE LEARNERS

Reinforce new vocabulary by helping students understand relationships between words. Help students link new words to familiar synonyms. Guide students to see that some of the new words have similar meanings and can therefore be grouped together with a common synonym.

STRUGGLING READERS

Provide pictures of different plants and animals and give students examples of shapes to look for in the pictures. Suggest that they look for shapes like circles, squares, rectangles, triangles, and spirals. Ask students to describe the shapes they find.

LANGUAGE CONVENTIONALITY AND CLARITY

PREVIEW VOCABULARY Use the Learn New Words Routine in Part 3 to assess what students know about the following words: *swirl*, *spiral*, *coiled*, *expand*, *curl*, *curves*, *protect*, *defend*, *exploring*, *winds*, *clings*, *grasping*, *clever*, *graceful*, *bold*, *twists*, *sparkling*, *expanding*.

Use the Vocabulary Activities and Games in Part 3 to provide practice with the vocabulary words in meaningful contexts.

KNOWLEDGE DEMANDS

ACTIVATE BACKGROUND KNOWLEDGE Use the Tell What You Think Routine in Part 3 and have students write or dictate opinion sentences about shapes found in nature. Remind students to think of illustrations from previous texts in the unit as they brainstorm shapes found in nature. Ask: What are some shapes that appear in nature? Which shapes do you find interesting and why?

Interact with Text

LEVELS OF MEANING

As you read *Swirl by Swirl,* periodically stop to assess students' level of understanding of how and where spirals appear in nature. Ask: Where might you find spirals in nature? (sleeping animals, leaves and flowers, tails of animals, spider webs, waves) Remind students to reference the illustrations in the text to guide their responses. Have students use the text to help them understand how the shape is helpful, protective, and strong.

STRUCTURE

The text in *Swirl by Swirl* utilizes both ellipses and multiple line breaks within a sentence, creating one-word lines. Model reading the text aloud fluently, pausing for each ellipsis and reading one-word lines with correct rate and enunciation.

Explain to students that authors sometimes use an ellipsis at the end of a page to show that they have not finished a thought. When this happens, authors also use an ellipsis at the beginning of the next page, where they finish writing their thought. This occurs on pp. 29–30 and 41–42. Work with students to examine the text on these pages. Point out what an ellipsis means and the effect it has on the text.

As you read p. 34, model reading at the correct rate and with enunciation. Form a fist and slowly open your hand as you read the lines of text. Next, tell students you are going to read the text again as if there are no line breaks. Form another fist, and open your hand faster as you read the text. Explain how reading the text one line at a time allows for a deeper understanding of the way a fern's leaves would slowly unwrap themselves.

If . . . students are unfamiliar with the word *unwraps* and have difficulty comprehending how the fern moves,

then . . . use a shoelace to form the shape of a fern. As you read the text once more, ask a student to slowly uncoil the spiral. Explain that the shoelace is unwrapping, just as the fern does.

ENGLISH LANGUAGE LEARNERS

When referencing the illustrations in the selection, be sure to provide proper pronunciation of the labeled items. Help students categorize words as a plant, animal, or thing. Use the Three-Column Chart Graphic Organizer in Part 3 to help students sort the new vocabulary.

STRUGGLING READERS

Create a word wall that separates the action words and describing words the author uses to tell about spirals in *Swirl by Swirl.* Include simple sketches to support meaning. Have students identify these words as they are encountered in the text and add them to the appropriate category on the word wall.

LANGUAGE CONVENTIONALITY AND CLARITY

Students may struggle with the figurative language in *Swirl by Swirl.* However, the illustrations may aid their comprehension. First, establish with students that a spiral is a shape, like a triangle, a circle, or a square. Ask: Are triangles, circles, and squares living things? How do you know? (No, they are not living things because they do not breathe, think, use energy, or move without assistance.) Explain that in *Swirl by Swirl,* the author uses words that give the spiral shape the qualities of a living thing.

Read and display the text on p. 43. Have students find and point to the spirals in the illustration. Ask: What do you see that has a spiral shape? (an elephant, a monkey) What are the animals with the spiral shape doing? (The elephant is holding a tree branch. The monkey is hanging from a tree branch.) Explain that the author is describing the spiral of the monkey's tail and the elephant's trunk as if the spiral shape is performing the action of the animal.

KNOWLEDGE DEMANDS

As you read, begin by pointing out the spiral shape on the snail's shell shown on the title page. Trace the spiral with your finger and describe how the shape starts small in the middle and then continues to curl around, making the outside wider than the inside. As you progress through the book, have students find and trace the spiral shapes. Monitor their understanding of the shape by ensuring students recognize the shape. Ask questions such as: How many spirals do you see on this page? Are the spirals on this page larger or smaller than the spirals on the previous page?

Express and Extend

LEVELS OF MEANING

EXPRESS One of the most important ideas in *Swirl by Swirl* is that a spiral shape is a strong shape. Ask: What makes a spiral strong? How does the spiral shape help different living things? Create a list of action verbs the text attributes to the spiral. (Spirals reach, grasp, move, protect, defend, and cling.) Discuss how these abilities give the living things that can form spirals strength.

EXTEND Lead students to name spiral patterns they have seen in everyday life. (Sample responses: spiral staircases, rotini pasta, parking ramps, bread rolls, springs) Discuss with students ways the shape is helpful. For example, a spiral staircase is strong and fits in a small space; rotini pasta can hold more sauce than flat pasta.

STRUCTURE

EXPRESS Explain that *Swirl by Swirl* makes use of certain text features to enhance the meanings of the words on the page. Refer students to the labels on the illustrations and ask: How does the placement of each label help you determine which part of the illustration it is referring to? (Each label is written next to or on top of the object, insect, plant, or animal and written in the direction the object is moving.) Have partners or small groups determine how the labels in the illustrations help the reader better understand the text. (They help the reader name the objects in the illustrations that have spirals on them.)

EXTEND Review text structures that have been discussed in earlier lessons of this unit, such as table of contents, glossary, index, and headings. Have partners decide whether any of the discussed text features would have been helpful in this selection and why.

MORE SUPPORT

ENGLISH LANGUAGE LEARNERS

To help students name the spiral objects shown on each page of the text, provide the sentence frame: This spiral is a ___. Point to and say the name of the object, such as: This spiral is a horn. Have students practice saying the sentence with a partner to increase fluency.

STRUGGLING READERS

To help students recognize the strategic placement of the labels in the illustrations, have them trace the words. Ask: As you trace the words, what else is your finger tracing? Help students see that they are also tracing the object that is labeled as they trace the words of the label.

LANGUAGE CONVENTIONALITY AND CLARITY

EXPRESS Talk about Sentences and Words

Display these sentences from *Swirl by Swirl* and read them aloud to students:

> A spiral reaches out, too, exploring the world. It winds around and around and clings tight, grasping what it needs.

Discuss the meaning of the sentences above. Ask: What actions does the spiral perform in these sentences? (It reaches, winds, clings, and grasps.) How do these words make it seem like a spiral is a living thing? (They are all actions that only living things can do.)

> **If . . .** students have difficulty understanding the descriptive vocabulary,
>
> **then . . .** use the Act Out or Draw Meaning Routine and Graphic Organizer in Part 3 to help students better understand the vocabulary.

TEAM TALK Have students look at the illustrations on pp. 40–41. Ask: What actually reaches and winds? (octopus's tentacles; seahorses' tails) Have partners analyze the illustrations together and then share their answers with the class.

EXTEND Ask students to give their ideas as to why the spirals in this text are described in a way that makes them seem like living things. (Sample response: The author wanted to show that spirals are an important pattern in nature.)

KNOWLEDGE DEMANDS

EXPRESS Have partners share examples of what they learned about spirals from the text. Then have students write or dictate a sentence telling about the features of a spiral, using vocabulary from the text. For example: A spiral can protect an animal. A spiral can cling to a tree branch. Have students draw a picture to represent their sentence.

> **If . . .** students have difficulty formulating sentences either for sharing examples with a partner or writing their sentence,
>
> **then . . .** provide students with sentence frames, such as: A spiral can ___. A spiral has ___. A spiral looks like ___.

EXTEND Have students use what they learned from the text to think about other places they might find spirals. Have small groups brainstorm ideas and write or draw them in a list. Have groups share their lists with the class.

ACCELERATED LEARNERS

Have students create a shape book, listing the shapes they see in the classroom or at school. Each page should include a picture and a sentence in a format similar to: I see a ___ in the ___. For example: I see a circle in the clock. I see a spiral in the slide on the playground. Have partners exchange books and discuss the shapes in each.

MORE SUPPORT

UNIT 6

Exploring Communities

TEXT SET

ANCHOR TEXT
On the Town

SUPPORTING TEXT
Places in My Neighborhood

TEXT SET

ANCHOR TEXT
Neighborhood Walk: City

SUPPORTING TEXT
While I Am Sleeping

Unlock the Text

QUALITATIVE MEASURES

Levels of Meaning	explicit: a boy explores his town for a classroom assignment; implicit: the importance of community helpers
Structure	illustrations support understanding of text and aid in implicit purpose; ongoing notebook included in illustrations
Language Conventionality and Clarity	domain-specific vocabulary; context clues and illustrations help define challenging words; use of symbols and illustrations to help convey meaning
Knowledge Demands	community workers and locations

ReadyGEN
Text Collection

On the Town, pp. 4–32

Prepare to Read

LEVELS OF MEANING

In *On the Town,* readers spend a day with Charlie, a boy whose teacher has assigned his class the task of getting to know their community. With his mother to guide him, Charlie explores familiar places in his neighborhood with new eyes. He realizes that the neighborhood businesses and the people who work in them are interconnected. Most importantly, Charlie discovers his own place in his community, both as a good citizen and as a person who makes his home there.

ENGLISH LANGUAGE LEARNERS

Show students examples of common jobs by holding up pictures of people in different uniforms doing different kinds of work. Point to each picture and say: This person is a ___. What do ___ do?

STRUGGLING READERS

Remind students that organizing new vocabulary into groups is helpful for remembering definitions. Have students sort vocabulary into words related to people and words related to places. Have students create groups for any remaining uncategorized vocabulary words.

STRUCTURE

PREVIEW Have students preview the selection, looking at the illustrations to help make a prediction of the story's events. Ask: Can you tell who the main characters are by looking at the cover and the illustrations in the text? (a boy and his mother) What are the boy and his mother doing? (They are visiting many places in their neighborhood. It looks like the boy is drawing pictures of each place.) Do the places the boy and his mother stop at have anything in common? (The places all seem to be near one another.) Can you predict what we will learn from this text?

LANGUAGE CONVENTIONALITY AND CLARITY

PREVIEW VOCABULARY Use the Learn New Words Routine in Part 3 to assess what students know about the following words: *community*, *explore*, *notebook*, *teacher*, *garbage collector*, *recycle*, *police officer*, *barber*, *genius*, *bank teller*, *badge*, *waitress*, *librarian*, *train conductor*, *florist*, *bouquet*, *mailman*, *plumber*, *gardener*, *neighbor*.

CRITICAL VOCABULARY Use the Vocabulary Activities and Games in Part 3 to develop students' understanding of domain-specific vocabulary, such as *town*, *school*, *park*, *police station*, *barber shop*, *post office*, *pharmacy*, *bank*, *luncheonette*, *library*, *fire station*, *train station*, *flower shop*, and *pizza parlor*.

KNOWLEDGE DEMANDS

ACTIVATE BACKGROUND KNOWLEDGE Explain to students that in this story, the boy and his mother visit many different places in their community. Ask students what they know about community workers. Create a class list of community workers. Say: Think of someone you know well, such as an older family member or adult. What is his or her job? How does that job help the community? Post the completed list on the wall to refer to as you read about the jobs mentioned in the selection.

Interact with Text

LEVELS OF MEANING

Since *On the Town* is a narrative about a boy and his mother, students may think the author's main purpose for writing the story is to entertain. As a class, discuss how the story also provides information about community jobs and workers.

Refer to the list of community workers the class created. Ask: What are some of the community workers from our list that are mentioned in the story? Circle community workers on the class list as you encounter them in the story. Explain that authors usually have one main purpose for writing a selection, but sometimes their writing serves other purposes. Ask: What are two purposes for writing *On the Town?* (to tell a fun story and to inform about community workers)

STRUCTURE

As you read each page, point out the illustration Charlie draws in his notebook. Compare the community workers listed in Charlie's notebook with the class list created during the Activate Background Knowledge activity. Point out that Charlie's list only includes a person's name and the place where he or she works. Extend students' understanding of Charlie's list by asking: What is the job of the person Charlie just added to his notebook?

If . . . students have difficulty identifying jobs,

then . . . refer to the illustrations and the text to help students determine the task each worker does. For example, on p. 17, review with students why Mama and Charlie go to the bank and what happens while they're there. (Mama needs money; the bank teller gives Mama money.)

ENGLISH LANGUAGE LEARNERS

Help students use context clues to infer that Mama's expressions, "Bingo!" and "You're a whiz," are Mama's way of telling Charlie he is smart. Have students share and discuss other known expressions of praise.

STRUGGLING READERS

Have partners discuss how the text and illustrations are related. For example, after reading p. 10, have partners review the illustrations depicting police officers and decide how they show that police officers are "a good part of [the] community."

LANGUAGE CONVENTIONALITY AND CLARITY

Ask: If you are reading and come across a word you don't know, what can you do? (Look at the pictures and read the words around the new word.) Words and pictures that help you tell the meaning of a new word are called context clues. Ask students to describe times when they have used word or picture clues to help them understand an unfamiliar word. Then help them use context clues to define words from *On the Town.* For example, students may have difficulty with the word *luncheonette.* After reading p. 18, ask: Based on the pictures and the words we read, is a luncheonette a person, place, or thing? (place) What do Charlie and his mom do at this place? (They drink.) What is another word we use to name a place where people go to eat and drink? (*restaurant*) What is a luncheonette? (A luncheonette is a place that serves food and drinks, or a restaurant.)

If . . . students need additional practice using context clues,

then . . . reread *On the Town* and have students stop you when you read an unfamiliar word. Walk them through the process of finding clues in the text or in the pictures to help them figure out the word's meaning.

KNOWLEDGE DEMANDS

Some students may have limited knowledge of professions, such as florist and barber. When a new profession is encountered in the reading, help students use information from *On the Town* to complete the sentence frame: A ___ works in a ___. (For example, A florist works in a flower shop.) Write the completed sentence on chart paper or poster board that can be displayed in the classroom. Then discuss some duties of the profession, and have students think of a picture they can draw next to the sentence to give clues about the job title's meaning.

Express and Extend

LEVELS OF MEANING

EXPRESS Have students share facts they have learned about communities from *On the Town.* Provide the sentence frame: I learned that a ___ works in a ___. (For example, I learned that a florist works in a flower shop.) Have students recall what Mama and Charlie do at each place in the community. Then discuss with students what their families might do at each place in the community. Remind students to look at the pictures for clues.

> **If . . .** students confuse community workers,
>
> **then . . .** refer them to the chart they created earlier. Remind students that they can use the sentences and picture clues on that chart to help them remember the different community workers and what they do.

EXTEND Have groups of students discuss what would happen if neighborhoods didn't have community workers. Ask: What would a community be like without police officers? Would people in the community feel safe? Why or why not? Have groups share their thoughts with the class. Repeat the exercise with other community workers.

STRUCTURE

EXPRESS The illustrations in *On the Town* help convey the meaning of the text by displaying the various community locations and workers in the town. In addition to the community workers Charlie adds to his notebook, many other workers are shown throughout the illustrations. Have groups of students review the illustrations and create a list, using words or pictures, of the additional community helpers they find in the illustrations. Once completed, have groups compare their lists.

EXTEND Help students use their lists of community workers and the knowledge they gained from the text to create a map of Charlie's town, including the locations mentioned in Charlie's notebook. Lead students to include the school, police station, library, and other locations mentioned in Charlie's notebook as well as locations of the workers students identified in the above activity.

MORE SUPPORT

ENGLISH LANGUAGE LEARNERS

Write the dollar symbol ($) on the board and explain that it is a way to show and say *dollar.* Write *$10* and say: ten dollars. Write some additional dollar amounts, such as $1 and $5, and have students practice saying the amounts using the word *dollars.*

STRUGGLING READERS

Students may be confused by the word *teller* because it is based on the word *tell,* which commonly means "to say." Explain that *tell* is a multiple-meaning word that can also mean "to count." Ask: What is something a bank teller counts? (money)

LANGUAGE CONVENTIONALITY AND CLARITY

EXPRESS Talk about Sentences and Words

Display the following passage from *On the Town,* and read it aloud with students:

"I'm running out of money," Mama said to Charlie. "Bank!" said Charlie. "Bingo!" said Mama. Charlie read the badge on the bank teller's blouse. Her name was Ms. Chung, and she gave Mama money while Charlie wrote her name with a long line of dollar signs.

Discuss the meaning of the passage. Ask: What is a bank? (a place where people give and receive money) Who works at the bank Charlie and Mama go to? (Ms. Chung) What is the name of Ms. Chung's job? (bank teller)

TEAM TALK   Have partners discuss their ideas about the answer to the following question: Why do you think Charlie writes Ms. Chung's name with "a long line of dollar signs"? (The dollar signs remind him that Ms. Chung's job is to help customers get money from the bank.)

If . . . students are unable to answer the question,

then . . . reread the passage and ask: How does Ms. Chung help Mama? (She helps Mama get money, or dollars, from the bank.)

EXTEND Have students review other symbols and illustrations Charlie uses in his notebook. Then have students decide on and draw symbols or illustrations for the mailman, plumber, and gardener mentioned on p. 32 of the text.

KNOWLEDGE DEMANDS

EXPRESS Create a matching game using index cards. Students will match the community workers with the locations of their jobs. For example, write a location such as *bank* under a picture of a bank on one card, and write *bank teller* under a picture of a bank teller on another card to serve as its match. Have students place the cards face down and select two cards at a time to find a match. Have students keep matched cards in a personal pile and return cards that do not match. The student with the most matches at the end of the game wins.

EXTEND Have students demonstrate their knowledge of community workers and their important roles in the community by writing a sentence telling which community job they would like to have. Use the sentence frame: I want to be a ___ to help people ___.

ACCELERATED LEARNERS

Have students think about the community workers that perform important jobs in your school. Have students create a minibook, modeled after Charlie's notebook, of the community workers in the school. For example, students should include teachers, cafeteria staff, custodians, secretaries, and nurses.

MORE SUPPORT

Unlock the Text

QUALITATIVE MEASURES

Levels of Meaning	explicit: an informational text about the places that make up a neighborhood and their functions
Structure	headings; photographs; glossary
Language Conventionality and Clarity	domain-specific vocabulary defined with the help of photographs and glossary
Knowledge Demands	neighborhood and neighbors; categorizing

ReadyGEN
Text Collection

Places in My
Neighborhood, pp. 33–52

Prepare to Read

LEVELS OF MEANING

Places in My Neighborhood is an informational text that tells the reader what a neighborhood is as well as the functions of the buildings that make up a neighborhood.

STRUCTURE

PREVIEW Have students preview the text features in the selection. Prompt students to recall from previous readings text features and the purposes they serve. Ask: What do you see on pages 36 and 40 that help you know what the text is about? (headings) What information do the headings provide? (the main idea of the section) What is the main idea of a section of text? (what a section of text is mostly about) Does this selection have a text feature that will help me if I am not sure about the meaning of a word? If so, what is it? (Yes, it has a glossary.)

ENGLISH LANGUAGE LEARNERS

Prior to reading the text, have partners identify common places in their neighborhood. Show pictures of places, such as a park, school, library, or hospital. Say the name of a place aloud and have students identify the correct picture.

STRUGGLING READERS

Help students relate the meanings of the words *neighbor* and *neighborhood*. Explain that a neighbor is a person who lives or works nearby and that a neighborhood is made up of people, houses, and buildings that are nearby.

LANGUAGE CONVENTIONALITY AND CLARITY

PREVIEW VOCABULARY Use the Learn New Words Routine in Part 3 to assess what students know about the following words: *neighborhood*, *community*, *purpose*, *city*, *apartment*, *house*, *town*, *station*, *firefighters*, *police officer*, *strangers*, *clinic*, *nurse*, *bandage*, *library*, *grocery store*.

Use the Vocabulary Activities and Games in Part 3 to provide practice with the vocabulary words in meaningful contexts.

KNOWLEDGE DEMANDS

ACTIVATE BACKGROUND KNOWLEDGE Ask students what they know about neighborhoods. Use the Web Routine and Graphic Organizer in Part 3 to record students' responses. Ask: What places in your neighborhood do you and your family frequently visit? Why do you go to those places? Who are the people in your neighborhood? How would you describe your neighborhood? Display the web on a wall in the classroom to refer to as you read the text.

Interact with Text

LEVELS OF MEANING

As you read, monitor students' understanding of the purpose of the text. Students may struggle to understand that this text is nonfiction. Although names are mentioned in the text, there are no characters. Ask: Is this text a story with events or a text that gives information? (a text that gives information) Are the names the author mentions in the text characters in a story? (No. This is an informational text, not a story.) Why do you think the author chose to include names in an informational text? (to give examples)

> **If . . .** students have difficulty understanding that the names in the selection are not names of characters,
>
> **then . . .** help students understand that the author is not telling a story about the children named in the text going on an adventure. Ask: Is the author telling us about a day in Lila's life or simply that Lila received a shot? (simply that Lila received a shot) What else does the author tell us about Lila in the book? (nothing else) Why does the author tell us about Lila? (to use her as an example)

STRUCTURE

As you read each section, remind students to read the headings and look at the photographs. Pause after reading each section to have partners relate the information they read in the text to the heading. For example, after reading "Places to Live" on pp. 36–39, have partners tell each other an example of a place to live in a neighborhood. Ask: The heading of this section is "Places to Live." What are some examples of places to live that we just read about in this section? Remind students to use the photographs as well as the text to guide their answers.

MORE SUPPORT

ENGLISH LANGUAGE LEARNERS

Encourage partners to draw pictures on index cards of the places mentioned in *Places in My Neighborhood*. Have them draw one place on each index card. Then have them use the index cards to quiz each other on the name and purpose for each place. For example, the police station's purpose is to help keep people safe.

STRUGGLING READERS

Provide sentence frames to help students describe the sections of text. For example: A ___ is a place to live. A ___ is a place to keep people safe. A ___ is a place to find things.

LANGUAGE CONVENTIONALITY AND CLARITY

Students may struggle with domain-specific vocabulary in *Places in My Neighborhood.* Ask clarifying questions to guide students' independence in determining the meaning of challenging vocabulary. For example, as you read p. 36, ask: What can you do to find the meaning of the word *apartment* if you don't know what this word means? (Sample responses: Use context clues; the text says an apartment is a kind of home. Use the photograph; the photograph shows what apartment buildings look like.) Aside from the photographs and text, does the selection offer another feature that tells the meanings of challenging words? (Yes, the selection has a glossary.) Have students explain how to use a glossary, and offer guidance as needed.

If . . . students are not familiar with glossaries,

then . . . walk them through how to use one. For example, read p. 48 and stop at the words *grocery store*. Show students *grocery store* in the glossary and read aloud the definition. Return to p. 48 and ask: What is sold in a grocery store?

KNOWLEDGE DEMANDS

Though most students will be familiar with places mentioned in *Places in My Neighborhood*, the idea of categorizing these places may be new.

Display a large three-column chart in the classroom. Label the columns *Places to Live, Places to Keep Us Safe,* and *Places to Find Things*. On index cards, write the following words and phrases: *apartment, house, fire station, police station, clinic, library, grocery store*. Work together to sort the words into the appropriate categories on the chart, using the text as a reference.

Express and Extend

LEVELS OF MEANING

EXPRESS Remind students that the main purpose of *Places in My Neighborhood* is to give information. Have students share some examples of information they learned about neighborhood places from reading the book. Provide sentence frames for student responses, for example: A ___ is a person who keeps us safe. I can find ___ at the ___. I live in a ___.

EXTEND Review the concept of main idea and details with students. Use the Main Idea and Details Routine and Graphic Organizer in Part 3 to guide students in writing the main idea and details of the "Places to Live" section. Then have students use the graphic organizer to write the main idea and details of the "Places to Keep Us Safe" section. Remind students that identifying the main idea and details in a selection is a good strategy to use when reading nonfiction texts.

STRUCTURE

EXPRESS Review the structure of the previous text, *On the Town*. Then discuss the structure of *Places in My Neighborhood.* Use the Venn Diagram Routine and Graphic Organizer in Part 3 to compare the structures of the two texts.

> **If . . .** students have difficulty recalling the structure of *On the Town*,
>
> **then . . .** lead students on a picture walk through *On the Town* to review the structure of the selection.

EXTEND Review the table of contents in *Plant Patterns* to remind students of the purpose of the text feature. Help students create a table of contents for *Places in My Neighborhood*, using the headings from the text as a guide. Remind students to include the glossary as well as page numbers.

MORE SUPPORT

ENGLISH LANGUAGE LEARNERS

Use the photographs in the selection to review the names of community workers and where they work. Lead students to point and say the sentence frames: This is a [nurse]. He works at a [clinic].

STRUGGLING READERS

Review how to categorize the places listed in the text prior to asking students to categorize places from the web. Help students understand the common characteristics among the places in each category.

LANGUAGE CONVENTIONALITY AND CLARITY

EXPRESS Talk about Sentences and Words

Have students use context clues to determine the meaning of unfamiliar words. Display and read aloud this passage from *Places in My Neighborhood*.

> At the clinic, a nurse gives Lila a shot. She feels better when she gets a bandage.

Discuss the meaning of the passage. Ask: What is a nurse? (a person who works with a doctor to help people when they are sick or injured) What is the nurse doing? (He is giving Lila a shot.)

TEAM TALK Ask partners to answer the following question: A bandage is something that makes Lila feel better. What is a bandage? (a covering to put over a wound) Why do you think the nurse put a bandage on Lila? (to cover the area where he gave her the shot)

EXTEND On index cards write sentences that contain one unfamiliar word. In each sentence, underline the unfamiliar word and make sure the sentence has clear context clues. On separate index cards, write one familiar word that is a synonym for each one of the unfamiliar words, creating matching pairs of cards. Have students read the sentences and use the context clues to pair the underlined, unfamiliar word with its matching synonym card.

KNOWLEDGE DEMANDS

EXPRESS Display the chart you made with the three categories from the text for places found in neighborhoods (Places to Live, Places to Keep Us Safe, Places to Find Things). Review the web students created at the beginning of the unit. Read aloud the neighborhood places from the web, and have students dictate in which category each place belongs. Add students' responses to the chart to create a master list.

EXTEND If there are places remaining in the web that do not fit into one of the three categories, have students determine new categories for the remaining locations. Alternately, have students think of a new set of category names that could be used to divide the entire list of neighborhood locations. Use a graphic organizer to sort the list of places into their categories.

ACCELERATED LEARNERS

Have students create a minibook modeled after *Places in My Neighborhood*. Have them use the same headings, but have them write sentences and draw pictures that relate to them personally. For example, under the heading "Places to Live," students should draw a picture of their home and write a sentence about it, such as this: I live in an apartment.

MORE SUPPORT

Unlock the Text

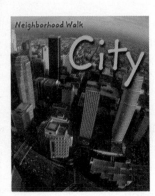

QUALITATIVE MEASURES

Levels of Meaning	explicit: to convey factual information about living in cities
Structure	main ideas and details; table of contents; headings; graphics/pictures to convey meaning; picture captions; glossary; index
Language Conventionality and Clarity	complex sentences containing lists; domain-specific vocabulary
Knowledge Demands	general understanding of neighborhoods and communities; basic understanding of the large number of people and locations in a city

Prepare to Read

LEVELS OF MEANING

Neighborhood Walk: City is an informational text that gives readers a detailed look at the various people and locations typically found in a city neighborhood.

STRUCTURE

PREVIEW The information in *Neighborhood Walk: City* is organized by main idea and details and includes many useful text features. Show students the table of contents and preview the headings. Ask: What does the table of contents show us? (a list of the headings) What do the headings tell us? (main ideas) What is a main idea? (what a section of text is mostly about) Have students preview the text and photographs. Point out that the thick, black words are vocabulary words found in the glossary.

ENGLISH LANGUAGE LEARNERS

Students can preview the information in the text by taking a picture walk. Have students look at the pictures in the book with a partner and predict what the book will be about.

STRUGGLING READERS

Much of the vocabulary in this text has been taught in previous texts in this unit. Remind students to review strategies for remembering familiar vocabulary to help them succeed in reading this selection. Use the Vocabulary Activities and Games in Part 3 for more practice.

Ask: How does a glossary help readers? (It tells the meanings of important words from the book.)

LANGUAGE CONVENTIONALITY AND CLARITY

PREVIEW VOCABULARY Use the Learn New Words Routine in Part 3 to assess what students know about the following words: *neighborhood*, *community*, *downtown*, *town houses*, *subways*, *crowded*, *government*, *patrol*, *emergency*, *ambulances*, *department stores*, *products*, *farmers' markets*, *cafés*, *vendors*, *programs*, *branches*, *city hall*, *hospital*, *museums*, *aquariums*, *arenas*.

Use the Vocabulary Activities and Games in Part 3 to review domain-specific vocabulary related to community locations and jobs from previous texts in the unit.

KNOWLEDGE DEMANDS

ACTIVATE BACKGROUND KNOWLEDGE Review the concept of neighborhoods and communities with students. Have students activate background knowledge by recalling information they learned in previous texts. Ask: What are some buildings you would typically find in a neighborhood or community? Who are some of the people that live and work in your neighborhood? To help students recall information they learned in previously read texts, ask: What are some places Charlie and his mother visit in *On the Town?* What places do you remember seeing pictures of in *Places in My Neighborhood?*

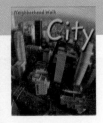

Interact with Text

As you read, ensure students understand the information by pausing after each section to allow students to summarize the information. For example, after reading pp. 10–11, ask: What can you tell me about schools in a city? How do students in the city get to school each day? Create sentence frames based on the headings for students to summarize the sections. For example, the headings are italicized in the following sentence frames: *Schools* in a city are ___. People in a city can get *food* from ___. ___ is a type of *home* in a city.

Neighborhood Walk: City contains many photographs with captions that help add meaning to the main text. Refer students to the photographs and ask: What is next to all of the photographs in the book? (captions) When do we read captions? (when we are looking at photographs) What do captions help us understand? (what is shown in a photo or how a photo relates to the text)

As you read through the sections, have students explain how the pictures and captions help them better understand the text. Ask questions to help students relate the main text to what is shown in the photographs. For example, on pp. 18–19, ask: What do you see in the photographs that helps you understand where people in cities get their food? (The photographs show a grocery store where people buy food and a café where people go to eat food.)

If . . . students have difficulty connecting the photographs and captions to the main text,

then . . . review the photographs, captions, and main text on a specific page, and guide students in understanding how they are all related. For example, read aloud the text on p. 16. Then point to the photo and read aloud the caption. Explain that both the main text and the caption tell about department stores, but the caption provides additional information. Repeat with another page as needed.

MORE SUPPORT

ENGLISH LANGUAGE LEARNERS

Display pictures of vocabulary related to city housing, transportation, and locations. Point to the specific images as you discuss the vocabulary to provide a visual reference for students.

STRUGGLING READERS

Students may struggle with how to begin expressing their ideas about a text. Provide sentence frames for them to use during discussion, such as these: The heading says the main idea is ___. The photo shows ___. The caption tells about ___.

LANGUAGE CONVENTIONALITY AND CLARITY

Remind students that if sentences are too long for them to understand, they can break up the sentences to look or listen for smaller phrases or sections. Display the following sentence from p. 7, and read it aloud with students:

People live in houses, apartment buildings, or town houses.

Tell students that this sentence includes a list. Point out the commas that separate each item in the list. Explain that a list names three or more things, one after the other. Writers use commas to separate items in a list. Say: This sentence tells the names of three kinds of places where people live. Reread the sentence and ask: What are the three types of places mentioned in the sentence? (houses, apartment buildings, and town houses) As you reread the sentence with students, underline and number each separate place.

If . . . students have difficulty understanding the concept of listing items in a sentence,

then . . . provide the following sentence frame for students to tell a partner their three favorite colors: My three favorite colors are ___, ___, and ___. Have students count with their fingers as they list the three colors. Explain that the three items listed are related, which is why they are able to be listed in one sentence.

KNOWLEDGE DEMANDS

As you are reading, relate the information presented in the text to students' background knowledge and personal experiences. Ask: Which of these places have you heard of before? Have we read about any of these places in previous texts? Have you ever been to one of these places in your community? As you read pp. 14–15, students may respond by telling about information they learned in On the Town or Places in My Neighborhood, or they may share information they learned during a field trip to a local fire station.

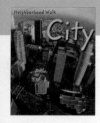

Express and Extend

EXPRESS The purpose of *Neighborhood Walk: City* is to inform the reader about the many people and places one might see in a city. Have partners review the table of contents, the text, and the photos. Then have them discuss what information in the book they found most useful and why. Ask: If you were visiting a new city, what information from this book would be most useful to you? Have partners share their responses with the class.

EXTEND Have partners write an informational paragraph about the information from the book that they found most useful. In their paragraphs, have students tell about the people, places, or things someone who has never visited a city before might need to know. Use the Informative/Explanatory Writing Routine and Graphic Organizer in Part 3.

STRUCTURE

EXPRESS Show and read aloud pp. 12–13. Then have students identify and explain three features of nonfiction text found in this section of *Neighborhood Walk: City*.

If . . . students have difficulty pointing out text features,

then . . . give them a definition or clue for each text feature, and have them tell you the name of the feature based on its definition. For example, ask: What tells the main idea of a section of text? (heading) What shows an example of words from the text? (photo) What tells what you see in the photo? (caption)

EXTEND Review the purpose of the glossary and the index with students. Then have students explain how the glossary and the index are helpful features for the reader. (The glossary tells the meaning of words. The index tells where to find information.) Lead students in finding *zoo* in the index and then finding the page about zoos. Then read aloud the text on p. 27 and lead students in looking up *aquarium* in the glossary.

MORE SUPPORT

ENGLISH LANGUAGE LEARNERS

Remind students to review the photographs and text to remember the people, places, and things found in a city. Provide sentence frames for students to complete, for example: I think the information about ___ is most useful because ___.

STRUGGLING READERS

Students may require help recalling the various people, places, and things in a city. Use the Web Routine and Graphic Organizer in Part 3 to help activate students' memories.

EXPRESS Talk about Sentences and Words

Display and read aloud this sentence from p. 26 of *Neighborhood Walk: City*.

Most cities have parks, playgrounds, and gardens for people to enjoy.

Discuss the meaning of the sentence. Say: This sentence includes a list. What is a list? (a series of related words) What three places that people can find in cities are included in the list in this sentence? (parks, playgrounds, gardens)

TEAM TALK Have partners discuss the answer to the following question: People go to parks, playgrounds, and gardens to have fun. To what other places in the city do people go to have fun? Have them share their ideas by adding them to the list above.

EXTEND Have students choose their favorite three places from *Neighborhood Walk: City* and complete the following sentence: My favorite places are ___, ___, and ___. Have them write their sentence using the text as a guide.

KNOWLEDGE DEMANDS

EXPRESS Have students tell the names of some city places they learned about from *Neighborhood Walk: City*. Discuss the similarities and differences between towns and cities. Use the Venn Diagram Graphic Organizer in Part 3 to organize student information. Students should understand that towns and cities are very similar; however, cities have more locations because they are much larger.

If . . . students have difficulty determining differences between towns and cities,

then . . . help students compare the knowledge gained from *On the Town* with the new information in *Neighborhood Walk: City*. For example, ask: What is a new vocabulary word that describes small locations in a city that are part of one main location? (branches) Name places in a city where people might get food. (cafés, farmer's markets, street vendors)

EXTEND Have students use information learned from the text, as well as from other texts in the unit, to determine whether they live in a city or a town. Have students write a sentence supporting their response. Provide students with the following sentence frame: I know I live in a ___ because ___.

ACCELERATED LEARNERS

Have students categorize places in their own town or city under the headings used in the text. Students should decide which heading within the text each place would fit. For example, their favorite pizza parlor would be categorized under the heading Food.

Unlock the Text

QUALITATIVE MEASURES

Levels of Meaning	story setting, exploring a city to learn about the people who work at night when others are sleeping, what nighttime workers do during the day.
Structure	roles of author and illustrator, illustrations directly support text; rhyming and repetitive verse
Language Conventionality and Clarity	domain-specific vocabulary; synonyms, rhyming words, short verb phrases
Knowledge Demands	first-person narrator, a large city; nighttime workers; jobs, times of day

While I Am Sleeping

WRITTEN BY MALAIKA ROSE STANLEY
ILLUSTRATED BY RACHAEL SAUNDERS

Prepare to Read

LEVELS OF MEANING

While I Am Sleeping is about the people who are working while a child is asleep at night. The text and the illustrations take readers on a tour of a large city, identifying workers and how they are busy during the nighttime.

STRUCTURE

PREVIEW Read the title of the book and the names of the author and the illustrator. Point out that the author, Malaika Rose Stanley, wrote the words for the story and the illustrator, Rachael Saunders, drew the pictures. Explain that the author's words and the illustrator's pictures work together to tell the story.

ENGLISH LANGUAGE LEARNERS

Because the word *while* has multiple meanings, students may not be sure of its meaning in the title *While I Am Sleeping*. Discuss the story's title, guiding students to understand that in the story the word *while* means "during the time that" or "when."

STRUGGLING READERS

The names of the workers are multisyllabic words that may be unfamiliar to students. Reinforce workers' names by relating them to the pictures of the workers. For example, after reading about the baker on pp. 4–5, point to the picture of the bakers and discuss what each is doing. Guide students to use the pictures as visual prompts for the workers' names.

Help students use the title and the cover illustration to establish the story setting.

- Look at the title of the book and the cover illustration. During what time of day does the story take place? (nighttime)
- What clue does the title give about the time? (The word *Sleeping* is a clue that the story takes place at night because most people sleep at night.)
- What clues does the illustration give about the time of day? (The sky is black with a few stars shining, and lights glow from the windows of some buildings.)
- Where does the story take place? (in a city) How do you know where the story takes place? (The cover illustration shows a city scene.)

LANGUAGE CONVENTIONALITY AND CLARITY

PREVIEW VOCABULARY Use the Learn New Words Routine in Part 3 to assess what students know about the following words: *scrubs, flames, rush, bright, pumps, doze, sirens, packets, diner, snoozing, snoring.*

DOMAIN-SPECIFIC VOCABULARY Use the vocabulary Activities in Part 3 to preteach the following domain-specific vocabulary terms: *bakers, market sellers, garage attendant, janitor, security guards, taxi.*

KNOWLEDGE DEMANDS

ACTIVATE BACKGROUND KNOWLEDGE Guide students to understand who the storyteller of *While I Am Sleeping* is. Explain that the storyteller is the person who is telling the story, and sometimes the storyteller is a character in the story. Remind students that the title of the story is *While I Am Sleeping* and the title is a clue that the storyteller is someone who is sleeping while others are busy. Have students look through the pictures to identify who is sleeping. Help them conclude that the boy in bed is the storyteller. He is telling us what happens when he is in bed sleeping.

Interact with Text

LEVELS OF MEANING

The main purpose of the story is to identify people who work during the night when most other people are sleeping. Ask: *What is the main purpose of While I Am Sleeping?* (to name nighttime workers) As you read, make a list of the nighttime workers and discuss why they work during the night. Help students understand the reasons that the workers do their jobs at night. For example, bakers bake at night so people can buy fresh bread and other baked goods the next day. Janitors clean at night, so they do not interrupt workers during the day. Guide students to discuss why firefighters, doctors, and ambulance drivers must work at night even though they also work during the day.

If . . . students have difficulty identifying the jobs nighttime workers do,

then . . . revisit the illustrations. Point to and identify each worker.

STRUCTURE

The story of the nighttime workers is told through *repetition* and *rhyme*. After reading page 3 aloud, point out to students that this sentence is repeated throughout the text. Then guide students to identify the rhyming structure of the text. Remind them that words that rhyme have the same ending sounds. Read a verse, emphasizing the rhyming words, and help students identify the words that rhyme. Read pp. 3–6 aloud, modeling the rhythmic structure of the text established by the repetition and rhyme.

If . . . students have difficulty hearing the rhythmic structure,

then . . . clap the rhythm as you read the lines.

ENGLISH LANGUAGE LEARNERS

Students may be familiar with synonyms or words with similar meanings in their home language. Guide students to understand that different English words can be used to describe the same general action in the same way.

STRUGGLING READERS

Use the repetitive text to encourage students to read aloud with you. Begin by pointing to each word of the repeating verse as you and students read the verse together. After they have read the verse with you several times, encourage students to read the verse on their own as you point to the words.

MORE SUPPORT

LANGUAGE CONVENTIONALITY AND CLARITY

The text uses several words that are related to the action of sleeping. Read through the text and help students identify words used in place of the word *sleep* or *sleeping*. (*doze*, p. 8; *snoozing* and *snoring,* p. 24) Discuss how the meanings of the words are alike and different. Both *doze* and *snooze* can mean "to sleep," but they can also mean "to sleep lightly." *Snore* means "to breathe noisily while sleeping." Ask questions to help students understand how the words are related to sleeping. Which words are words that can mean "to sleep"? (*doze* and *snooze*) Which word is something people might do when they sleep? (*snore*)

If . . . students have difficulty understanding that the words have similar meanings,

then . . . use actions or pictures to reinforce the meanings of the words.

KNOWLEDGE DEMANDS

Guide students to relate the name of each worker to the job that worker does. Make a T-chart with the labels *Worker* and *Job*. Have students page through the book, identifying each worker. Write the names of the workers in the chart. Then name a worker, and help students use the information in the words and pictures of the text to tell what the worker's job entails. For example, a baker's job is to make bread and other baked goods and a janitor's job is to clean. List the worker's job in the second column of your chart. Help students understand that the text does not tell all the jobs that each worker does.

Express and Extend

LEVELS OF MEANING

EXPRESS Remind students that the story tells what nighttime workers do when the boy is sleeping. Turn to p. 24. Read the text and have students examine the picture. What is the boy doing now? (He is awake and looking out a window.) What are the nighttime workers doing? (sleeping) When do the nighttime workers sleep? (during the day) Why do they sleep during the day? (They work at night.)

EXTEND Have each student choose one of the nighttime workers and draw a picture showing that worker sleeping during the day. Display their pictures on a board labeled *Bedtime for Nighttime Workers*.

STRUCTURE

EXPRESS Remind students that the rhyming verses and the illustrations work together to tell the story. Discuss the illustrations on pp. 8–9. Read the first verse. Which picture supports this sentence? (picture of the boy in bed) What details does the picture show that the words do not tell? (The picture shows the boy holding a stuffed rabbit.) Read the second verse. Which pictures support this sentence? (picture of firefighters fighting a fire; picture of a hospital) What do the pictures show that the words do not say? (The picture of firefighters shows the firefighters are on ladders and one is rescuing a cat. The picture of the hospital shows a doctor talking to a patient, patients sleeping, and a man walking past the hospital.)

EXTEND Have partners choose an illustration in the book and tell which words of the text it supports and the additional information the picture gives. Have the partners share their information with others.

ENGLISH LANGUAGE LEARNERS

Some verb phrases have meanings that cannot be determined from the literal meanings of the words. Help students use context and pictures to discern the meanings of phrases such as *take care of* (give care to), *watch over* (guard), and *fill up* (fill completely).

STRUGGLING READERS

The illustrations not only support what the words say but also help establish the time and place of the story. The illustration on pp. 12–13 shows the middle of the night, the one on pp. 22–23 shows the dawn, and the one on p. 24 shows the early morning.

EXPRESS Talk about Sentences and Words

Display and read aloud the following sentence from *While I Am Sleeping.*

> Delivery drivers in trucks and
> in vans
> drop off papers and food in
> packets and cans.

Briefly discuss the rhyming words in the sentence. Underline the word *vans*, reread the passage, and ask: What word in this text rhymes with *vans*? (cans) Then focus on the words *drop off*. The words *drop off* are a short verb phrase. I know that the word *drop* can mean "let fall," but letting something fall off does not make sense in this sentence. I will look for clues in the sentence to help me understand what *drop off* means. The word *delivery* is a clue to the meaning of *drop off*. I know that sometimes we use the words *drop off* to mean "to deliver." That meaning makes sense in this sentence.

TEAM TALK Have partners discuss what the sentence is saying the delivery drivers do.

EXTEND Ask students to turn to pp. 18–19. Read the verses aloud and point to the verb phrase *pick up*. Then have pairs of students discuss the meaning of *pick up*. Encourage them to use clues in the picture or words to help them figure out the meaning.

EXPRESS Discuss the time frame of the story, guiding students to understand that the story begins in the dark of night and ends in daylight. Guide students to explain why most of the story takes place during the night. Students should be able to relate the purpose of the text to the time frame of the text.

> **If . . .** students have difficulty understanding why the time frame focuses on the nighttime,
>
> **then . . .** ask them to tell when the people featured in the text are working.

EXTEND Reread p. 24 and have students examine the picture. Remind them that the story tells about people who work at night while the boy is sleeping. Ask partners to tell why the last page shows the boy awake.

ACCELERATED LEARNERS

Help students identify other night workers, such as nurses, police officers, airline workers, and restaurant workers. Have students draw a picture of one of the workers and write or dictate a sentence telling what he or she does.

Unlock the
Writing

Part 2 **Unlock the Writing**

Scaffolded Lessons for the Performance-Based Assessments

Scaffolded Lessons for the Writing Types

Scaffolded Lessons for the Performance-Based Assessments

Unlock the Task: Write About Animal Homes

Distribute copies of the task found on page 146 of the Teacher's Guide and read it aloud. Create a class T-chart to list the animals and homes in *Where Is Home, Little Pip?* and *A House for Hermit Crab.* As students name an animal or a home, display its illustration in the text and ask questions such as: What animal is this? Where does it live? What does its home look like? Discuss the answers with students.

Read aloud the task. Work with students to name and highlight the important points in the task.

> Choose an animal from *Where Is Home, Little Pip?* or *A House for Hermit Crab.* Draw a picture of the animal and its home. Draw, dictate, or write something that could happen in the home.

ANSWER QUESTIONS ABOUT THE TASK

Display the questions below about the task and discuss them together. Read each question aloud. Work together to answer the questions.

- **What will I be writing?** (an event)
- **What texts or books will I use?** *(Where Is Home, Little Pip?* or *A House for Hermit Crab)*
- **What will my event be about?** (something that could happen in an animal's home)
- **What do I need to include in my writing?** (a picture of the animal and its home plus drawn, spoken, or written sentence(s) telling something that could take place in the home)

RESTATE THE TASK

Have students restate the task in their own words. Check for possible misunderstandings or missing elements.

ENGLISH LANGUAGE LEARNERS

If . . . students have difficulty naming animals in English,

then . . . together, create a T-chart. In the first column, place a simple drawing or picture of the animal. In the second column, write the animal's name in English. Say the animal's name and have students repeat it several times.

STRUGGLING WRITERS

If . . . students have difficulty understanding the task,

then . . . reread the task. Ask questions to help students understand the task. For example, ask: What will you write? (one thing that could happen in an animal's home) What stories can you use to help you get ideas? (the stories we read together) What details will you include? (the name of the animal, the kind of home it lives in, and something that happens there)

Prepare to Write

Once students clearly understand the writing task, have them review the stories *Where Is Home, Little Pip?* and *A House for Hermit Crab* as well as the T-chart you created as a class. When students have chosen an animal to write about, have them use sticky notes to mark pages in the selection that tell about the animal. Provide students with the Story Map B Graphic Organizer from Part 3 and model how to fill it out. Point to the Characters box. Review with students that characters are the people or animals in a story. Work with students to use pictures or words to name their animal in the Characters box. If students have difficulty choosing between two animals, have them choose the animal they like best.

Point to the Setting box in the graphic organizer. Tell students that the setting of their story is going to be where the animal lives. Display the class T-chart and help the students find their animal's home on the chart. Then work with them to use pictures or words to name their animal's home in the Setting box of the story map.

GATHER IDEAS

Help students begin to put together ideas for an event they could write about by drawing pictures in their graphic organizer. Encourage students to find pages about their animal's home in the appropriate selection. These pages may help them think of an event that could take place in the home. Also ask questions, such as: What could happen in your animal's home? How does this make your animal feel? Point to the Events box in the story map. Guide students to record their ideas here.

You may wish to talk about an event and record your ideas as pictures in a chart as a model. For example, say: My animal's home is the pebbly nest of a penguin. A baby penguin hatches from an egg in the nest. The penguin mother and father will be happy. Draw a cracked egg and two penguins.

ACCELERATED WRITERS

If . . . students write more than one event that could happen in the animal's home,

then . . . remind them that they are telling about only one event. Help them identify a single event to write about and encourage them to add details about that event.

MONITOR AND SUPPORT

TALK IT THROUGH

Display the questions below and read them aloud. Talk through them with students, explaining that writers can get valuable information if they talk about their writing ideas with a partner or classmates. Then have partners take turns talking through their ideas for an event and asking each other these questions to see if others understand. Circulate among the pairs and provide support as they present their ideas and ask questions of their partners. You may prefer to do this as a whole group activity and have students take turns asking the group their questions.

Questions a Writer Might Ask

- Which animal am I writing about?
- Where does the animal live?
- What should my picture of the animal and its home include?
- What could happen at the home?
- What words or pictures should I use to tell what happens?
- What else can I add?
- Is there anything I should leave out?

Encourage students to ask partners questions of their own.

GET ORGANIZED

Work with students to think about any part of the event that their partner did not understand. Remind them that what was unclear for their partner might confuse another reader too. Guide students to clear up confusing ideas and details.

If students are having difficulty determining an event to write about, talk about their animal, its home, and something the animal might do at its home. If students' events lack details, have them look back at the texts for pictures that show the animal and its home.

ENGLISH LANGUAGE LEARNERS

If . . . students have difficulty choosing words for their events,

then . . . have students draw their animal, its home, and elements for an event in one column. Then write English words for each picture across in the other column. Help students use their charts as they write.

STRUGGLING WRITERS

If . . . students find it difficult to write about how an animal feels about an event,

then . . . talk about their events and ask questions about how the animals involved would feel. For example, if an event is a baby penguin hatching from an egg, ask how the parents of the baby would feel when they see it. Help students draw conclusions about the feelings.

Write

Display the chart below and illustrate it with pictures or clip art that students can associate with the words. Review with students that their writing should include characters, setting, and an event. Review the definitions of each element and answer any questions students may have about them. Then work with students to provide the examples for the last column using their own writing or ideas from texts you have read together. Help students use the chart as they write.

Element	Definition	Example
Characters	• The people or animals in the story	penguin, whale, bird, dogs, hermit crab, starfish, sea urchin, snail, lanternfish
Setting	• Where the story takes place • When the story takes place	Antarctica, a pebble nest, a shell, the ocean, the present time
Event	• What happens • Details about what happens and how the characters feel	Penguins slide down icy hills in their cold Antarctic home. A whale and its babies leap in the ocean. Hermit crab gets too big for his shell. Snails keep the ocean floor clean.

ENGLISH LANGUAGE LEARNERS

If . . . students have difficulty writing or dictating about what happens in an animal home, because of their lack of language skills,

then . . . have students draw detailed pictures of the events. Using the pictures as visual prompts, use words to describe the events. Record your descriptions in notes and read them aloud to confirm that they tell what the students wanted to say.

STRUGGLING WRITERS

If . . . students have difficulty providing details for an event,

then . . . ask questions to help them identify details related to the events. For example, ask: What happens? Who does it happen to? Where is the animal? What does that place look like? What does the animal do? How does the animal feel?

Look Closely

UPPERCASE AND LOWERCASE LETTERS Review with students the uppercase and lowercase forms of the letters. Hold up an Alphabet Card for a letter, such as *Mm.* Name the two forms of the letter and have students name the letters as you point to them. Continue with other letter cards. Then write a row of mixed uppercase and lowercase letters, such as *A, a, M, m, T, t, R, r, E, e,* and *F, f.* Name a specific letter, such as uppercase *T,* and have a volunteer circle it.

END PUNCTUATION Write each punctuation mark: period, question mark, and exclamation point. Explain that these marks are used to end sentences. Write the following sentences: *Whales live in the ocean. Where do whales live? Whales are huge!* Read aloud the first sentence and circle the period. Tell students that the first sentence ends with a period because it is a telling sentence. Read the second sentence and circle the question mark. Explain that the sentence ends with a question mark because it is an asking sentence, or a question. Read the third sentence and circle the exclamation mark. Explain that the sentence ends with an exclamation mark because it shows strong feeling. Write short sentences from the selections and have student volunteers identify the end marks.

LOOK AT CRAFT

SENTENCES Write the sentence *Penguins slide on the snow.* Read aloud the sentence. Circle the *P* in the the word *Penguins.* Review with students that the uppercase *P* is used because the first word of a sentence always begins with an uppercase letter. Then write the sentence *The bear is sleeping.* Read aloud the sentence. Point to the uppercase *T* that begins the sentence. Ask: Why is this an uppercase *T*? (It is the first letter of the first word in the sentence.) Provide other examples. Have students circle the uppercase letter that begins each sentence.

CAPITALIZATION OF I Write the following sentence: *My friend and I play in the park.* Circle the word *I.* Explain that the word *I* is always written with an uppercase letter *I.* Write these sentences: *May i have a snack? Now i am ready to go.* Read each sentence and work with students to correct the capitalization of the word *I.*

ENGLISH LANGUAGE LEARNERS
If . . . students have trouble punctuating sentences in English,

then . . . provide each student with a template of simple sentences correctly punctuated with periods, question marks, and exclamation marks. Discuss how the sentences are punctuated in English and how the punctuation may differ from that of the students' home language. For example, in Spanish, question marks and exclamation marks are used at the beginning and the end of sentences. Encourage students to refer to their template when punctuating their own sentences.

STRUGGLING WRITERS
If . . . students have difficulty forming letters correctly,

then . . . provide practice in writing uppercase and lowercase letters. Write dotted letters on the board. Model how to trace the dots to form the letters. Give students a page with a dotted letter on each line. Guide them to trace the first letter and then write a row of the letter. Monitor students' printing as they trace and write the other letters on their own.

MONITOR AND SUPPORT

Name_____

Title_____

Write About Animal Homes
Writing Checklist

Work with your teacher to complete this writing checklist.

❏ I chose one animal and its home to write about.

❏ I drew a picture of the animal and its home.

❏ I drew, dictated, and/or wrote something that could happen in the animal's home.

❏ I used uppercase and lowercase letters correctly.

❏ I ended each sentence with the right punctuation mark.

❏ I reread my writing to see if it makes sense.

Unlock the Task: Write About a Special Home

BREAK APART THE TASK

Distribute copies of the task found on page 286 of the Teacher's Guide and read it aloud to students. Have students recall information about the animals and their homes from *Life in a Pond* and *A Bed for the Winter.* Create a list with pictures of the animals and their homes for students to use as they write. If students have difficulty recalling the names of the animals and their homes, review the selections together.

Read aloud the task. Work with students to name and highlight the important points in the task.

> Choose one animal or plant from *Life in a Pond* or *A Bed for the Winter.* Tell something about the animal's or plant's home. Draw a picture of the animal or plant in its home. Then draw, dictate, or write a sentence explaining something about the home.

ANSWER QUESTIONS ABOUT THE TASK

Display the questions below, read them aloud, and discuss them together. Work together to answer the questions.

- **What will I be writing?** (a sentence explaining something about the home of an animal or a plant)
- **What texts or books will I use?** (*Life in a Pond, A Bed for the Winter*)
- **What will I tell about?** (the name of an animal or plant, the kind of home it has, and details explaining something about the home)
- **What do I need to include in my writing?** (pictures and/or words in sentences)

RESTATE THE TASK

Have students restate the task in their own words. Check for possible misunderstandings or missing elements.

ENGLISH LANGUAGE LEARNERS

If . . . students have difficulty naming animals and their homes in English,

then . . . make flashcards for students to use as they write about animals and their homes. On one side of the card, include an image of the animal. Below it, label the name of the animal in English and in the students' home language. On the other side, include an image of the animal's home. Label the name of the home in English and in the students' home language. Help students practice saying the names of the animals and their homes.

STRUGGLING WRITERS

If . . . students have difficulty understanding what they will explain in their writing,

then . . . provide an example. Draw a picture of bats in a cave. Write a sentence saying *Bats spend the winter sleeping in their dark cave.* Once students understand the task, have them move on to gather ideas.

Prepare to Write

DETERMINE FOCUS

Once students clearly understand the task, have them review the selections *Life in a Pond* and *A Bed for the Winter.* Help students decide which one animal home or one plant home they want to write about. Explain that this is their topic. If necessary, tell students that where the animal or plant lives is its home. For example, if a tree lives in a forest, the forest is the tree's home. Guide students to look through the selections and mark pages about their topic with sticky notes. Provide each student with the Main Idea and Details Graphic Organizer or a web from Part 3. Work with students to write the names of the plant or animal and its home or draw pictures of them in the Main Idea box or in the center of the web. Students may also dictate the names of the plant or animal and its home for you to write.

If students have difficulty choosing a topic to write about, have them choose the plant or animal home they like best or the one they want to learn more about.

GATHER IDEAS

Help students begin to gather information for their explanations. Have them look back at the pages in the selection that they marked with sticky notes. Ask: What is this home like? Have students write, dictate, or draw facts in the detail boxes of the Main Idea and Details graphic organizer or in the ovals of the Web.

If writers become stalled, encourage them to show you the pages they marked. Reread the pages. Then ask questions: What is the home of the animal [plant]? What do the words say about this home? What do the pictures show about this home? Help students include the information in their graphic organizer.

ACCELERATED WRITERS

If . . . students want to find out more about the animal or plant and its home,

then . . . provide additional nonfiction texts or resources for students to use for gathering more facts and details about the animal or plant and its home.

TALK IT THROUGH

Display the questions below and read them aloud. Talk through them with students, explaining that writers can get valuable information if they talk about their writing ideas with others. Then pair students and have them take turns talking through the ideas for their explanations to see if their partners understand what they plan to write. Circulate among students and provide support as they ask each other questions about their writing ideas. You might wish to work as a group and have students take turns asking and answering these questions.

Questions a Writer Might Ask

- Which animal or plant did I choose?
- What kind of home does it have?
- What is its home like?
- What pictures should I draw?
- What else can I add?
- Is there anything I should leave out?

GET ORGANIZED

Work with students to think about which ideas their partner did not understand. Remind them that what was confusing for their partner will probably be confusing for other readers too. If they work to clear up confusing parts of their explanations now, their writing will be better.

Help students think about what they can improve in their explanations. If naming a clear topic was difficult, provide them with a sentence frame: A ___ makes its home in a ___. Work with students to fill in the blanks with words or pictures. If their explanation does not explain something about the home, review information about the home and guide students into telling what the home is like.

ENGLISH LANGUAGE LEARNERS

If . . . students have difficulty choosing English words to use in their explanation,

then . . . have them share their pictures of the animals and their homes with you. Talk together about what the pictures show. Some students may prefer to first explain in their home language what they want to write about.

STRUGGLING WRITERS

If . . . students are able to discuss a topic but have difficulty with an explanation or with staying on topic,

then . . . together, talk through their ideas. Write or draw a list of important words and phrases as students discuss their explanations. Then give your list to students and suggest they use it to draw their own pictures for their explanations or to label their pictures.

MONITOR AND SUPPORT

Write

BREAK IT DOWN

Display the chart below. Point out the following elements of the task and remind students that these elements need to be included in the explanations they write. Review the definitions of these elements and answer any questions students have about them. Together with students, provide and talk about examples for the last column, such as those listed below. Help students use this chart as they write.

Element	Definition	Example
Topic	• Main idea • What the information in your writing is about	A fish lives in a pond. A bat lives in a cave. A rabbit lives in a burrow.
Explanation	• A sentence explaining something about the topic • Facts and details to support the explanation	A pond is the best home for a fish because a fish needs water to live. Bats sleep upside down clinging to rocks in their cave. A lot of rabbits may crowd into an underground burrow.

ENGLISH LANGUAGE LEARNERS

If . . . students have difficulty providing an explanation in English,

then . . . have students draw a picture of their explanation. Discuss the picture, identifying words for the features that students may want to use when dictating or writing their sentence.

STRUGGLING WRITERS

If . . . students have difficulty getting started,

then . . . have students look through the selections to find a picture of the animal or plant home they want to write about. Have them draw their own picture of the plant or animal and its home. Then encourage students to tell you about the home. Record the information they provide. Help them use that information to complete this sentence frame in pictures or words. The ___ (kind of home) of a ___ (plant or animal name) is ___ (something about the home).

Look Closely

LOOK AT CONVENTIONS

SENTENCES Review with students that a complete sentence tells who or what the sentence is about and what that person, animal, or thing is or does. Write the following example of a complete sentence and read it aloud: *The bear sleeps.* Work with students to identify the parts of the complete sentence. Listen to this sentence: *The bear sleeps.* Ask questions such as Who is doing something? (the bear) What does the bear do? (sleeps) Explain that this is a complete sentence because it tells who does something and what it does. Finally read aloud the following sentence: *I rolled the ball.* Guide students to identify it as a complete sentence.

NOUNS Review with students that a naming word, or noun, names a person, a place, a thing, or an animal. Display pictures of singular nouns, such as *bed, farm,* and *girl.* Point to each picture and have students name the noun shown. Explain that each of these nouns name one, but sometimes nouns name more than one. Explain that we can make many nouns mean more than one by adding *-s* to the ends of the words. Show pictures of plural nouns, such as *beds, farms,* and *girls.* Have students name the plural noun shown in each picture; then write its picture name on the picture.

LOOK AT CRAFT

QUESTION WORDS Write these words: *who, what, where, when, why, how.* Read the words aloud as you point to them. Review with students that we often use these words at the beginning of questions, such as *Where does a frog live?* *Why does a fish live in a pond?* Display each sentence and ask a volunteer to circle the question word. Then have students use each question word in a sentence.

SENTENCES Write a sample sentence, such as *Ducks swim in the pond.* Remind students that the first word of a sentence begins with a capital letter and the sentence ends with a period, a question mark, or an exclamation mark. Write the following sentences without capitalization or end punctuation: *The fish lives in a pond. What do ducks eat?* Work with students to correct the sentences.

ENGLISH LANGUAGE LEARNERS

If . . . students have difficulty with the English names for picture names or objects in the classroom,

then . . . have them point to the picture or the object and say the word for the object in their home language. Then say the English word and have students repeat it.

STRUGGLING WRITERS

If . . . students have trouble understanding what a complete sentence is,

then . . . remind them that a complete sentence tells who or what the sentence is about and what that person, animal, or thing is or does. Have students practice constructing oral sentences about pictures. Hold up a picture and identify what it shows. For example, hold up a picture of a ball and say *The ball.* Then write the sentence frame The ball ___. Have students complete the sentence frame by telling something about the ball. If necessary, model a sentence, such as *The ball rolls on the floor.* Continue with several other pictures.

Name_____

Title_____

Write About a Special Home Writing Checklist

Work with your teacher to complete this writing checklist.

- ❏ I chose the home of one animal or plant to explain about.

- ❏ I used information from *Life in a Pond* or *A Bed for the Winter.*

- ❏ I drew a picture of the animal or plant and its home.

- ❏ I explained something about the home.

- ❏ I drew, wrote, or dictated a sentence about the home.

- ❏ I reread my writing to see if it makes sense.

Unlock the Task: Write About Changes

BREAK APART THE TASK

Distribute copies of the task found on page 146 of the Teacher's Guide. Read the task aloud and talk about it with students. Read and discuss the task, pointing out that students will be writing a personal narrative, or a story about themselves. Analyze the task, identifying the two kinds of products students will create: pictures and dictated or written sentences. Also identify the story topic, something the students did when they were younger that they do differently now. Highlight the key words and phrases, explaining that the highlighted text identifies the words and phrases that are most important.

Read aloud the task below. Have students name and highlight the important parts of the task.

> Think about something you did when you were younger that you do differently today. Write a story about how you changed. Draw a picture showing something you did when you were younger and a picture showing what you do today. Dictate or write sentences that begin "Then I" and "Now I" about your pictures.

ANSWER QUESTIONS ABOUT THE TASK

Display the questions below about the prompt and discuss them together. Read each question aloud and work together to answer the questions.

- **What will I write?** (a story about myself)
- **What will my story be about?** (something I did in the past that I do differently now)
- **What do I need to include in my story?** (pictures and words)

RESTATE THE TASK

Have students restate the task in their own words. Check for possible misunderstandings or missing elements.

ENGLISH LANGUAGE LEARNERS

If . . . students have difficulty understanding the terms *then* and *now,*

then . . . remind students that *then* tells about things that happened in the past—yesterday, last week, or years ago. *Now* tells about things happening in the present—right now, today. If possible, relate the words *then* and *now* to equivalent words in students' home languages.

STRUGGLING WRITERS

If . . . students have difficulty restating the task,

then . . . restate each part of the task and guide them to respond to questions about that part of the task. For example, say: This part of the task says to draw a picture showing something you did when you were younger and a picture showing what you do today. What are you supposed to do—write or draw pictures? Will you draw one or two pictures? If one picture shows you crawling as a baby, what might the picture show you doing today?

Prepare to Write

DETERMINE FOCUS

Once students clearly understand the writing task, remind them that they need to identify the kinds of things they did when they were younger as babies or very young children. Help them think of things people do, such as move around, eat, sleep, and play. Encourage them to think of how babies or young children do these things.

GATHER IDEAS

Draw a two-column chart with one column labeled Then and the other labeled Now. Ask questions to help students focus on how babies and very young children do things. For example, ask: Do babies feed themselves or does someone else feed them? How do little babies move around before they learn to walk? Can very young children ride bikes? What can they ride? Can babies dress themselves, or does someone else dress them? Do babies sleep in a bed or a crib? What kind of swing do babies swing in? Can babies go down slides by themselves? As students respond to the questions, draw simple pictures on the chart to represent the responses. Encourage students to suggest other things babies and younger children can or cannot do. Add their ideas to the chart.

After you have a number of activities on the Then side of the chart, point to the first activity and encourage students to tell what they do now that is different. Provide an example. For example, a baby would move by crawling and a student would move by walking. Draw simple pictures to complete the second column of the chart as students tell how they do the activity differently today.

Post and review the chart. Tell students they can choose ideas from the chart for their stories. Provide students with sticky notes that they can attach to ideas they want to write about.

ACCELERATED WRITERS

If . . . students choose more than one activity from when they were younger,

then . . . guide them to select the one activity they most want to write about. Encourage them to add details to their drawings and sentences to make their personal narratives more interesting.

Once students have chosen what they want to write about, have them make quick sketches of themselves doing something when they were younger and doing a related activity now. Ask the questions below and talk through them with students, explaining that writers can get valuable information from classmates if they talk together and ask questions about their writing ideas. Have partners discuss the sketches and the writing task. Provide support as they present their ideas and ask questions.

Questions a Writer Might Ask

- What activities am I writing about?
- What should I include in my pictures?
- What should my "Then I" sentence say?
- What should my "Now I" sentence say?
- What else can I add?
- Is there anything I should leave out?

GET ORGANIZED

Work together with students to think about the parts of their writing that confused others. Ask questions that will help them clear up confusing ideas and details. For example, if their Then and Now activities are not related, guide them to identify activities that belong together and to use those for their stories. If their narratives lack details, have them add details to their pictures and sentences.

ENGLISH LANGUAGE LEARNERS

If . . . students have difficulty choosing words to explain their then-and-now pictures,

then . . . have them show you the picture. Discuss the picture, using terms students can use in their dictated or written sentences.

STRUGGLING WRITERS

If . . . students have difficulty staying on topic,

then . . . use questions or comments to redirect the focus. For example, you can ask about what the picture shows and urge students to use that information in their sentences.

MONITOR AND SUPPORT

Write

Display the chart below. Talk with students about the elements of a personal narrative. Review with students that their writing should include pictures depicting what they could do when they were younger and what they can do today as well as dictated or written sentences that tell about their pictures. Work with students to suggest examples for the last column. Guide students in using this chart as they write.

Element	Definition	Example
Personal Narrative	• A story about yourself • Pictures and sentences that tell about something you did in the past that you do differently now	When I was a baby, I could only crawl. Now I can walk.
Drawings	• Show what I did in the past • Show what I do now	picture of me as a baby crawling picture of me as I am now walking
Sentence Starters	• "Then I . . ." tells about the past • "Now I . . ." tells about the present	Then I crawled to get around. Now I walk to get around.

ENGLISH LANGUAGE LEARNERS

If . . . students have difficulty understanding the terms for the elements in their then-and-now narrative,

then . . . provide a visual and example of each. For *narrative*, use examples from Lessons 6 and 7.

STRUGGLING WRITERS

If . . . students are intimidated by the task,

then . . . encourage students to work on one section at a time—drawings, narrative. Provide direction for each part and have students show you their work on each part before they move on. Breaking the task into smaller, more manageable pieces can remove some of the anxiety and make the task seem more achievable.

Look Closely

SENTENCES Remind students that a sentence begins with an uppercase letter and ends with a punctuation mark. Review end punctuation for each sentence type—periods for telling sentences, question marks for asking sentences, and exclamation marks for sentences showing strong feelings. Provide and discuss examples, such as: *The seasons change. How are things different now? I can ride my bike by myself!*

VERBS Remind students that verbs are action words. They tell what someone or something does. Write the word *verb* for students and provide examples. Then say the following sentences and have students name the verb: The dog <u>barks</u> loudly. I <u>tie</u> my shoe. We <u>eat</u> lunch. Remind students to include verbs in their own writing.

SPELLING Remind students that we use letters to spell the sounds in words. Say *tap*. Write the word as you segment its sounds: /t/ /a/ /p/. Spell the word aloud as you point to the letters and say it again: *t-a-p, tap*. Work with students to identify the letters that spell each of the following words: *sit, pat, map*.

SENTENCES Review with students that a complete sentence has two parts: a subject that names someone or something and a predicate that tells what that person or thing did. Provide an example of a complete sentence and identify its parts: *Keela played on the swings. Keela* is the subject, or the person who did something, and *played on the swings* is the predicate, or what she did. Write the following sentence frame: Jaz ___. Have students add predicates to complete the sentence.

DETAILS As students write, remind them that details can make their pictures and sentences more interesting. Draw a picture of a baby sitting on a floor. Ask how you could make your picture more interesting. Guide suggestions, such as showing the baby in a colorful shirt or reaching for a toy. Encourage students to add details to their pictures.

ENGLISH LANGUAGE LEARNERS

If . . . students have difficulty naming and using English verbs,

then . . . make a poster or set of picture cards depicting verbs that show daily actions. Write the verb in English below each picture. You may also include the verb written in students' home language. Make the pictures and cards available for students' reference.

STRUGGLING WRITERS

If . . . students have difficulty understanding what a complete sentence is,

then . . . write and read examples of sentence fragments and explain why they are not sentences: *Arie and Ella.* (lacks a predicate); *rode bikes.* (lacks a subject). Then combine the examples into a sentence: *Arie and Ella rode bikes.* Explain that the sentence is complete because it has both a subject and a predicate.

Name_____

Title_____

Write About Changes
Writing Checklist

Work with your teacher to complete this writing checklist.

❏ I wrote about something I did when I was younger that I do differently now.

❏ I drew pictures of what I used to do and what I do now.

❏ I wrote a "Then I" sentence to tell what I did in the past.

❏ I wrote a "Now I" sentence to tell what I do now.

❏ I used an uppercase letter at the beginning of each sentence and end punctuation.

❏ I reread my writing to see if it makes sense.

Unlock the Task: Write About Life on a Farm

BREAK APART THE TASK

Distribute copies of the task found on page 286 of the Teacher's Guide and read it aloud to students. Recall with students the details they learned about farm life from *Farming Then and Now.* Create a class list to record details about farm life including working hours and chores. The list might include working from sunrise to sunset, milking cows, feeding the animals, growing and harvesting crops, and shearing sheep.

Read aloud the task below. Together, name and highlight the important parts of the task.

> Think of what you learned about farm life from *Farming Then and Now.* Would you like to live on a farm? Draw, dictate, or write your opinion and one reason for it.

ANSWER QUESTIONS ABOUT THE TASK

Display the questions below and discuss them together. Read each question aloud. Work together to answer the questions.

- **What will I write?** (my opinion about living on a farm)
- **What texts or books will I use?** (*Farming Then and Now*)
- **What will my opinion be about?** (whether I would like to live on a farm)
- **What do I need to include in my opinion?** (pictures or words telling my opinion and one reason for it)

RESTATE THE TASK

Have students restate the task in their own words. Check for possible misunderstandings or missing elements.

ENGLISH LANGUAGE LEARNERS

If . . . students are unsure about what an opinion is,

then . . . define opinion as "what someone thinks or feels about something" and provide examples, such as *My favorite color is blue. I think that is the best song.*

STRUGGLING WRITERS

If . . . students have difficulty identifying which book to use as a writing resource,

then . . . display the selections *Farming Then and Now* and *The Old Things.* Read the titles, show several pictures inside each book, and ask which book tells about farming.

Prepare to Write

Once students clearly understand the task, have them review *Farming Then and Now* and the class list. Have students place sticky notes on any pages of the selection that they want to come back to during their writing. Tell students that they will use the list and pages to help them decide whether they would like to live on a farm.

GATHER IDEAS

Tell students they should answer the opinion question to themselves. Then help them begin to gather support for their opinions. Tell students that a good place to begin gathering ideas is from the class list or the pages they marked with sticky notes. Ask: Is there anything from the story that helped you answer the question? If you decided you would or would not like to live on a farm, then you need to ask yourself why. The answer to that "Why" question will be the reason that supports your opinion. Make a list with simple pictures of reasons students give in support of each opinion. Students may choose from these reasons or write their own.

Remind students that when they write their opinion about living on a farm, their reasons for their opinions can come from ideas in the selection or from what they already know about farms.

ACCELERATED WRITERS

If . . . students offer more than one reason for their opinions,

then . . . have them consider each reason and choose the one reason that they think is most important. They should use that reason in their writing.

MONITOR AND SUPPORT

TALK IT THROUGH

Display the following questions and read them aloud. Talk through the questions with students, explaining that writers get valuable information about their writing ideas by talking with and asking questions of others. Have students take turns reading, showing, and talking through the ideas for their opinion writing with a partner. They can use these questions. Circulate and provide support as needed.

Questions a Writer Might Ask

- What is my opinion?
- What reason do I give for my opinion?
- What pictures would help make my opinion stronger?
- What else can I add?
- Is there anything I should leave out?

GET ORGANIZED

Work with students to think about how they can improve their writing. What did others find confusing? Help students use the feedback they received from their classmates as they continue the writing process. If students need help writing a reason for their opinion, provide them with a sentence frame: I would/would not like to live on a farm because ___. If their reason does not support their opinion, direct them to the list you created earlier or the selection with sticky notes. Ask: Is there a detail here that tells more about why you have the opinion you do?

ENGLISH LANGUAGE LEARNERS

If . . . students have difficulty understanding the term *reason* and its meaning,

then . . . provide a simple explanation, such as a reason tells why you want to do something. If possible, help students relate the term *reason* to the comparable word in their home languages. For example, the Spanish word for *reason* is *razón*.

STRUGGLING WRITERS

If . . . students have difficulty providing reasons for their opinions,

then . . . ask questions to help them identify reasons that support their opinions. For example, ask: Do you like cows? Do you think it would be fun to live on a farm?

Write

Display the following chart. Review the elements and their definitions and answer any questions students may have about them. Remind students that these elements need to be included in their own opinion writing. Help students provide examples for the last column and encourage them to use this chart as they write.

Element	Definition	Example
Topic or Question	• The subject of your writing • What you will have an opinion about	Would you like to live on a farm?
Opinion	• What you think or feel about the topic or question	I would like to live on a farm. I would not like to live on a farm.
Reason	• Tells why you think or feel the way you do	There are many animals on a farm, and I like animals. I would get to grow food for people. It would be hard work to live on a farm and take care of animals and crops.

ENGLISH LANGUAGE LEARNERS

If . . . students have difficulty stating in English their opinions and reasons for them,

then . . . have them draw pictures that show them either doing something on a farm or doing something somewhere else. Ask questions to help them indicate why they want to live in that place. For example, if a picture shows a student petting a farm animal, ask: Would you like to live on a farm because you like animals?

STRUGGLING WRITERS

If . . . students are overwhelmed by the task,

then . . . have them draw pictures of where they would like to live and then discuss with you why they want to live there. Write their responses at the bottom of their pictures.

Look Closely

SENTENCES Remind students that a complete sentence begins with an uppercase letter and ends with the correct punctuation mark. Write the following sentences without capitalization or end punctuation: *I like cows. What do sheep eat? I see a barn. Where do you live?* Work with students to correct the sentences.

SPELLING Discuss how students can use letter-sounds to spell words. Remind them to listen to the sounds they hear in the word and write a letter for each sound. Demonstrate with the word *cat.* Write the letters as you say each sound aloud: /k/ /a/ /t/. Then point to the letters as you spell and say the word: *c-a-t, cat.* Practice with other words, such as *sit, map,* and *tip.*

PREPOSITIONS Make a list of common prepositions, such as *in, to, with, from,* and *on.* Remind students that prepositions are words that usually come before a naming word and show a connection to another word in the sentence. Point out the preposition in a few sample sentences: *The man sat <u>in</u> the boat. Put the plate <u>on</u> the table. I go <u>to</u> the park <u>with</u> my friend.*

SENTENCES Remind students that a sentence provides a complete thought by telling who or what does something and what is done. Write the following example and read it aloud: *The farmer grows corn.* Discuss the parts of the sentence. *The farmer* tells who is doing something and *grows corn* tells what is done. Write the following sentence frame: *The farmer ___.* Ask students to complete the sentence. If necessary, provide examples, such as *The farmer lives in a white house. The farmer is on the tractor.* Then remind students that they can expand sentences by adding details. Write and read aloud the following sentence: *I saw a cow.* Ask: What can we add to make this sentence tell more? Work with students to expand the sentence. (I saw a big brown cow. I saw a cow on the farm.) Continue expanding additional sentences by having students include nouns to provide more information.

ENGLISH LANGUAGE LEARNERS

If . . . students have difficulty understanding English prepositions,

then . . . use pictures to illustrate common prepositions. For example, show a picture of a bowl *on* a table, a child *at* the bus stop, and a fish *in* a bowl. Ask questions and have students respond using the preposition: Who is at the bus stop? (The child is at the bus stop.) Where is the fish? (The fish is in the bowl.) What is on the table? (The bowl is on the table.)

STRUGGLING WRITERS

If . . . students have trouble understanding the features of a complete sentence,

then . . . display a chart that provides models of complete sentences with labels for its distinguishing features: initial uppercase letter and end punctuation. Encourage students to refer to the chart when they are writing.

MONITOR AND SUPPORT

Name_____

Title_____

Write About Life on the Farm
Writing Checklist

Work with your teacher to complete this writing checklist.

❏ I told my opinion about living on a farm.

❏ I gave a reason for my opinion.

❏ I used information from *Farming Then and Now*.

❏ I used uppercase letters at the beginning of sentences.

❏ I ended each sentence with a punctuation mark.

❏ I used letter-sounds to spell words.

❏ I reread my writing to see if it makes sense.

Unlock the Task: Create a Story

Distribute copies of the task found on page 146 of the Teacher's Guide and read it aloud to students. Have them think about what Tessie does during the rainstorm in *Come On, Rain!* Discuss how she reacts to the storm. Then ask: What does Tessie do when she sees the rain clouds? What does she do when it is raining? Is Tessie happy about the rain? Have students share the events in the order they happen. Ask questions about the events if students' responses lack details. Discuss how Tessie and the other characters react to the storm. Tell students that they will use what they learned about Tessie and what she does during the rainstorm to write a story about what Tessie might do in a snowstorm.

Read aloud the task below. Have students name and highlight the important parts of the task.

> Think about Tessie, the main character in *Come On, Rain!* What might she do in a snowstorm? Draw, dictate, or write a story about what Tessie does in a snowstorm. Tell how she reacts to the snow.

ANSWER QUESTIONS ABOUT THE TASK

Display the questions below and talk about them together. Read each question aloud and work together to answer it.

- **What will I be writing?** (a story)
- **What texts or books will I use?** *(Come On, Rain!)*
- **What will my story be about?** (what Tessie does during a snowstorm)
- **What do I need to include in my story?** (details about what Tessie does and feels during a snowstorm.)

RESTATE THE TASK

Have students restate the task in their own words. Check for possible misunderstandings or missing elements.

ENGLISH LANGUAGE LEARNERS

If . . . students have difficulty understanding the word *reacts*,

then . . . review the meaning of the word *reacts* ("acts in response to something that happens"). Talk about how Tessie reacts to the rain in the story—what she does and how she feels. Explain that for their own stories, students should tell what Tess does in the snowstorm and how she feels about the snow.

STRUGGLING WRITERS

If . . . students have difficulty understanding the task,

then . . . review the task with them and have students say one sentence about each question. Example: I will write a story. I will use the book *Come On, Rain!* to learn about the character for my story. I will tell about something that changes for a character or for me. I will write what happens in order.

Prepare to Write

DETERMINE FOCUS

Once students clearly understand the task, provide each student with a Story Map B graphic organizer from Part 3. Remind students that they will be writing about what Tessie will do in a snowstorm. Guide students to complete the first two boxes in the graphic organizer. In the Characters box, they should identify Tessie and any other characters, such as Mamma and Tessie's friends, they want to include in their story. In the Setting box, they can draw, dictate, or write a description of the setting. Remind them that the setting should be Tessie's neighborhood on a snowy winter day. You may want to have students review the illustrations in the text to help them visualize the setting.

GATHER IDEAS

Now help students begin to gather ideas for their stories. Remind them that the main character in their story is doing something during a snowstorm. Then have students begin to fill in the Events box on their graphic organizer using pictures, dictation, or writing. Remind students that they should show their events, or what happens, in order so that readers can understand what is happening.

Remind students that they will also need to tell how the character reacts to the snowstorm. Discuss the kinds of reactions Tessie might have. For example, she might be happy or excited about the snowstorm because she and her friends will be able to play in the snow. If students have difficulty identifying how Tessie might react to the snowstorm, help them think about her reactions to the rainstorm in *Come On, Rain!* Ask: What does Tessie feel and do when she sees rain clouds? What do Tessie and her friends do and feel when it is raining hard?

MONITOR AND SUPPORT

Display the questions below and read them aloud. Talk through them with students, explaining that writers get valuable information by asking questions of others. Have pairs of students take turns talking about their stories using these questions to see if their partner understands. Circulate and provide support as needed.

Questions a Writer Might Ask

- What is my story about?
- What is Tessie doing?
- How does Tessie respond to the snowstorm?
- Are the events in the right order?
- What pictures would be good to include?
- What else can I add?
- Is there anything I should leave out?

Have students think about the things in their stories that were difficult for their partner to understand. Remind them that what was hard for their partner to understand might also confuse another reader. Ask questions that will help students clear up confusing ideas.

Have students think about how they can improve their stories. If students' stories are ordered illogically, help them number events or use sequence words, such as *first, next, then,* and *last* in their graphic organizer. If students' story ideas do not include Tessie's reactions to the snowstorm, discuss what Tessie does during the storm and what her actions show about her feelings. Then have students describe Tessie's feelings and encourage them to draw, dictate, or write their descriptions. Work with students individually and in small groups to organize and plan their stories. Some students may also benefit from working with a partner.

ENGLISH LANGUAGE LEARNERS

If . . . students have difficulty choosing words to use in their stories,

then . . . have them begin by drawing pictures to illustrate what happens in the story. Then, ask students questions about the pictures, and help them formulate short sentences or phrases for each picture. Some students may explain their story in their home language first to build confidence.

STRUGGLING WRITERS

If . . . students have difficulty ordering the events of their story,

then . . . model filling in the Events box of their graphic organizer in the correct order using *Come On, Rain!* For example: *First, Tessie is hot because there is no rain. Next, Tessie sees rain coming. Then Tessie puts on her bathing suit and goes outside. Last, Tessie, Mamma, and their friends dance in the rain.* If necessary, provide additional examples using other familiar texts.

Write

Display the chart below. Point out to students the elements of a story and their definitions. Remind them that these elements need to be included in their own stories. Review the definitions of each element and answer any questions students may have. Together, help students provide examples for the last column. Help students use this chart as they write.

Element	Definition	Example
Characters	• The people in a story	Tessie Mamma
Setting	• Where the story takes place • When the story takes place	Tessie's neighborhood on a winter day during a snowstorm
Events	• What happens in the story • Events written in the order they happen • Details telling more about the characters, setting, and events • Character's response to events	Tessie looks outside her window. She wishes it would snow. She sees one snowflake and then another. Soon it is snowing hard. Tessie is happy. She asks Mamma if she can put on her snowsuit and go out and play.

ENGLISH LANGUAGE LEARNERS

If . . . students do not have the vocabulary to describe Tessie's feelings about the snowstorm,

then . . . generate an illustrated list of feeling words, listing each word and a simple drawing of a face showing that feeling. Students can use the chart to help them.

STRUGGLING WRITERS

If . . . students are intimidated by the task,

then . . . have students focus on writing one event at a time. Ask questions about the first story event and use students' responses to help them draw, dictate, or write their first story events. Continue working with students to help them write every event and Tessie's reaction to the snowstorm.

MONITOR AND SUPPORT

Look Closely

LOOK AT CONVENTIONS

SENTENCES Remind students that sentences begin with an uppercase letter and end with a punctuation mark. Write a sentence using proper capitalization and punctuation. For example: *We played in the snow.* Point out the uppercase letter that begins the sentence and the period at the end of the sentence. Then have students review their own sentences for correct capitalization and end punctuation.

SPELLING As students write and want to spell unknown words in their stories, remind them to listen to the sounds they hear in a word and then write the letter(s) for each sound. Practice this with the word *sat.* Say: /s/ /a/ /t/. The first sound in *sat* is /s/. I will write *s.* The next sound is /a/. I will write *a.* The final sound is /t/. I will write *t.* The word *sat* is spelled *s-a-t.* Write each letter as you say its name. Practice spelling more words, such as *mop* and *tin,* with students.

PROPER NAMES Remind students that people's names, including the names of story characters, begin with an uppercase letter. Have students practice writing their own names and the name *Tessie* from the story *Come On, Rain!*

LOOK AT CRAFT

SENTENCES Write this sentence: *The friends play in the rain.* Ask: Who or what is this sentence about? (the friends) What do the friends do? (play in the rain) Remind students that every complete sentence tells who or what does something (subject) and what is done (predicate). Work with students to complete these sentence fragments: *played in the snow* (Tessie played in the snow.); *Mamma and Tessie* (Mamma and Tessie walked home.)

DETAILS Remind students that their stories should use details to make their writing more interesting for readers. Write several sentences and have students add details. For example: *I rode my bike.* (I rode my new bike down the street to the corner.) Then help students add details to their own stories.

ENGLISH LANGUAGE LEARNERS

If . . . students have difficulty adding details to their sentences,

then . . . model how to add words and phrases to sentences. For example, *Tessie built a snowman.* (Tessie and her friends built a big snowman.) Then help students identify words or phrases they can add to their own sentences.

STRUGGLING WRITERS

If . . . students do not use uppercase letters to begin sentences or people's names,

then . . . provide several model sentences and point out the uppercase letters in each. Then write several sentences that are missing uppercase letters. For example: *peter made tracks in the snow; snow fell on peter's head; mamma and tessie danced in the rain.* Have students explain how to correct them.

MONITOR AND SUPPORT

Name_____

Title_____

Create a Story
Writing Checklist

Work with your teacher to complete this writing checklist.

❏ My story tells what Tessie does in a snowstorm.

❏ I told how Tessie feels about the snowstorm.

❏ I wrote events in order.

❏ I used details in my story.

❏ I wrote complete sentences that begin with uppercase letters and end with end punctuation marks.

❏ I used uppercase letters for names of people.

❏ I used letter-sounds to spell words.

❏ I reread my writing to see if it makes sense.

Unlock the Task: Predict the Weather

BREAK APART THE TASK

Distribute copies of the task found on page 286 of the Teacher's Guide and read it aloud to students. Have students recall what they learned in *What Will the Weather Be?* and *Weather Words and What They Mean.* Make a list of students' ideas, including weather vocabulary. If students have difficulty recalling content vocabulary used to describe the weather, then review the selections together. Remind students that weather forecasts tell people what they can expect. Ask: How are weather forecasts helpful? (They tell us how to dress.)

Read aloud the task below. Work together to name and highlight the important parts of the task.

> Think of what you learned about weather from *What Will the Weather Be?* and *Weather Words and What They Mean.* Write a weather forecast. Draw pictures of two kinds of weather. Label the pictures *Today* and *Tomorrow.* Write a sentence about the weather in each picture.

ANSWER QUESTIONS ABOUT THE TASK

Display the questions below and talk about them together. Read each question aloud and help students answer it.

- **What will I be writing?** (weather forecast)
- **What texts or books will I use?** (*What Will the Weather Be?* and *Weather Words and What They Mean*)
- **What will my writing be about?** (the weather forecast for today and tomorrow)
- **What do I need to include in my weather forecast?** (pictures of the weather, labels, weather words, sentences)

RESTATE THE TASK

Have students restate the task in their own words. Check for possible misunderstandings or missing elements.

ENGLISH LANGUAGE LEARNERS

If . . . students have difficulty understanding what a weather forecast is,

then . . . provide a simple definition of *forecast,* such as "telling what might happen in the future." Explain that a weather forecast tells what the weather might be like. Then show examples of online or newspaper weather forecasts or dramatize a meteorologist delivering a weather forecast.

STRUGGLING WRITERS

If . . . students have difficulty accessing the content vocabulary needed to complete this task,

then . . . help students make a weather dictionary. Have them review the selections and choose a few weather words they would like to use in their writing. Have students write and illustrate each word. They can use the selections or a classroom pictionary as they complete the task.

MONITOR AND SUPPORT

Prepare to Write

DETERMINE FOCUS

Once students clearly understand the task, have them name different types of weather. Make a list with words *(sunny, rainy, cloudy, snowy, windy)* and simple pictures for students to use as they write. Have students choose two types of weather to include in their forecasts. Then instruct students to review the selections *What Will the Weather Be?* and *Weather Words and What They Mean.* Suggest that students use sticky notes to mark pages that include the weather they wish to write about.

GATHER IDEAS

Now help students begin to gather ideas and details for their weather forecasts. They can use the pages they marked with sticky notes. Provide a T-chart with the headings *today* and *tomorrow* for each student. If necessary, review the meanings of the words *today* and *tomorrow*. Then have students use pictures or words to record in their charts the weather information they gather for their writing.

Remind students that their writing will need to include a picture, a label, and a sentence to tell about the weather for each day. Explain that each picture and sentence should match. For example, if they draw a picture of a sun, their writing should be about sunny weather.

ACCELERATED WRITERS

If . . . students are comfortable drawing and writing to explain the weather,

then . . . encourage them to expand the information they are explaining by including daytime and nighttime weather forecasts for today and tomorrow. In this way, students can include more details in their weather forecasts. Have them draw a horizontal line across each column of their T-chart to create two boxes each for Today and Tomorrow. Suggest that they add labels to the top and bottom boxes for each day. They should label the top box Day and the bottom box Night.

TALK IT THROUGH

Display the questions below and read them aloud. Talk through them with students, explaining that writers can get help with their writing ideas by talking to others and asking questions. Have pairs of students take turns talking through their weather forecasts using these questions to see whether others understand their ideas. Provide support as you circulate among the pairs.

Questions a Writer Might Ask

- What weather am I describing for each day?
- Are my descriptions and details clear?
- What weather do my pictures show?
- What should my sentences tell about the weather in the pictures?
- What else can I add?
- Is there anything I should leave out?

GET ORGANIZED

Work with students to think about the things in their weather forecasts that were difficult for their partner to understand. Remind them that what was hard for their partner to understand would probably confuse other readers too. Help them fix these things so that their writing will be better.

Have students think about how they could make their weather forecasts clearer and more interesting. If students need to add words to describe the weather in their pictures, help them use the selections and the list you created as a class to write words that tell about each picture. If students need to add more details to their pictures, help them find pages in the selections to use as examples.

ENGLISH LANGUAGE LEARNERS

If . . . students have difficulty choosing words to describe the weather,

then . . . work with students to pronounce and understand the meanings of the following weather words: *sunny, rainy, snowy, cloudy, windy.* Make a set of weather cards that include the English word, a picture illustrating the word, and if necessary, the word in the students' home language. Practice using the weather words in sentences, for example: *Today is sunny.*

STRUGGLING WRITERS

If . . . students are able to discuss what they want to write but have difficulty staying on topic,

then . . . have students draw pictures of the weather first. Then provide the following sentence frame: It is ___. Have students complete the sentence frame by dictating or writing words to describe each kind of weather.

Write

Display the chart below. Point out to students the elements of a weather forecast and their definitions. Review the definitions and answer any questions students may have about them. Remind students that these elements need to be included in their own weather forecasts. With students, provide examples for the last column. Help students use this chart as they write.

Element	Definition	Example
Weather Words	• Words that describe the weather	sunny cloudy snowy rainy windy cold warm
Sentences	• Tell details for the weather shown in the pictures	Wear your hat and coat today because it will be cold. It will be cold and snowy tomorrow.
Labels	• Identify the day for the forecast	today tomorrow
Pictures	• Show the forecasts	picture of snow falling from the sky and covering the ground picture of clear sky with snow on the ground

ENGLISH LANGUAGE LEARNERS

If . . . students have difficulty using English words to describe the pictures,

then . . . have them work with a student who has the same home language but is more proficient in English. The students can discuss the pictures in their home language. Then they can work together to identify English words for the sentences.

STRUGGLING WRITERS

If . . . students are overwhelmed by the task,

then . . . break the task into easy steps. Have them produce the weather forecast for today first. They should (1) draw the picture, (2) label it, and (3) dictate or write a sentence about the picture. They then can repeat the steps to produce the weather forecast for tomorrow.

MONITOR AND SUPPORT

Look Closely

SENTENCES Review writing sentences correctly. Write the following example: *The sun is in the sky.* Ask: What should we remember to do when we write a sentence? (Begin with an uppercase letter; end with a punctuation mark.) Display incorrect sentences and help students identify and correct the errors. For example: *it will rain tomorrow; the clouds are gray; When will it rain.* (It will rain tomorrow. The clouds are gray. When will it rain?)

SPELLING As students write, remind them to listen for the sounds they hear in the words they want to spell. Remind them to write the letter(s) for each sound they hear. Practice with the word *not.* Say: /n/ /o/ /t/. Write each letter as you say its sound. The letters *n-o-t* spell the word *not.* Practice with more words, having students write the sound as you say it.

PREPOSITIONAL PHRASES Remind students that a preposition is a word that tells how a noun is related to another word in the sentence. Write and say this sentence: I put the book on my desk. Circle *on.* The word *on* is a preposition that tells where the book is. Where is the book? It is on the desk. Write and read aloud several sentences that include prepositional phrases. Identify each preposition and discuss what information the prepositional phrase provides readers.

SENTENCES Remind students to add details to their sentences to provide more information and make their writing clear. Write the following sentence: *Today it is sunny.* Have students suggest details to add to the sentence. (Today it is sunny and windy.) Have students add details to their own weather forecasts.

WEATHER WORDS Tell students that when they work on an informative or explanatory writing task, they will use words that are specific to the topic. Review weather words in *Weather Words and What They Mean.* Encourage students to use words from the text, such as *flurries, sleet, snow, snowstorm,* and *blizzard* in their own sentences.

ENGLISH LANGUAGE LEARNERS

If . . . students have difficulty using prepositional phrases,

then . . . review by giving simple commands for students to follow. For example, say: Place the book on the shelf. Put your paper by the basket. Write the prepositional phrase from each sentence and point to the preposition. Have students say the prepositional phrase. Then have students give a few commands that include prepositional phrases.

STRUGGLING WRITERS

If . . . students have difficulty adding details to their weather forecasts,

then . . . make a T-chart that lists the weather words in the first column and details in the second column. Details can be in the form of pictures or words. For example, details for *sunny* might include *hot, warm, bright,* and so on.

Name_____

Title_____

Predict the Weather
Writing Checklist

Work with your teacher to complete this writing checklist.

❏ I wrote a weather forecast for today and tomorrow.

❏ I used information from *What Will the Weather Be?* and *Weather Words and What They Mean.*

❏ I drew pictures with labels to show the weather for each day.

❏ I used weather words to tell about each picture.

❏ I wrote sentences that began with an uppercase letter and ended with the right punctuation mark.

❏ I used letter-sounds to spell words.

❏ I reread my writing to see if it makes sense.

Unlock the Task: Write About a Day with My Friend

BREAK APART THE TASK

Distribute copies of the task found on page 146 of the Teacher's Guide and read it aloud to students. Have students pretend they are friends and spending the day with the main character in either *I Love Saturdays y domingos* or *Apple Pie 4th of July*. Work with students to generate a list of activities that friends can do together. Have students choose three activities and tell which one they would do first, next, and last. Then have students think about how they feel about their day with their friend. Remind students they can use ideas from what they learned from reading and also their own experiences.

Read aloud the following task. Work with students to name and highlight the important points in the task.

> Pretend you are friends with the main character in *I Love Saturdays y domingos* or *Apple Pie 4th of July*. Write a story about three things you do together. Use the words *first, then,* and *last* to tell the events in order. Tell how you and your friend feel about your day.

ANSWER QUESTIONS ABOUT THE TASK

Display the questions below about the task. Read them aloud and discuss them together.

- **What will I be writing?** (a narrative in order)
- **Which text or book will I use?** (*I Love Saturdays y domingos* or *Apple Pie 4th of July*)
- **What events will I describe?** (three things friends do together)
- **What do I need to include in my writing?** (three events, the words *first, then,* and *last,* and my feelings about the day)

RESTATE THE TASK

Ask students to restate the task in their own words. Check for possible misunderstandings or missing elements.

ENGLISH LANGUAGE LEARNERS

If . . . students have difficulty using the time-order words to order their events,

then . . . label the sections of their Story Map A graphic organizer. Label the first section 1. *First,* the second section 2. *Then,* and the third section 3. *Last.* Guide them to put their events in 1, 2, 3 order. Then when they draw, dictate, or write each event for the story, they can use the word next to the number.

STRUGGLING WRITERS

If . . . students have difficulty rewording the task,

then . . . review the task with them and help them restate each part of the task. Example: I need to pretend I am a friend with one character from a story. Then I will write three things that my friend and I do together. I will use time words *first, then,* and *last* to show when we do each thing. Finally, I will tell how my friend and I feel about our day together.

Prepare to Write

Once students clearly understand the writing task, have them review the selections *I Love Saturdays y domingos* and *Apple Pie 4th of July.* Refer students to the class list of activities friends do in a day. Guide students to choose three and to put the three events in the order they would do the events. Remind students that they will use the time-order words *first, then,* and *last* to tell when the events happen.

GATHER IDEAS

Help students begin to gather information for their narrative. Some students may benefit from looking through the selection in which their character is featured. They can mark pages that tell about activities the character enjoys. Students could use these activities or ones like them in their own story. Once they choose three events, students can use the Story Map A graphic organizer in Part 3 to record the events in order. Remind them that the first box should tell the event that happens first. The middle box should tell what happens next. The last box should tell what happens last. Allow students to draw, dictate, or write the events in the organizer.

Remind students that in a narrative, events are told in the order they happen. To help them record events in order, ask questions such as: What do you and your friend do first? What do you and your friend do next? What is the last thing you and your friend do?

ACCELERATED WRITERS

If . . . students have included more than three activities,

then . . . have them review the activities they selected and choose the three that they would most enjoy doing. Suggest that students review their writing to add descriptive details about each activity. Remind students to tell how they and their friend from the story enjoy their day together.

Display the questions below and read them aloud. Talk through them with students, explaining that writers can get valuable information by asking questions of others. Have students work in pairs, taking turns talking through their story ideas using these questions to see if their partner understands. Circulate among the pairs and provide support as needed.

Questions a Writer Might Ask

- Which three activities am I writing about?
- Which activity do we do first?
- Which activity do we do next?
- Which activity do we do last?
- Do the order of the events make sense?
- Have I used the words *first, then,* and *last?*
- What do I say about how my friend and I feel about our day together?
- What pictures would be good to include?
- Did I forget anything?
- Is there anything I should leave out?

GET ORGANIZED

Have students think about the parts of their narrative that their partner did not understand. Remind them that what was hard for their partner to understand might also confuse another reader. Ask questions that will help students clear up confusing ideas.

Together, help students determine which parts of their narratives they need to improve. If putting the activities in order was difficult for students, refer them to their Story Map A organizer and remind them to use the time-order words *first, then,* and *last.* If students are having difficulty describing their reactions to the activities, have them think about the activities and how they feel after each activity.

ENGLISH LANGUAGE LEARNERS

If . . . students have difficulty choosing words to use in their narratives,

then . . . have them draw pictures to show the activities. Then use guiding questions about the pictures to help students select words to use. For example, if a student has a picture that shows the friends with a ball, ask questions, such as *Are you playing basketball? Are you playing ball at your home? In a park?*

STRUGGLING WRITERS

If . . . students are able to discuss what they want to write but have difficulty writing their narratives,

then . . . have students either dictate their narratives to you or have them draw illustrations to depict the three events and their reaction to them.

Write

Display the chart below. Point out to students the elements of a narrative. Remind them that these elements need to be included in their own writing. Review the definitions of each element and answer any questions students may have about them. Work together with students to provide the examples using their own writing or ideas from texts you have read together. Help students use this chart as they write.

Element	Definition	Example
Characters	• The people or animals in a story	the girl from *I Love Saturdays y domingos* myself
Setting	• Where the story takes place • When the story takes place	a park a sunny day after lunch
Plot/Events	• What happens in the story or event • Events are written in the order they happened. • Time-order words are used to tell the order of events: *first, next, then, finally, after, before, last.* • Details tell more about the characters, setting, and events.	My friend and I play together for a whole day! First, we played on the swings and slides. Then, we kicked my soccer ball. Last, we ate a snack.
Reaction	• How characters feel about the events	We had fun. We want to play together again.

ENGLISH LANGUAGE LEARNERS

If . . . students are intimidated by the task because of their lack of language skills,

then . . . have students work with an ESL assistant or a partner who is more proficient in English. They can tell their narratives in their home language and the assistant or partner can help them choose English words to use in their narratives.

STRUGGLING WRITERS

If . . . students have difficulty organizing their narratives,

then . . . have them begin by sequencing illustrations that they want to include in their narratives. Encourage students to number their drawings and tell about the image numbered *1* first. Then they should dictate or write a sentence to accompany it before telling about the next image.

MONITOR AND SUPPORT

Look Closely

SENTENCES Remind students that they have worked on writing sentences correctly using uppercase and lowercase letters, proper spacing between letters and words, and correct punctuation at the end of each sentence. Write a few sentences that are missing uppercase letters at the beginning, punctuation marks at the end, or that have problems with spacing. Have students tell what is wrong with each sentence. Rewrite the sentence correctly, and have students copy the correct sentence.

SPELLING As students write, tell them to listen to the sounds they hear in the words they want to spell. Model how to use letter-sounds to spell CVC words, such as *cat* and *fan*. Remind students to write the letter(s) for each sound they hear. Encourage students to review their writing to find words that may be missing sounds. Students may also use a word wall, word journal, their *Reader's and Writer's Journal,* or the text to help them spell unknown words.

NOUNS Remind students that nouns are words that name people, places, things, and animals. Have students share some of the nouns they used in their writing. Help students check the sentences in their narratives for the proper use of nouns.

LOOK AT CRAFT

SENTENCES Remind students that in a narrative, the sentences should be in the order that the events take place. Tell students to review their writing to make sure they also included at least one sentence about how they feel at the end of the day.

VERBS Remind students that every sentence has at least one verb. Review with students that verbs are action words that tell what someone or something is doing or what someone or something is like. Provide an example of a sentence with a general verb and the same sentence with a more descriptive verb, such as *We go down the slide. We speed down the slide.* Ask which verb helps students visualize the action better. Then guide students to evaluate their own sentences for verb choice. If needed, help them identify and select more descriptive verbs.

ENGLISH LANGUAGE LEARNERS

If . . . students have difficulty using nouns and verbs,

then . . . make a T-chart labeled Nouns and Verbs and guide students to name nouns and verbs to list in the chart. You might also provide noun and verb picture flash cards that students can use to create sentences. For example, a noun card might show a picture of a girl with the word *girl* written under the picture. A verb card might show a picture of a child running with the word *run* written under it.

STRUGGLING WRITERS

If . . . students have difficulty writing complete sentences,

then . . . remind students that a complete sentence tells who or what does something and what the person or thing does. Provide and discuss example sentences, such as *The friends run to the swings.* Then help students check their writing and revise any sentences that are incomplete.

Name_____

Title_____

Write About a Day with My Friend Writing Checklist

Work with your teacher to complete this writing checklist.

❏ I chose the main character from either *I Love Saturdays y domingos* or *Apple Pie 4th of July* to be my friend.

❏ I described three activities my friend and I do together.

❏ I used the words *first, then,* and *last* to tell the events in order.

❏ I told how we felt at the end of the day.

❏ I wrote sentences that begin with uppercase letters and end with the right punctuation marks.

❏ I sounded out words to spell them.

❏ I reread my writing to see if it makes sense.

Unlock the Task: Write Questions and Answers

Distribute copies of the task found on page 286 of the Teacher's Guide and read it aloud. Together with students recall and list information about music from *Making Music*. Then make a separate list of information about clothing given in *Clothes in Many Cultures.* If students have difficulty recalling information from the texts, have them look through the selections for word and picture clues. As needed, ask questions to elicit further details about the information in each selection.

Read aloud the task below. Work with students to name and highlight the important points in the task.

> Think of two questions about the selections *Making Music* and *Clothes in Many Cultures.* Use evidence from the texts to answer the questions. Write or dictate one question about music and one question about clothing. Draw, dictate, or write the answer to each question, using facts from the texts.

ANSWER QUESTIONS ABOUT THE TASK

Display the questions below and discuss them together. Read each question aloud and work together to answer it.

- **What will I be writing?** (questions and answers)
- **What texts will I use?** *(Making Music* and *Clothes in Many Cultures)*
- **What will my questions and answers be about?** (about music and clothing)
- **What do I need to include?** (questions about music and clothing, answers with facts from the texts)

RESTATE THE TASK

Ask students to restate the task in their own words. Check for possible misunderstandings or missing elements.

ENGLISH LANGUAGE LEARNERS

If . . . students are unfamiliar with the term *text evidence,*

then . . . model asking a question and using the text to find the answer. For example, to answer the question, *How do some children play ankle bells?,* turn to p. 8 and read the second paragraph. Then say: The text says that children play ankle bells by moving their feet. This is the text evidence I need to answer my question.

STRUGGLING WRITERS

If . . . students have difficulty trying to understand what should be included in their writing,

then . . . review the task with them and have students reread a bulleted question and then provide the answer. For example: My writing will include two questions and two answers. I will use facts from the texts *Making Music* and *Clothes in Many Cultures.* My writing should have questions and answers with facts.

Prepare to Write

DETERMINE FOCUS

Once students clearly understand the task, have them review the selections *Making Music* and *Clothes in Many Cultures.* Work with students to record information about music and clothing. Students may benefit from putting sticky notes on the text pages that have interesting information about music or clothing.

GATHER IDEAS

Guide students in gathering facts for their questions and answers by reviewing the pages on which they put sticky notes. Give each student a graphic organizer to use to sort his or her information. Write *Music* in one column and *Facts* in the next. Do the same for clothing. Model how to identify a detail about music and facts that support it. For example, identify a musical instrument, such as panpipes. Then identify facts about panpipes in the words and the pictures. (You blow across the top of the pipes to play them. The pipes are different lengths.) Have students record information in their charts that they may want to ask questions about. They can then use their charts to generate questions and develop answers based on text evidence. Suggest that students circle the information in each chart that they will write about.

Remind students to choose just one musical instrument and just one piece of clothing to write their questions and answers about. If students are having difficulty choosing just one item for each question, encourage them to create a two-column chart with their choices. Students should list instruments that interest them in one column and then clothing that interests them in the other column. Tell students to choose just one item from each column.

ACCELERATED WRITERS

If . . . students provide more than two questions and answers about music and clothing,

then . . . review the task, noting that it states to provide only one question for music and one for clothing. Have students evaluate their questions and answers for completeness and accuracy and choose the two best ones. Encourage them to use as many details from the text as possible to make their answers complete.

TALK IT THROUGH

Display the following questions and read them aloud. Talk through the questions, explaining that writers can get valuable help and improve their writing by discussing their ideas with others. Then have students work in pairs, taking turns asking each other questions about the ideas for their questions and answers. In this way, students will see whether others understand what they want to write about. Circulate among the pairs and provide direction as needed.

Questions a Writer Might Ask

- What is my question about music?
- What is the answer to my question?
- Have I included facts from *Making Music* in my answer?
- What question do I ask about clothing?
- What is the answer to my question?
- Have I included facts from *Clothes in Many Cultures* in my answer?
- What else can I add?
- Is there anything I should leave out?

Encourage students to ask partners questions of their own.

GET ORGANIZED

Work with students to think about the questions or answers that their partner did not understand. Point out that what was confusing for their partner will likely be confusing for other readers as well. Have students work on revising their questions and answers for clarity.

Have students gather all the facts they can use to answer a question and determine which facts they will use. Remind students that their answers should be based on evidence, or facts from the words and photos, in the two selections.

ENGLISH LANGUAGE LEARNERS

If . . . students have difficulty choosing words to write their questions and answers,

then . . . have them begin by drawing or gathering pictures and other images they can use to ask and answer questions. These can be drawn, selected from magazines or newspapers, or taken from clip art software. Talk together about what the selected images tell about the music or clothing. To build confidence, some students may want to tell their questions and answers first in their home language.

STRUGGLING WRITERS

If . . . students are having difficulty focusing on generating two questions with answers,

then . . . help them work on generating a question and an answer for each selection separately. Guide them as they look for information in *Making Music* to ask about. Help them identify the text evidence that answers the question. After they write their question and answer for *Making Music,* repeat the process for *Clothes in Many Cultures.*

MONITOR AND SUPPORT

Write

Display the chart below. Review with students the elements of questions and answers that they need to include in their writing. Remind them to use words that ask questions, such as *who, what, when, where, why,* and *how*. Review the chart below and answer any questions students may have. Then work with students to provide examples of questions and answers based on text evidence for the last column. Help students use this chart as they write.

Element	Definition	Examples
Question	• Asks something • Uses a question word, such as *who, what, where, when, why,* or *how* • Ends with a question mark	• What are chapchas made from? • How can you make music without instruments? • Why do people wear parkas? • What do office workers in Asia wear to work?
Answer	• Response to a question • Provides information • Uses text evidence	• Chapchas are made from the toenails of goats. • You can clap, stomp your feet, hum, sing, or whistle to make music without instruments. • People wear parkas to stay warm when it is cold. • Office workers in Asia wear business suits.

ENGLISH LANGUAGE LEARNERS

If . . . students misunderstand the directions and write two questions about one selection,

then . . . provide a sheet of paper for each title. Label the selection's title at the top of the page. Divide the sheet in half, and then label one half *1 Question* and the other half *1 Answer*. Have students use these sheets for their writing.

STRUGGLING WRITERS

If . . . students have difficulty thinking of questions to ask,

then . . . have them look through each selection to find a fact that they think is interesting. Help them convert the fact into a question. For example, for the fact "A group of singers is called a choir," you can guide them to ask, *What is a choir?*

MONITOR AND SUPPORT

Look Closely

SENTENCES Remind students that when writing a sentence that is a question, they use an uppercase letter at the beginning and a question mark at the end. Share examples of questions as models. Then write incorrect questions for students to identify and correct the errors.

SPELLING As students write, have them listen to the sounds they hear in the words they want to spell. Remind them to write the letter(s) for each sound they hear. Have students who struggle dictate words to you, and guide them in identifying the letters that correspond to the sounds in the words. Students may also use a word wall, word journal, or the texts to help them spell difficult words.

CAPITALIZATION Remind students that their questions and answers should begin with an uppercase letter. Have partners review each other's writing to check for uppercase letters at the beginning of questions and answers.

SENTENCES Remind students that their answers should be written in complete sentences that tell who or what does something and what the person or thing does. The beginning word in their answer should start with an uppercase letter. The answer should end with a period. Share examples of statements that students can use as models. Have students check that their answers are complete sentences.

END PUNCTUATION Display example questions and answers with correct end punctuation and have students tell which punctuation mark is used in each question and answer. Discuss the differences between a period and a question mark and review when each is used. Have students check for correct punctuation in their writing.

ENGLISH LANGUAGE LEARNERS

If . . . students have difficulty understanding some conventions,

then . . . help them participate in the discussion by providing sentence starters to use when forming answers about the conventions: Every sentence begins with ___. Every question always ends with a ___. Every answer ends with a ___. Allow children to complete the sentence frames using words or written symbols.

STRUGGLING WRITERS

If . . . students have difficulty using correct end punctuation,

then . . . remind them that every question should end in a question mark and every answer should end with a period. Show students several examples of each. Post a reminder that students can refer to, such as:

question = ?

answer = .

Name_____

Title_____

Write Questions and Answers Writing Checklist

Work with your teacher to complete this writing checklist.

❏ I wrote one question about music.

❏ I wrote one question about clothing.

❏ I used *Making Music* and *Clothes in Many Cultures* to find facts to use in my answers.

❏ I used uppercase letters to start each question and answer.

❏ I used question marks to end my questions and periods to end my answers.

❏ I reread my questions and answers to see if they make sense.

Unlock the Task: Write About My Favorite Book

BREAK APART THE TASK

Distribute copies of the task found on page 146 of the Teacher's Guide and read it aloud to students. Hold up *The Tiny Seed* and *Jack's Garden* and have students share what they remember about each story. Ask questions about the stories if students' responses lack details. Make a list or draw simple pictures of the ideas shared. Tell students that in this writing task, they will tell their opinion about one of these texts. That is, they will tell which story they like better and why they like it better. Remind students that when they give their opinion, they tell what they think about something and then they tell the reasons they think the way they do.

Read aloud the following task. Help students name the important points in the task. Talk about each part and highlight each as you discuss it.

Choose which story about plants you like better, *The Tiny Seed* or *Jack's Garden.* State your opinion about the story you like better. Tell the name of the story you are writing about. Draw, dictate, or write at least two reasons to support your opinion.

ANSWER QUESTIONS ABOUT THE TASK

Display the following questions. Read and discuss the key points of each question. Then work with students to answer each question.

- **What will I be writing?** (my opinion about a story)
- **What texts or books will I use?** (*The Tiny Seed* or *Jack's Garden*)
- **What will I write about?** (which story I liked better and why I liked it better)
- **What do I need to include in my opinion?** (the book title, my opinion, and at least two reasons)

RESTATE THE TASK

Have students restate the task in their own words. Check for possible misunderstandings or missing elements.

ENGLISH LANGUAGE LEARNERS

If . . . students have difficulty understanding what an opinion is,

then . . . define *opinion* as "what you think or feel about something" and provide an example, such as *I like the color yellow best because it is the color of the sun.* Students practice stating an opinion about something they are familiar with, such as a sport or a school subject. For example: I like soccer because it is good exercise.

STRUGGLING WRITERS

If . . . students have difficulty forming an opinion about which book they preferred,

then . . . use a Venn diagram to help students compare the books. Point out differences in the books and ask questions: Which book taught you a new fact? Which book was fun to read? Which book uses rhyme? Which book had pictures you liked? Guide students to form an opinion based on their answers.

Prepare to Write

Once students clearly understand the task, have them review the selections *The Tiny Seed* and *Jack's Garden.* Remind students that they are to choose which story they like better. Have students look through both stories and decide which one they prefer.

If students have difficulty choosing between the two stories, instruct them to think about the text features, illustrations, and the things they learned in each. If both stories seem about equal, have students think about which story they would want to share with a friend.

GATHER IDEAS

Help students begin to gather support for their opinion. Some students might use sticky notes to mark pages that support their opinion. Other students may benefit from filling in a concept web by drawing, dictating, or writing their ideas with teacher support. Explain to them that they are to tell what they like about the book and why they like that. Remind them that they are to identify at least two reasons that support their opinions. Encourage students to gather as many reasons as possible, even though they might not use all their ideas in their final opinion piece.

Remind students that when they write an opinion about a story, their reasons, support, and examples should come from that story. For example, if some students like *Jack's Garden* better, remind them to use that story when gathering ideas to support their opinion.

ACCELERATED WRITERS

If . . . students have too many examples and reasons for their opinion,

then . . . have them determine which ones best support their opinion about the story. Suggest that they cross out ideas that provide little or no support of their opinions.

TALK IT THROUGH

Display the following questions and read them aloud to the class. Talk through the questions, explaining that writers get valuable information by asking questions of others. Tell partners to take turns asking each other these questions. Circulate among partners and provide support.

Questions a Writer Might Ask

- What is my opinion?
- Which story am I writing about?
- What reasons do I give for my opinion?
- How do my reasons support my opinion?
- What else can I add?
- Is there anything I should leave out?

GET ORGANIZED

Work with students to think about the parts of their opinions and reasons their partner did not understand. Remind them that what was hard for their partner to understand will probably confuse other readers too. Encourage students to fix these confusing parts, so that their writing will be better.

Direct students to review their sticky notes or concept webs. Have them draw a line through any ideas that do not support their opinion about the story. If students do not have at least two reasons to support their opinion, guide them to go back to the book they have chosen and look for more ideas.

ENGLISH LANGUAGE LEARNERS

If . . . students have difficulty choosing the words to explain their opinion,

then . . . then have them point to the parts of the story or the pictures that they like best. Talk together about what is happening in that part of the story or in the picture. If necessary, allow students to use their first language to describe their reasons. Then help them restate their reasons in English.

STRUGGLING WRITERS

If . . . students have difficulty organizing reasons that support their opinion,

then . . . have them restate their opinion. Then ask: What do you like best about this story? Why do you like this so much? What else do you like about this story? You might also ask very specific questions about the story's structure, illustrations, and so on.

Write

Display the chart below. Review these elements of opinion writing and their definitions. Answer any questions students may have about them. Remind students that these elements need to be included in their own opinion writing. Together, help students provide examples for the last column using their own writing or texts you have read together. Then help students use this chart as they write, dictate, or draw their opinions.

Element	Definition	Example
Topic	• What you are writing about	*The Tiny Seed* *Jack's Garden*
Opinion	• What you think or how you feel about the topic	I think *The Tiny Seed* is a better story. I liked *Jack's Garden* the best.
Reasons or Support	• Tells why you think or feel the way you do • Includes examples from the story	The pictures in *The Tiny Seed* are more colorful. The labels on each page in *Jack's Garden* helped me learn about the things that Jack needed to plant a garden. *Jack's Garden* has repeating and rhyming words that help me read and understand the story.

ENGLISH LANGUAGE LEARNERS

If . . . students are intimidated by the language demands of the task,

then . . . break the task into smaller, more manageable pieces. First have students write or dictate a sentence stating which story they liked better. Then have them write or dictate a sentence that gives one reason they preferred that story and then repeat for a second reason. If students have additional support for their opinion, have them continue adding reasons, focusing on one sentence at a time.

STRUGGLING WRITERS

If . . . students have difficulty organizing their opinion and reasons,

then . . . provide sentence frames: I liked ___ better because ___. My favorite story was ___ because ___.

Look Closely

SENTENCES Remind students that they have worked on writing sentences that begin with uppercase letters and end with punctuation marks. Review with students the three kinds of sentences and their end marks. Then write a few sentences that are missing uppercase letters and/or use incorrect end punctuation marks. Guide students to identify and correct the mistakes they see. Then have them review their own writing to make sure each sentence begins with an uppercase letter and ends with the correct punctuation mark.

SPELLING Remind students that when they spell a word, they should write the letter(s) for each sound they hear. Choose words from the texts, say the words one at a time, and have students write the letters they hear. For example, say: Spell *wet, /w/ /e/ /t/.* Spell *hot, /h/ /o/ /t/.*

PRONOUN I Remind students that they should always use an uppercase letter when they write the word *I.* Instruct students to check their writing for the correct capitalization of the word *I.* Have them correct any sentences in which they wrote a lowercase *i* when talking about themselves.

SENTENCES Remind students that their reasons should support their opinion. Have students review their writing and revise or remove sentences that do not support their opinion.

DETAILS Review with students that details can help make the reasons that support their opinions stronger. Help them add details or examples to strengthen their writing. For example, if they are writing about the labels in *Jack's Garden,* guide them to name some of the tools or plants identified with labels in the story.

ENGLISH LANGUAGE LEARNERS

If . . . students have difficulty with English spelling,

then . . . review the letter-sounds in the word they are trying to spell. Sound out each letter-sound and help students identify the letter or letters that stand for that sound. Write the letter and continue until you have written the entire word. Then have students write the word as they say the sounds.

STRUGGLING WRITERS

If . . . students' writing lacks detail,

then . . . remind students that when they use detail words, their writing is clearer and gives more information. Model adding detail words to a sentence. Example: *I swam in the clear, blue ocean* instead of *I swam.* Discuss how adding detail words helps the reader. Guide students to add detail words as they revise their sentences.

MONITOR AND SUPPORT

Name_____

Title_____

Write About My Favorite Book
Writing Checklist

Work with your teacher to complete this writing checklist.

- ❏ I chose a story and told my opinion about it.

- ❏ I used the name of the story.

- ❏ I gave at least two reasons for my opinion.

- ❏ I used information from the story to support my opinion.

- ❏ I used uppercase letters at the beginning of sentences and punctuation marks at the end.

- ❏ I reread my writing to see if it makes sense.

Unlock the Task: Create a Did You Know? Book

Distribute copies of the task found on page 286 of the Teacher's Guide and read it aloud to students. Have students describe the patterns in nature they learned about in *Plant Patterns* and *Swirl by Swirl: Spirals in Nature.* As students recall the patterns, show the images in the text and add each pattern to a class list. Ask questions about the pattern if students have difficulty articulating their thoughts. Then ask: Why is it important to have a picture to go along with the text? (The picture shows what the pattern looks like. It gives the reader more information.)

Read aloud the following task. Help students name and highlight the important parts of the task.

> Look at patterns in nature using *Plant Patterns* and *Swirl by Swirl: Spirals in Nature* and other sources. Write your own Did You Know? book about patterns in nature that includes information learned from your research. Name what you are writing about, give information about your topic, and include an ending for your book.

ANSWER QUESTIONS ABOUT THE TASK

Display the following questions and read them aloud. Discuss the key points of each question to ensure that students fully understand the task.

- **What will I be writing?** (a Did You Know? book about patterns in nature)
- **What will that book look like?** (a short book with facts and pictures)
- **What texts or books will I use?** (*Plant Patterns* and *Swirl by Swirl: Spirals in Nature;* other books)
- **What information will be in my book?** (the name of my topic, facts about the patterns, a conclusion)

RESTATE THE TASK

Ask students to restate the task in their own words. Check for possible misunderstandings or missing elements.

ENGLISH LANGUAGE LEARNERS

If . . . students have difficulty understanding what a Did You Know? book is,

then . . . bring in examples of Did You Know? books and lead a discussion about what makes Did You Know? books different from other kinds of books.

STRUGGLING WRITERS

If . . . students struggle to understand what information will be in their book,

then . . . have students recall the information about patterns that was given in the selections. Guide them to see that the books told what the patterns looked like, where they could be found, and how they could be helpful. Tell students that they should look for these facts to include in their book.

Prepare to Write

DETERMINE FOCUS

Once students clearly understand the task, guide the shared research project by working with students as they look through the selections and other books. Help them choose patterns in nature they would like to write about. If students have difficulty choosing patterns, remind them that they can write about more than one pattern.

Have students work in small groups to review the selections *Plant Patterns* and *Swirl by Swirl: Spirals in Nature.* Have students use sticky notes to mark the pages that tell about the patterns they want to write about. Create a T-chart, and label each column with the title of a text. Distribute these to students.

GATHER IDEAS

Have students in each group work together to gather facts and details for their Did You Know? books. Direct students to review the book pages they marked to find information about the patterns they selected. Provide additional sources that students can use to research information as well. Work with students to take notes on the facts or details they find. Have them dictate, draw, or write facts or details in their T-charts. Encourage groups to gather as many ideas as possible now, even though they may not use them all in their books.

Remind students that their Did You Know? books should include facts about the patterns in nature. It should not include their opinions. If students struggle to find facts, guide them to identify a pattern in one of the selections and tell what the source says about it. Ask: What does this selection say about (name of pattern). Where do you find the pattern? What is the pattern like? How is it like other patterns? How is it different?

MONITOR AND SUPPORT

ACCELERATED WRITERS

If . . . students have many more facts than needed for their Did You Know? book,

then . . . tell them to circle the facts that describe the patterns best or the ones that have the most detail. Remind students that each fact must be about the patterns they are writing about. Suggest that they include pictures of their patterns.

Display the following questions. Read and discuss them together. Explain to students that talking through their ideas with a classmate will help them identify ways to make their writing better. Instruct students to take turns asking questions about their Did You Know? books with a partner. Circulate among pairs and provide direction and support as needed.

Questions a Writer Might Ask

- Which patterns am I writing about?
- What did I learn about these patterns?
- What information is most important?
- Where did my information come from?
- What pictures would be good to include?
- What else can I add?
- Is there anything that I should leave out?

GET ORGANIZED

Help students think about the parts of their book that their partner did not understand. Remind them that what was hard for their partner to understand will probably confuse other readers too. Ask students how they think they can improve their writing.

Have students review their T-chart and choose only the information that is most important for their books. Have them draw a line through any facts that would not be helpful to the reader. If they are missing important facts, guide students to use the texts to find a few more details about the patterns they chose. Students should also decide whether to include pictures or drawings to ensure that the reader will understand the patterns and what they look like.

ENGLISH LANGUAGE LEARNERS

If . . . students have difficulty using pattern-related vocabulary,

then . . . work with them to find and read descriptive words in the selections, such as *stripe, row, spiral, ring,* and place a sticky note under each word. Then have students draw pictures of each pattern-related word and label each picture. They may want to label the pictures in both English and their home language.

STRUGGLING WRITERS

If . . . students are able to discuss what they want to write about but have difficulty choosing the facts that are most important,

then . . . work with students to identify the most important facts about the patterns. Guide them to list these facts and refer to the list as they write.

Write

Display the chart below. Review these elements and their definitions. Answer any questions students may have about them. Remind students that these elements need to be included in their own writing. Work with students to provide examples for the last column using their own writing or other texts you have read together. Help students use this chart as they write.

Element	Definition	Example
Title	• Names the topic • Catches the reader's interest	*Did You Know There Are Patterns in Nature?*
Text	• Provides facts and details about the topic • May use pictures to show the patterns	Corn is planted in rows. It looks like stripes when you look at it. Corn has rows of kernels that make a pattern. Tree trunks have a pattern of rings. Each year, a new ring is added to the trunk. The needles on a cactus make a pattern. They look like a star.
Conclusion	• Is the last part of the book • May summarize the informatiion or make a suggestion	Every kind of flower has its own shape pattern. You can name the flower by its pattern. Be a pattern spy! Go outdoors. Look around. Find patterns of colors or shapes.

ENGLISH LANGUAGE LEARNERS

If . . . students are intimidated by the language demands of the task,

then . . . encourage students to focus on writing and illustrating one fact at a time. Work with students to write a fact from their two-column chart and then add a picture. Have them write one sentence telling a fact about the pattern and then label their drawing with other words they have learned but are uncertain of using in a sentence.

STRUGGLING WRITERS

If . . . students have difficulty organizing their Did You Know? book,

then . . . have them begin by writing the name of each pattern on a sheet of paper. Then have students place each fact from their T-chart onto the page with the name of the corresponding pattern.

Look Closely

LOOK AT CONVENTIONS

SENTENCES Remind students that they have worked on writing sentences correctly using uppercase and lowercase letters and end punctuation marks. Using selections you have read, write examples of incorrect sentences and have students identify and correct the mistakes. Then have them review their Did You Know? books to make sure each sentence begins with an uppercase letter and ends with the correct punctuation mark.

SPELLING As students write, tell them to listen to the sounds they hear in the words they want to spell and write the letter(s) for each sound they hear. Post words students might use in their writing, such as *corn, plant, flower,* and *garden*, on the word wall. Say each word and have students identify the letter for each sound as you write it. Remind students to refer to a word wall, word journal, their *Reader's and Writer's Journal,* or the texts to help them spell words.

VERBS Remind students that verbs can tell about the present, the past, and the future. Guide students to provide examples of phrases that use verbs for now (*I run, she swims*), verbs for the past (*I ran, she swam*), and verbs for the future (*I will run, she will swim*). Have students review their writing for their use of verbs.

LOOK AT CRAFT

SENTENCES Remind students that each of their sentences should tell about the nature patterns they have chosen. Have students exchange books with a partner. Does each sentence tell about the nature pattern on that page? Have students review their writing and remove sentences that do not belong.

NOUNS Review singular and plural nouns. Display singular nouns such as *tree, pattern, seed, petal.* For each noun, ask: How many does this noun name? (one) What do I need to add to this noun to make it name more than one? (-s). Have students check their writing to make sure they used nouns correctly.

ENGLISH LANGUAGE LEARNERS

If . . . students have difficulty with nouns that name one and more than one,

then . . . help students make a two-column chart showing words or pictures for nouns that name one and nouns that name more than one. Examples: *tree, trees; flower, flowers; color, colors; garden, gardens.* Try to include nouns students are using in their own writing.

STRUGGLING WRITERS

If . . . students are having difficulty writing sentences,

then . . . remind students that a sentence begins with an uppercase letter, tells a complete thought, and ends with a punctuation mark. With students, review the sentences they are writing. Ask: Does this sentence begin with an uppercase letter? Does it tell a complete thought? Does it end with the correct end punctuation mark? Continue asking questions to help students revise as necessary.

Name_____

Title_____

Create a Did You Know? Book Writing Checklist

Work with your teacher to complete this writing checklist.

❏ My book is about patterns in nature.

❏ My book has a title that names what it is about.

❏ I used *Plant Patterns* and *Swirl by Swirl: Spirals in Nature* and other books to find facts.

❏ All the facts in my book are about the patterns.

❏ I used nouns and verbs correctly.

❏ My book has an ending.

❏ I reread my writing to see if it makes sense.

Unlock the Task: Write a Book Review

BREAK APART THE TASK

Distribute copies of the task found on page 146 of the Teacher's Guide. Read the task aloud to students. Hold up *On the Town: A Community Adventure* and *Places in My Neighborhood*. Have students recall what they read about and enjoyed in each text. Record the ideas students share. Tell students that in this writing task, they will tell their opinion about which selection they liked better and support that opinion with reasons. Remind students that an opinion tells what they think or how they feel.

Read aloud the task below. Help students name the important parts of the task. Highlight each part as you talk about it.

State and support an opinion about which selection you like better, *On the Town: A Community Adventure* or *Places in My Neighborhood*. You will write a book review. Tell what you are writing about, give your opinion, and support your opinion by saying "I like this book because . . . ."

ANSWER QUESTIONS ABOUT THE TASK

Display the following and read them aloud. Discuss the questions as a group so that students fully understand the task.

- **What will I write?** (an opinion)
- **Which selections will I use?** (*On the Town: A Community Adventure* and *Places in My Neighborhood*)
- **What will I include in my writing?** (the name of the book I like better and a sentence telling why I like the book)

RESTATE THE TASK

Have students restate the task in their own words. Check for possible misunderstandings or missing elements.

ENGLISH LANGUAGE LEARNERS

If . . . students have difficulty understanding what "support your opinion" means,

then . . . explain that when you support an opinion, you give a reason for the opinion. Remind students that they are to tell which book they like better and why they like the book. Then focus on this sentence frame: I like this book because ___. Tell students that they can use this frame to begin the sentence that supports their opinion.

STRUGGLING WRITERS

If . . . students have difficulty understanding how to begin the writing task,

then . . . help them focus on choosing a book to write about. You have read *On the Town: A Community Adventure* and *Places in My Neighborhood*. Look through the selections. Tell which selection you like better. This is the book you are going to write about. In your writing, you will name this book and tell why you like it.

Prepare to Write

Once students clearly understand the task, have them review the selections *On the Town: A Community Adventure* and *Places in My Neighborhood*. Have students look through each selection and decide which one they want to write about. Have them write or dictate the title of the selection in the middle circle of a concept web. Then have them look through the book to find parts or features that they really like.

If students have difficulty choosing a book, tell them to think about which book they like and identify each book's genre, topic, and text features. Ask questions to help them note differences in the selections and to choose the text they prefer. For example, ask Which selection is a made-up story? Which selection uses photographs? and Which book would you be able to convince a friend to read?

GATHER IDEAS

Help students begin to gather support for their opinion. As they look through the book they have chosen, instruct them to use their concept web to record or dictate reasons to support their opinion. Remind students that they will need good, strong reasons to support their views. These reasons might be about the characters in the book, the plot, the illustrations, or the ending. Encourage students to write or dictate as many reasons as possible now, even though they may not use them all in their book review.

Remind students that when they write their opinion, they should support it with features from the book they chose. For example, if some students are writing about *On the Town,* remind them to use that text when gathering ideas to support their opinions.

ACCELERATED WRITERS

If . . . students have many more reasons to support their opinion than are needed,

then . . . guide them to rate their reasons from most to least important. They can then choose the top two or three reasons for liking the text.

TALK IT THROUGH

Display the following questions and read them aloud. Talk through them with students. Remind students that these questions will allow them to get helpful information from others about their writing plans. Have pairs take turns talking through their book reviews with each other. Circulate among partners and provide support.

Questions a Writer Might Ask

- Which book am I writing about?
- What is my opinion of the book?
- Why do I like it?
- What can I add to my opinion?
- Is there anything I should leave out?

GET ORGANIZED

Work with students to think about what was confusing for their partner. Remind them that what was hard for their partner to understand would probably confuse readers too. Ask questions that will help students clear up confusing ideas.

Direct students to the sentence frame they should use as they support their opinions: *I like this book because ___.* Have students copy the sentence onto their concept web. Then instruct them to use the information on their web to complete the sentence. Encourage students to include at least two reasons to support their opinion. If necessary, students may dictate their ideas or draw pictures.

ENGLISH LANGUAGE LEARNERS

If . . . students have difficulty choosing the words to explain their opinion,

then . . . help them talk through their opinion in the form of a conversation. For example, ask: Which book did you like better? (I liked *On the Town: A Community Adventure.*) Why? (I liked learning about the places and things in Charlie's community. I liked the pictures that showed where Charlie went.)

STRUGGLING WRITERS

If . . . students have difficulty finding reasons to support their opinion,

then . . . suggest some text features to think about, such as the photographs or illustrations, the characters, and the setting. It may also help to model reasons that support an opinion. For example, say: I like *On the Town* because Charlie's notebook teaches me about community jobs.

Write

Display the chart below. Review the elements of opinion writing and their definitions. Answer any questions students may have about them. Remind students that these elements need to be included in their own writing. Work with students to provide examples for the last column using their own writing or other texts you have read together. Help students use this chart as they write.

Element	Definition	Example
Topic	• The title of the text you are writing about	*On the Town: A Community Adventure* *Places in My Neighborhood*
Opinion	• Which book you like better	*On the Town: A Community Adventure* is a great book.
Reasons	• Tell why you think or feel the way you do • Include examples from the text to support the opinion	It's exciting when Charlie visits the police and fire stations. Charlie visits places in his neighborhood and draws pictures about them. He goes to many places I have visited. The illustrations are very colorful. They make the text interesting and fun to read.

ENGLISH LANGUAGE LEARNERS

If . . . students have difficulty writing the *I like* construction in English,

then . . . have them practice saying sentences beginning with *I like.* For example, ask: What is your favorite fruit? Have students respond: I like ___ .

STRUGGLING WRITERS

If . . . students have difficulty focusing on the writing task,

then . . . break the task into pieces. Encourage students to write their topic sentence first. Provide a sentence frame for them to use, such as ___ *is a good book.* Then have students use their charts to write their reason for liking the book, using the sentence frame *I like this book because ___ .* Breaking the task into smaller, more manageable pieces can make the task seem more achievable.

Look Closely

SENTENCES Remind students that they have worked on writing complete sentences with correct capitalization, spacing, and end punctuation. Review declarative and interrogative sentences and their features. Then write the following sentences without uppercase letters or end punctuation: *Charlie learns about his town. Who is your teacher?* Help students identify and correct the mistakes in capitalization and punctuation. Then encourage students to review their own writing to make sure each sentence begins with an uppercase letter, has proper spacing between letters and words, and ends with the correct punctuation mark.

SPELLING Remind students that when they spell a word, they should write the letter(s) for each sound they hear. Have them practice spelling long-vowel words with the vowel-consonant-*e* (VC*e*) pattern. Say the following words and have students write them: made, like, name, time. Remind students that in these words the VC*e* pattern is used to spell the long vowel sound.

SENTENCES Remind students that they need to write sentences that support their opinions. Provide examples of sentences that do and do not support an opinion. Read aloud the following opinion: I like dogs. Then read aloud the following sentences: Dogs are fun to play with. Dogs can do tricks. I like cats too. Dogs are smart. Have students identify the sentence that does not support the opinion. (I like cats too.) Then have students review their writing and revise or remove sentences that do not support their opinion.

DETAILS Remind students that they can expand their sentences by adding details. Explain that added details can make their writing clearer and more interesting. Write this sentence: *Charlie got a haircut.* Ask: What details can be added to make this sentence clearer and more interesting? (*Charlie got a haircut from George at the barber shop.*) Practice with other sentences. Then guide students to add details to their own writing.

ENGLISH LANGUAGE LEARNERS

If . . . students have difficulty pronouncing and spelling words with the VC*e* pattern,

then . . . work with students to make a two-column chart. In one column, write the following short-vowel words: *rip, rat, not, cut.* In the second column, write the words *ripe, rate, note, cute.* Remind students that in English the final *-e* in a word with the VC*e* pattern is not pronounced; it is silent. Have students practice reading each word aloud, noting the difference between short- and long-vowel sounds and their spellings.

STRUGGLING WRITERS

If . . . students have difficulty expanding sentences,

then . . . remind students that detailed sentences are more interesting for readers. Write the sentence *She gave the children notebooks.* Then read aloud the following sentence from *On the Town:* She gave each of the children a black, speckled notebook. (p. 5) Compare and contrast the two sentences and help students identify the one that is more interesting to read.

MONITOR AND SUPPORT

Name_____

Title_____

Write a Book Review
Writing Checklist

Work with your teacher to complete this writing checklist.

❏ I named the book I chose.

❏ I gave my opinion about the book.

❏ I gave reasons for my opinion.

❏ I used information from the book to support my opinion.

❏ I wrote a conclusion by saying: I like this book because _____.

❏ I used complete sentences with correct end punctuation marks.

❏ I reread my writing to see if it makes sense.

Unlock the Task: Create a Travel Brochure

BREAK APART THE TASK

Distribute copies of the task found on page 286 of the Teacher's Guide. Read the task aloud to students. Hold up *Neighborhood Walk: City* and *While I Am Sleeping.* Have students discuss the details about city life that are included in each selection. Record the details students share, using words or pictures. Tell students that in this writing task, they will write their opinions about the city and use facts and details from the books to convince others to visit the city.

Read aloud the following task. Help students name the important points in the task. Highlight the points as you discuss them.

> Think about the books you read in this unit, *Neighborhood Walk: City* and *While I Am Sleeping.* Use facts and details from the books and your own words and pictures to make a travel brochure that convinces people to visit the city. As you write, tell your topic and your opinion about the topic, give reasons to support your opinion, and include a conclusion.

ANSWER QUESTIONS ABOUT THE TASK

Display the questions below and read them aloud. Discuss them together so that students clearly understand the task. Provide further direction if needed.

- **What will I be writing? Whom am I writing for?** (a travel brochure; people who want to know about the city)
- **What texts will I use?** (*Neighborhood Walk: City; While I Am Sleeping*)
- **What do I need to include in my brochure?** (an opinion about the city, reasons that support the opinion, pictures, and a conclusion)

RESTATE THE TASK

Have students restate the task in their own words. Check for possible misunderstandings or missing elements.

ENGLISH LANGUAGE LEARNERS

If . . . students have difficulty understanding what a travel brochure is,

then . . . provide samples of brochures for a variety of places or products. Point out elements the brochures have in common, such as pictures, captions, maps, descriptive text, and bulleted lists. Remind students that they should include some of these items in their own brochures.

STRUGGLING WRITERS

If . . . students are not sure what it means *to convince,*

then . . . review the meaning of *convince* with students. Say: When you convince someone, you cause that person to agree to do something or believe something. Remind students that when they write their travel brochures, they will be trying to convince readers to visit the city.

Prepare to Write

Once students clearly understand the task, have them review the selections *Neighborhood Walk: City* and *While I Am Sleeping.* Remind students that a city travel brochure tells readers why they should visit the city. Explain to students that a travel brochure should give an opinion and supporting reasons that will convince readers to visit the city. The reasons can include the fun and interesting things to see and do in the city. Have students look through the texts for information about cities that they might want to include in their brochures. Have them mark some of those pages with sticky notes.

Together with students, write a topic sentence that states an opinion about the city. If students have difficulty suggesting a sentence, tell them to think about what they might see on the cover of a brochure. If possible, have examples of city brochures that students can refer to throughout the task. You might also provide the following sentence frames: Visit the city because ___. The city is a great place to visit because ___.

GATHER IDEAS

Help students begin to gather facts and details for their travel brochures. They might use sticky notes to mark pages of the selections and write their ideas without putting them in any particular order yet. A concept web or T-chart might also be helpful. If necessary, students can dictate their ideas. Encourage them to gather as many ideas as possible now, even though they may not use them all in their brochures.

Remind students that a brochure includes only the most important and interesting facts. If writers become stalled, have them place themselves in the reader's shoes. Ask: What would the reader want to know about the city? What would the reader find most interesting? What information would convince the reader to visit in the city?

ACCELERATED WRITERS

If . . . students have many more ideas and details than needed for their brochures,

then . . . have them categorize the facts (places to visit, things to do, fun facts about the city, and so on) and then choose the best information from each category to include in their brochures. Remind students that a brochure usually uses short chunks of text with room for pictures.

TALK IT THROUGH

Display the following questions and read them aloud. Talk through the questions, explaining that students will take turns asking a partner these questions. The answers to the questions will provide students with important information about their writing plans.

Questions a Writer Might Ask

- What do I say about the city?
- What reasons do I give for people to visit the city?
- Do my reasons make you want to visit the city?
- What pictures or drawings should I include?
- What else can I add?
- Is there anything I should leave out?

GET ORGANIZED

Help students think about parts of their writing ideas that their partner did not understand. Remind them that what was hard for their partner to understand will probably confuse other readers too. Work with students to clear up confusing ideas and details.

Have students review their concept webs, T-charts, or sticky notes. Instruct them to draw a line through facts or details that will not convince the reader to come to the city or that are not important. Then tell students to think about what pictures or drawings they want to include. If possible, help students use digital tools to find pictures and prepare their brochures.

ENGLISH LANGUAGE LEARNERS

If . . . students have difficulty choosing the words to express their opinion and reasons,

then . . . have them begin by selecting the pictures they want to use in their brochure. Images can be drawn, selected from magazines or newspapers, or taken from clip art software. Talk together about what the selected images show about the city.

STRUGGLING WRITERS

If . . . students have difficulty finding reasons to support their opinion,

then . . . ask questions to guide them as they work. For example, ask: What did you find most interesting about the city? What would you want to do if you visited the city? How would you convince a friend to visit the city?

MONITOR AND SUPPORT

Write

Display the chart below. Point out to students the elements of a travel brochure and review their definitions. Remind students that these elements need to be included in their own brochures. Answer any questions students may have. Help students provide examples for the last column using information from the selections and their own writing. Help students use this chart as they write their travel brochures.

Element	Definition	Example
Title	• Gives the topic of the brochure	Visit the City! It's All Right Here!
Opinion	• Tells what you think or how you feel about the topic	The city is a great place to have fun.
Reasons	• Tell why you think or feel the way you do • Provide details to help convince readers of your opinion	There are many ways to get around in a city. You can ride buses, trains, subways, taxis, cars, and bikes to get places. There are many stores in the city. The buildings are really tall. You can learn about many things in a museum.
Illustrations	• Drawings or photographs • Support reasons and details • Catch the readers' attention	One illustration or photograph for each category or fact
Conclusion	• Gives a closing statement • May restate the opinion and an important reason • May summarize the ideas	Come to the city for fun, food, and amazing sights.

ENGLISH LANGUAGE LEARNERS

If . . . students have difficulty using precise vocabulary in their brochures,

then . . . work with them to create an illustrated list of city-related words, such as *skyscraper, subway, museum,* and *neighborhood.* Direct students to the list as needed. For example, if students write about "tall buildings" in their brochures, have them refer to the list and use the term *skyscrapers* instead.

STRUGGLING WRITERS

If . . . students are having difficulty beginning the task,

then . . . encourage them to work on one part of the task at a time. Have them begin by finding or drawing an image they want to include in their brochure. Then have them write or dictate text to support that image. Have students repeat this process, working on one image at a time.

MONITOR AND SUPPORT

Look Closely

SENTENCES Remind students that they have worked on writing sentences correctly using uppercase and lowercase letters. As students write, remind them that each sentence must begin with an uppercase letter. Remind them to review their brochure to make sure each sentence begins with an uppercase letter.

SPELLING Remind students that when they spell a word, they should write the letter(s) for each sound they hear. Have them practice spelling words with vowel-consonant-*e* (VC*e*) pattern. Say the following words and have students write them: home, like, cute, wave. Remind students that the VC*e* pattern in a word usually spells the long vowel-sound.

PLURAL NOUNS Review making singular nouns plural. Make a two-column chart. Title one column **-s** and the other **-es**. Remind students that *-es* is added to words that end with *s, x, sh,* or *ch* to make them mean more than one. Write singular nouns, such as *fox, car, lake,* and *bus.* Read a noun and guide students to say the plural form of the noun and tell in which column of your chart the plural noun should go. As students revise their writing, have them check to make sure their plural nouns are spelled correctly.

SENTENCES Remind students that as they revise their writing, they should look for ways to make it clearer and more interesting. Adding more details to their sentences is one way to do this. Write this sentence: *Cities have libraries.* Ask: What details can be added to make this sentence clearer and more interesting? (*Cities have libraries where you can read, use computers, and check out books.*) Practice with other sentences.

NOUNS AND VERBS Remind students that a noun is a word that names a person, a place, a thing, or an animal. A verb tells what the noun is doing. It is an action word. Write and read aloud sentences from the texts. Tell students to circle the nouns and underline the verbs. Have students reread their sentences to make sure they are using specific nouns and verbs.

ENGLISH LANGUAGE LEARNERS
If . . . students have difficulty reading and spelling words with the VC*e* pattern,

then . . . make a set of picture word cards that includes words with short and long vowels, such as *hat, tape, dig, kite, hop, robe, cup,* and *cube.* Have students look at each picture and read the word aloud, sorting the cards by long- and short-vowel sounds.

STRUGGLING WRITERS
If . . . students have difficulty writing or pronouncing plural words with -s and -es,

then . . . point out that adding *-es* to form the plural of a word adds a syllable to the word, such as in *speeches, dishes,* and *foxes.* But adding only *-s* usually does not add a syllable, such as in *cats, bikes,* and *pens.* Knowing these pronunciations can help students also avoid spelling errors.

Name_____

Title_____

Create a Travel Brochure
Writing Checklist

Work with your teacher to complete this writing checklist.

❏ I gave an opinion about the city in my brochure.

❏ I gave reasons for people to visit the city.

❏ I used information from *Neighborhood Walk: City* and *While I Am Sleeping* to support my opinion.

❏ I included pictures.

❏ I included a conclusion.

❏ I reread my brochure to see if it makes sense.

Scaffolded Lessons for the Writing Types

Unlock Opinion Writing

INTRODUCE

Ask students what their opinion or preference is on a topic that is familiar to them. *Do you like ___ or ___ more? Would you rather ___ or ___? What is your favorite ___?* Consider using a model sentence frame for them to use: *I think apples taste better than oranges.* Point out to students that they have different opinions about the topic. Remind them that we are all different in many ways. Not only do we look and act differently, we like and dislike different things as well. Tell students that in an opinion piece, a writer is telling his or her view, choice, or opinion about something. Lead them to understand that they can draw, dictate, or write to show their opinion about a topic.

Tell students that when they read opinion pieces, they may or may not agree with what the writer has to say. Some opinion pieces are based on the writer's feelings, or what the writer has heard or been told.

UNDERSTAND TASK

Tell students that in opinion pieces they may be asked to draw or write their thoughts or views about a topic. Remind them that before they begin writing, they must carefully read or listen to the assignment and understand all of its parts. Explain to students that even though they may get excited about their opinion, they need to remember to draw or write about the topic in a way that answers what they are asked. Remind students that others may have different feelings and opinions. As they listen to others share their opinions, they should be respectful and understand that differences in opinions are expected and accepted.

REFOCUS ON THE WRITING TYPE

Throughout the year as students read or are asked to write opinion texts, remind them of the key features of this text type. Opinion writing

- uses drawings and/or spoken and written words to share an opinion about a topic.
- tells the reader the topic, or what the opinion piece is about.
- gives an opinion about the topic.
- often tells what the writer likes or doesn't like about a topic.

Draw, Dictate, and Write

What Students Should KNOW	What Students Will DO
• Know basic sentence structure. • Identify opinions.	• Use drawings, dictating, and writing to compose opinion pieces.

MODEL AND PRACTICE

Help students understand that they can use drawings, as well as spoken and written words, to show an opinion about a topic. Use an opinion piece that you have already read to the class. Go through the piece together, identifying words and pictures that show the writer's opinion. Ask if the text tells a story, teaches about something by giving information, or tells what the writer likes or thinks about something.

MODEL I want to share my favorite thing to do after school. I'm going to draw a picture first. Can you tell that I drew a picture of me running? What could I say or write about my picture that tells my opinion? I don't want to tell a story about something that happened one day while I was running. I don't want to teach someone about running. I want to tell why running is my favorite thing to do after school.

PRACTICE Make a three-column chart with the column headings *Favorite, Best,* and *Like.* Ask students to draw a picture that would fit in one of the categories. Invite them to share their pictures and say a sentence to show in which column they want the picture placed. Model sentences such as the following: My favorite ___ is ___. ___ is the best ___. I like ___ very much.

DEEPER PRACTICE Encourage students to dictate or write a sentence about their picture. Students may want to make a picture for each column.

ENGLISH LANGUAGE LEARNERS
If . . . students have difficulty creating a sentence to go with their pictures,

then . . . repeat a sentence frame for the practice activity above. Ask students to repeat each sentence you model. Encourage them to suggest new key words to use in the sentence frame.

STRUGGLING WRITERS
If . . . students tell stories rather than give opinions,

then . . . remind them to tell about something they like a lot. Keep pulling students back to making a choice to help them focus on an opinion.

Tell the Topic

What Students Should KNOW	What Students Will DO
• Identify the title or topic of an opinion piece.	• Tell the reader the topic of an opinion piece.

MODEL AND PRACTICE

Work with students to pick a topic for an opinion piece. Talk about topics that interest them. You may wish to brainstorm a list of topics, and then go through each one to determine if it is a topic that will work for an opinion piece. Tell students that one way to figure out if a topic will work is to see if there are any choices people can make about the topic. Can you choose a favorite or choose which is better? Provide examples to work through with students. Write the sentences with the topic and opinion on the board. Then have students practice saying the sentences with you.

MODEL I am going to pick the topic of fun things to do after school and the opinion that running is my favorite. If my topic is fun things to do after school, I might want to say something like, "I have fun after school. Running is my favorite thing to do after school." I could even tell you more about why I like running so much.

PRACTICE Have partners look at a book they both enjoy. Ask the pair to choose a favorite part of the story or a favorite character. Have partners tell another pair what book they selected and then state an opinion. Listen for students who need more support.

DEEPER PRACTICE Have students work in pairs to draw a picture of a topic. Consider providing a topic or allowing them to pick from a list of possible topics. Encourage students to say the name of their topic and dictate or write a sentence about what they drew.

ENGLISH LANGUAGE LEARNERS
If . . . students confuse what a topic is,

then . . . go through one or two books that you read to them in the past. Have students do a picture walk to determine the topic of each book. Then model a complete sentence that states the topic.

STRUGGLING WRITERS
If . . . students confuse what the topic of the picture is,

then . . . help students tell what they are going to draw or write about before they begin. Help them write that as a title to help focus their work.

MONITOR AND SUPPORT

State an Opinion

What Students Should KNOW	What Students Will DO
• Form an opinion about a topic. • Use drawings, dictation, and writing to state an opinion about a topic.	• State an opinion about a topic.

MODEL AND PRACTICE

Tell students that an opinion piece should do more than tell about the topic; it must also state an opinion. In opinion writing, the writer should tell his or her opinion about the topic. Point out to students that they may use drawings, dictation, and writing to tell their opinion about a topic. Review with them what a complete sentence is, and explain to students that they should tell or write their opinion as a complete sentence.

MODEL I need to say more about my topic. I have said that running is my favorite thing to do after school. Next I will let readers know what my opinion about running is. I could say, "Running is my favorite thing to do after school. I like to run because I can get somewhere faster than if I walk." I clearly stated my opinion about the topic, and I even told one thing I like about running. If I write an opinion statement about liking dance class, this would not be sticking to my topic or my opinion about my favorite thing to do after school. I also need to make sure that my opinion sentence begins with a capital letter and ends with a period.

PRACTICE Work with students to practice stating an opinion about a topic. Hold up several photographs or illustrations. Ask them to pick their favorite and to work with a partner to state an opinion about why the picture is their favorite.

DEEPER PRACTICE Have students draw, dictate, or write an opinion statement about one of the pictures. Then invite students to share their opinion statements with the class.

ENGLISH LANGUAGE LEARNERS

If . . . students confuse what an opinion is,

then . . . have them draw a picture of a topic that you give them. Work with them to talk about the different opinions or thoughts they could have about the topic. Consider prompting them by saying, "I like ___" or "I do not like ___."

STRUGGLING WRITERS

If . . . students have difficulty understanding how to write a complete sentence,

then . . . show them a variety of complete and incomplete sentences on sentence strips. Have them use a marker or pen to trace capital letters and add punctuation to the ends of the sentences. Help them read aloud the sentences and check that they are complete.

Shared and Interactive Writing

Review with students how to do shared and interactive writing to produce an opinion piece. This type of writing involves both the teacher and students working together. Shared and interactive writing includes the ideas that are generated to get the writing process started. Students and teacher select or name the topic for the opinion piece together. Choosing the opinion for the opinion piece should also be a group effort. Since not all students are likely to have the same opinion, you may write several opinion pieces together on the same topic, but with different opinions.

PLAN THE WRITING Model how to choose a topic for an opinion that can be given. You might suggest several topics and have the group decide which would be most interesting to draw or write about. Write the name of the topic at the top of a chart or in the center of a web organizer.

ORGANIZE THE WRITING Ask each student to draw a picture of or write an opinion about the topic on a sticky note or small piece of paper. Invite students to share their opinions. Have students tape their picture or piece of paper on the board or wall in the classroom. Discuss with students how the opinions are the same or different. When all opinions have been placed, have students vote on which opinion to use. Model aloud how to introduce the topic and state the opinion. Work with the group to develop several options.

SHARE THE WRITING As you write in front of the group, find opportunities to share the writing by asking questions as you go. Consider asking questions that will encourage students to think of reasons for the opinion. For example: What can we write that will help people understand our opinion? Should I use an uppercase or lowercase letter here? Should I use a period or an exclamation mark? What's a good way to tell the reader why we have this opinion? Model how to "stretch out the word" to help children hear the sounds and write the letters they hear. These opportunities model the skills you want to reinforce.

FOCUS ON SENTENCES As you write with the group, look for opportunities to focus on what sentences are. Example: We want to say that running is fun. Can we just write *fun*? Would that be a complete sentence? Remind students that all sentences should begin with a capital letter. You might want to make an "intentional error" by using a lowercase letter to begin a sentence and help students catch the mistake.

Look Back at the Writing

CHECK FOR CONTENT When the shared writing is completed, have the group look back at your shared writing and the planning charts or graphic organizers you used in planning the opinion piece. Review what you set out to do when you started and planned your writing. You might have the group put a checkmark next to each element of the plan that was included in your final version.

USE A CHECKLIST Work with students to develop writing checklists. Help students review the shared writing text as a group. This type of modeling helps students understand that good writers go back into their work to make changes or strengthen what they have written. Work through a checklist similar to the one below. Invite volunteers to point to or highlight examples in the shared writing that shows an example of each item on the checklist.

Writer's Checklist

- Did we choose a topic and clearly state it?
- Did we use drawings and written words?
- Did we tell what our opinion is?
- Did we explain our opinion clearly so that the reader understands it?
- Did we use complete sentences?

CAPITALIZATION Model how to check and correct capitalization in their writing. Invite a volunteer to circle or highlight the first letter of the first word of each sentence to check that it is capitalized. If other capital letters are used, you might explain why they are used in that situation.

PUNCTUATION Model checking and correcting punctuation at the end of the sentences. Have students help you determine when a period, question mark, or exclamation point is needed. Demonstrate that punctuation helps determine how your voice changes when you read the sentences aloud.

SPELLING Show students how to check for misspelled, missing, or extra words. Encourage them to sound out some of the decodable words. Show students that all writers need to recheck their work to become good writers.

ACCELERATED WRITERS

If . . . students want to include additional information for their stated opinion,

then . . . have them check to make sure each statement relates to their topic and supports their opinion. Help them use a web organizer to draw or write their ideas in a circle around their topic and opinion, which should be in the center.

Unlock Informative/ Explanatory Writing

Explain to students that there are different types of text. Select books or texts that may already be familiar to students to illustrate the different kinds of text. Extend the conversation by saying that text can tell a reader how to do something. It may tell about a topic. It may also tell a story. It may even show the writer's opinion about something. These text types have different purposes. Explain to students that in informative/explanatory writing, the writer gives information or tells about a topic. When writing informative/explanatory texts, students should write or draw about something they know. Lead them to see that if they know a lot about a topic, they should be able to help others learn about it by drawing or writing.

Display for students pictures or diagrams that are informative/explanatory and that you have already shown to them or that may already be familiar to them. For example, point to a fire safety diagram in the classroom or hallway that shows where students should go and what they should do in a fire or during a fire drill. Read the diagram together. Then ask students what they learned about fire safety from the diagram and if they learned the meanings of any words. Ask students why this diagram is an informative/explanatory text. Take a walk around the classroom or school to identify other examples of texts that inform or explain, such as a list of classroom rules, a menu for the cafeteria, or a class newsletter.

UNDERSTAND PURPOSE

Explain to students that they will sometimes be asked to draw or write to give information or explain something. Tell students that they must first understand the task before they begin. What should they explain? What information do they need to share about the topic? Remind students that sometimes it helps to put the task in your own words before you start.

REFOCUS ON THE WRITING TYPE

Throughout the year as students read or are asked to draw or write informative/ explanatory texts, remind them of the key features of this text type. Informative/ explanatory writing

- gives information.
- explains something.
- helps the reader learn something.

Draw, Dictate, and Write

What Students Should KNOW	What Students Will DO
• Understand that words can be spoken and written. • Understand that information can be given in and obtained from drawings/pictures. • Attempt prewriting and writing that connects to the topic.	• Combine drawings, dictating, and writing.

MODEL AND PRACTICE

Remind students that they can use pictures, words they say, and words that are written to share what they know. Invite students to work in pairs to pantomime one person learning something from another. Have the group guess what is being learned and how it is being taught. Using a familiar informative/explanatory text, have students tell what information is being given and if the information is being shared in pictures, words, or both. Read aloud a selection from the text, and ask students to listen carefully. Have them raise their hands to tell what they learned by listening to the words.

MODEL I drew a picture of my neighborhood to show where different things are. I drew a picture of my apartment, the park, our school, and the grocery store. I can also write labels for each part of my drawing. Writing words and using pictures can help show and tell people about my neighborhood. I can also talk about my neighborhood and give more information than what I show in my pictures and labels.

PRACTICE Have students work with a partner to draw and dictate or write about what is inside the classroom. Remind students to use drawings, spoken words, and written words to tell about what objects and people are in the classroom and what happens there each day. Invite students to present their text and drawing to another pair of students.

DEEPER PRACTICE As a group, compose an informative/explanatory text about the different types of rooms in the school, such as classrooms, the lunchroom, the nurse's office, and principal's office. Invite students to suggest related words and pictures to include.

ENGLISH LANGUAGE LEARNERS

If . . . students have trouble naming objects in the classroom,

then . . . provide some rebus sentence models, such as "I see tables (picture of tables) and chairs (picture of chairs) in the classroom." Read the sentence aloud and ask students to repeat the sentence and point to the pictures and then "read." Invite students to suggest additional items to be used to create new sentences.

STRUGGLING WRITERS

If . . . students have difficulty contributing to group writing,

then . . . take a walk around the school with paper and pencils. Encourage students to draw pictures and write words as best they can about what they see and hear. Then return to the classroom and have them share what they recorded to add to the group writing activity.

Name the Topic

What Students Should KNOW	What Students Will DO
• Identify the topic in texts that students read or experience. • Focus writing or prewriting efforts on one topic or idea. • State the topic of the writing or prewriting efforts.	• Name what they are writing about.

MODEL AND PRACTICE

Naming what they are writing about helps keep young writers focused on one topic or idea. Show students a few familiar texts and go through the texts together to determine what the topics are. Invite students to explain how they knew what the topic was. Some students may notice that the title of the text often tells what the writer is writing about. Point out that when writing to teach or explain something, the reader or listener should be able to figure out quickly what the topic is.

MODEL We want to be ready to draw and write to share what we know about things. Let's start a list of things we know a lot about and can give information about. I'll write "We Know About ___" at the top of this chart. We know about our class and neighborhood. What could we explain to someone? I'll write "We Can Explain ___" at the top of this chart. We could explain about how to make a sandwich or how to take care of the fish in our aquarium.

PRACTICE Have students draw pictures of something they could add to the class chart of topics on sticky notes or on other pieces of paper. Encourage them to dictate or write the topic. As students bring the notes to the chart, ask if it is something they know and have lots of information about or something they can explain how or why about. Add to and use the chart throughout the year to give students ideas for topics.

DEEPER PRACTICE Have students look through informative/explanatory texts and name the topic. Ask students to work with a partner to get ideas from these texts for other topics to add to the chart. Encourage students to write or dictate titles for texts on these topics.

MONITOR AND SUPPORT

ENGLISH LANGUAGE LEARNERS

If . . . students have trouble naming a topic,

then . . . have them draw a picture of something they already know about. Help students name the items in the picture. Model a sentence that names the objects and topic. For example, you might say: You drew a cat, a dish, and a ball. You know about how to take care of a cat. Encourage students to use some of those words and create their own sentences about the pictures.

STRUGGLING WRITERS

If . . . students have little confidence in their knowledge and hesitate to name a topic,

then . . . ask students to think about what they see and do each day. Offer suggestions such as games they like to play, talents they have shown, or common classroom experiences or rules. Remind students that they are experts who know many different things and have a great deal to share with others.

Supply Information About the Topic

What Students Should KNOW	What Students Will DO
• Identify information in texts students have read or experienced. • Gain content knowledge on the topic. • Focus information on the topic. • Use complete sentences.	• Supply some information about the topic.

MODEL AND PRACTICE

Discuss with students information that tells about their topic. Explain that information comes in different forms, such as pictures, spoken words, and written words. Provide several examples from texts that are familiar to students. Point out that information needs to be focused only on their topic. Work together to find examples of information in the texts.

MODEL I'm thinking about the information I want to include when writing to give information about or explain a topic. My topic today is New York City. I should give only information about my topic, New York City. I know that New York City has a lot of buildings and people. A park. Oops. That's not a complete sentence. There is a big park and a zoo. My sister goes to college in New Jersey. Oh, this last bit of information is not about my topic. It is not about New York City. I will not use this information in my writing.

PRACTICE Have students work with a partner and decide together what one topic they want to give information about or explain. Have them each make a drawing and dictate or write sentences to go with the pictures. Ask the pairs to show the drawings to the class and invite others to guess the topic. Help students read the words as needed. Ask the group to tell if all the information is about the topic.

DEEPER PRACTICE Have students state a topic to a partner. Then ask them to take turns passing an object, such as a ball or marker, back and forth. When a student is holding the object, that student should say a complete sentence that gives information relating to the topic. Encourage students to pass the object back and forth at least five times before going to a new topic.

ENGLISH LANGUAGE LEARNERS

If . . . students have trouble stating a complete sentence related to a topic,

then . . . model a sentence frame that connects to their topic. For exmaple: "A cat needs a water dish. A cat needs food. A cat needs love." Encourage students to repeat each sentence and then add new details to create new sentences related to the topic.

STRUGGLING WRITERS

If . . . students have difficulty focusing information on one topic,

then . . . help students use a highlighter to circle topic-related items in their pictures or writing. Before they circle an item, ask students to tell how it connects to the topic. Then point to non-related items in students' pictures or writing. Ask: Is this related to your topic? Why or why not? Help students understand what makes these items unrelated.

Shared and Interactive Writing

Review with students how to do shared and interactive writing to produce an informative/explanatory text. This type of writing involves both the teacher and students working together. Shared and interactive writing includes the ideas that are generated to get the writing process started. Students and teacher name the topic together through brainstorming or using a web or diagram to generate ideas. Choosing the information to include in the informative/explanatory text should be a collaborative effort between students and teacher. At times you may choose to "make a mistake" or forget what to do next to draw attention to the decisions writers need to make or to check that students understand the process.

PLAN THE WRITING Model how to name a topic. You might use the lists the class created or suggest a few topics and have the group decide which topic would be most appealing or which topic the group is more of an expert on. Write the name of the topic at the top of a chart or in the center of a web diagram.

ORGANIZE THE WRITING Ask each student to draw or write information he or she already knows about the topic on a sticky note or a piece of scratch paper. Invite students to share what they know by telling the class about their picture or what they wrote. As students share their information, have the class help organize it by having students stand near one another if their information is related. Invite one volunteer to stand in the middle of the classroom to act as the topic. Invite the other students with information to stand in lines coming out of the topic. (The students should form the shape of the sun.) Have students check to see that all of the information connects to the topic.

SHARE THE WRITING As you write for the group, find opportunities to share the writing by asking questions as you go. For example: Which letter will come next? Should I use an uppercase or a lowercase letter here? Which word comes next? What punctuation should I use at the end of the sentence? Which question words could I use here? These opportunities model the skills you want to reinforce.

FOCUS ON SENTENCES TO STRENGTHEN WRITING As you write with the group, look for opportunities to focus on sentences. Remind students that a sentence tells a complete thought. Model some examples and some non-examples. Example: We are writing about the playground today. I could write *swings*. Is that a complete thought? What could we say about the swings? We could say, "The swings are near the balance bars. There are four swings in a row."

Look Back at the Writing

USE A CHECKLIST Work with students to develop writing checklists. Help students review the shared writing text. This type of modeling helps students understand that good writers go back into their work to make changes or strengthen what they have written.

Writer's Checklist

- Did we name what we are writing about?
- Did we draw and write about our topic?
- Did we supply some information and details about the topic?
- Did we use complete sentences?
- Did we capitalize the first word in our sentences?
- Did we put punctuation marks at the ends of the sentences?

CHECK FOR CONTENT When the shared writing is completed, have the group look back at your planning chart or graphic organizer. Ask: Did we name our topic? Did we stick to our topic? Is the information we included only about our topic? Did we use complete sentences? Will a reader learn about our topic? You may ask volunteers to point to examples to answer each question.

CAPITALIZATION Demonstrate for students how to check and correct capitalization in their writing. Remind them that sentences should begin with a capital letter. You may model this by having students use a highlighter to trace the capital letters on the shared writing text. Ask students to tell why each capital letter was used.

PUNCTUATION Demonstrate how to check and correct punctuation, such as commas and periods. You may have students use hand motions or sounds for each punctuation mark, for example, poking a finger for a period, outstretching palms and tilting their heads in a questioning pose for a question mark, and cupping their hands near the mouth in a yelling motion for an exclamation mark. Go back over the shared writing text and pause for students to show with an action which punctuation marks are used at the end of each sentence. Using colored highlighters, you might invite volunteers to highlight each type of punctuation in a different color and tell why that mark was used.

ACCELERATED WRITERS

If . . . students are comfortable drawing, telling, and writing about a topic,

then . . . encourage them to expand the information they share or explain by looking at related picture books for additional ideas. Tell students that even experts do research to learn more. Help students create topical collections of related books or organize your classroom library in a topical manner.

Unlock Narrative Writing

Talk with students about what a story is. Then talk with students about stories that people tell, and consider sharing a story with them. You may read a narrative in which the story is based on real events and people and also one that is based on imagined events and people. Work with students to help them identify the parts of the story, including the beginning, middle, and end. Help students tell who and what the story is about. Point out that stories include people or animals and things that happen to them. Then explain that writing stories, whether about real or imagined places, people, and events, is called narrative writing.

UNDERSTAND PURPOSE

Tell students that the purpose of narrative writing is to tell a story. Unlike writing that informs a reader or gives an opinion about something, a narrative does not tell facts or give an opinion about a topic. Narrative writing does not show that you are an expert on a topic the way an informational/explanatory text does. It also does not tell what you think, or your opinion, about a topic the way opinion writing does. Reinforce to students that narrative writing simply tells a story, which can be something that actually happened or something that is make-believe.

REFOCUS ON THE WRITING TYPE

Throughout the year as students read or are asked to write narrative texts, remind them of the key features of this text type. Narrative writing

- tells a real or make-believe story.
- tells about an event or events.
- includes people or animals that take part in the events or react to what happens.

Prepare to Tell a Story

What Students Should KNOW	What Students Will DO
• Identify events from narrative texts students have read. • Understand that information can be given in and obtained from spoken and written words and also from drawings/pictures. • Attempt prewriting and writing activities to tell about a single event or several loosely linked events.	• Use a combination of drawings, dictating, and writing to narrate a single event or several loosely linked events.

MODEL AND PRACTICE

Help students understand that narrative writing is storytelling and can use words and pictures to show how things happened in a story. Use a narrative text that you have already read to the class. Go through the text together, pointing out the words and pictures. Ask students if the things that happen relate to each other. Then have them take turns identifying various parts of the story.

MODEL I want to tell a story, but I can't decide what my story will be about. I could tell about the time I was on the playground and a fire engine went by. I could tell about an imaginary talking dog that likes to eat watermelon and goes to the store to buy one. Let's make a list of some stories we can write and tell. For each story, let's think about who is in the story and what events happen to make the story interesting.

PRACTICE Using a two-column chart, work with the group to create a story ideas chart. Write *Who and Where* at the top of one column and *What Happens* at the top of the other. Encourage students to suggest ideas for one or both columns. You might ask one student to make a suggestion for the first column and a different student to make a related suggestion for the second column.

DEEPER PRACTICE Ask students to draw pictures showing ideas they have for stories. Invite students to share their drawing and tell who might be in the story, where it might happen, and an event that might be part of the story.

ENGLISH LANGUAGE LEARNERS

If . . . students have trouble verbalizing information about their drawings,

then . . . have students point to an element in their drawing that shows who is in the story. Encourage them to tell who is pictured or one thing that happens. Model how to stretch that information into a complete sentence. For example, you might say: The story is about a boy. The story is about a boy who is on a swing. Encourage students to repeat the modeled sentences.

STRUGGLING WRITERS

If . . . students have difficulty thinking of a story idea,

then . . . have students help you create a story box with interesting photos from magazines or newspapers, or fill the box with other picture cards. Students can randomly select a picture to use as a story starter.

Use Sequence

What Students Should KNOW	What Students Will DO
• Identify and retell events from texts students read. • Retell events in the correct sequence.	• Tell about the events in the order in which they occurred.

MODEL AND PRACTICE

Remind students that narrative writing is the retelling of a story and that it can be something that really happened or something make-believe. Point out to them that the events or things that occur should be retold or written in the order in which they happened. Read aloud a narrative text that you have already read together as a class. As you read the text to the class, ask students to listen for the events in the story. Choose a certain number of events from the narrative and ask the same number of students to stand up. Assign each standing student an event from the narrative. Then have each student recite or retell his or her assigned event. When the student is finished retelling the event, have him or her link arms with the next student as he or she recites his or her event. Lead students to see that the things that happen in stories are often connected or linked.

MODEL I am thinking about the story that happens on the playground. I'll draw pictures of some things that happened. I need to put them together in the correct order. Something happens first, and then something happens second, and so forth. I need to put these in order so that the story makes sense.

PRACTICE Read aloud a narrative and pause between events that happen. At the end of the story, invite students to draw pictures to show different events that happened in the correct order. Ask students to retell the events in order.

DEEPER PRACTICE Ask students to fold a paper in half so that there is drawing space at the top and the bottom. Have students think of a story and draw what happens first at the top of the page and what happened next below it. Encourage students to dictate, write, or tell the group about their story.

ENGLISH LANGUAGE LEARNERS

If . . . students have difficulty retelling the events in their drawings,

then . . . encourage them to tell the first thing that happened. Model using the information in a complete sentence. Then ask a question that includes some of the words from the sentence. For example, you might ask: What did the boy on the swing do next? Did the boy on the swing run to the slide?

STRUGGLING WRITERS

If . . . students draw unrelated events for their story,

then . . . ask them to tell about the first picture. Ask questions about the characters or events in the first picture. When looking at the second picture, ask about the characters and events from the first picture to draw their attention to what may be missing and to connect the two drawings.

Include a Reaction

What Students Should KNOW	What Students Will DO
• Identify various emotions and words that were reactions to something that happened.	• Provide a reaction to what happened.

MODEL AND PRACTICE

Talk with students about what a surprise is and how they act when they learn about a surprise. Explain to them that not all stories have surprises, but people in the story may respond or react to an event that happened. Illustrate reactions and responses by using examples from narrative texts you have read with students. Read aloud the event and the reaction in the story. Point out to students which is the event and which is the reaction or response. Talk with students about the reaction or response. Ask: What feelings did characters have? Were they happy, glad, sad, mad, angry, or tired? Explain to students that reactions can often include emotions such as these.

MODEL When I think about the events or things that happen in my playground story, I also must think about what reaction there is to the event. For example, the fire engine was loud and I covered my ears. A reaction might be that I was worried about where the fire might be. Another reaction might be that one of the children on the playground started to cry.

PRACTICE Work together with students to talk about different reactions they might include in the playground story. Draw a chart that shows three different kinds of emotions that might be expressed for each event in the playground story. Select the emotions as a group, and then label each column of the chart with an emotion. Then work with students to list each story event in the appropriate column.

DEEPER PRACTICE Provide pairs of students with magazines or newspapers and have them cut out a picture that shows a reaction or an emotion. Encourage the pair to tell a story about what might have caused the reaction in the picture. You might ask students to draw, dictate, or write a story based on the picture.

ENGLISH LANGUAGE LEARNERS

If . . . students do not know the words to describe emotions,

then . . . show them simple drawings or photographs of students' faces. Say the name of the emotion that each picture shows, and invite students to repeat the name. Model a sentence frame and have students practice using the correct word: This boy is ___. This girl is ___. Encourage students to make a similar facial expression when saying the sentence.

STRUGGLING WRITERS

If . . . students don't include reactions when dictating or writing stories,

then . . . have them pantomime the reactions to the events as they retell their stories. Encourage them to be overly dramatic to make the reactions more memorable.

Shared and Interactive Writing

Review with students how to do shared and interactive writing to produce a narrative text. Students and teacher choose a topic for the story together. Selecting the events or things that happen in the narrative text should be a collaborative effort. At times you may choose to "make a mistake" or use a non-example to draw attention to the decisions writers need to make.

PLAN THE WRITING Model how to choose a story idea. Talk with students about whether they want to write a real or make-believe story. Decide together where the story happens and who is in the story. You might suggest several ideas and have the group make the final decision. Write the title for the story at the top of a chart or in the center of a web organizer.

ORGANIZE THE WRITING Ask each student to draw a picture of or write about an event or something that could happen in the story on a sticky note or small piece of paper. Students may also share their idea verbally. Have students share what they drew, wrote, or dictated with the class. Then move students to different parts of the classroom based on events that are related. Point out that grouping the things that happen will make the writing clearer and easier. Then tape the related pictures and pieces of paper on the board.

SHARE THE WRITING As you write in front of the group, find opportunities to share the writing by asking questions as you go. Consider asking questions that will encourage students to help put the events in the correct order. Ask: Does this event come before or after this event? Should this event come last? Do we have all of the events in the correct order? These opportunities model the skills you want to reinforce.

FOCUS ON REACTIONS As you write with the group, look for opportunities to focus on reactions to the events in the story. Example: I see that we included three events in the story, but we did not include reactions for each of these events. What reactions can we add to make the story more interesting? What words can we use that tell about the emotions the characters feel? Tell students that it is important to include reactions to events in a story to make their writing come alive and make it seem real. Invite students to act out the emotions in the story as they determine which ones to include.

Look Back at the Writing

USE A CHECKLIST Work with students to develop writing checklists. Help students review the shared writing text. This type of modeling helps students understand that good writers go back into their work to strengthen what they have written.

Writer's Checklist

- Did we draw and write about one or more related events in the story?
- Did we put the events in the story in the correct order?
- Did we provide reactions to the events that happened in the story?
- Did we use complete sentences?
- Did we capitalize the first word in our sentences?
- Did we put punctuation marks at the ends of the sentences?

CHECK FOR CONTENT When the shared writing is completed, have the group look back at your planning chart or graphic organizer. Ask: Did we tell about two or more events? Are the events in the story in the correct time order? Did we tell how the people or animals feel? You may ask volunteers to point to examples to answer each question.

CAPITALIZATION Demonstrate how to check and correct capitalization in your shared writing. Remind students that sentences should begin with a capital letter. You may have names in the story that need to be capitalized as well. Perhaps use a highlighter to trace the capital letters on the shared writing text. Ask students to tell why each capital letter was used.

PUNCTUATION Demonstrate how to check and correct punctuation at the ends of sentences. Have a volunteer use a highlighter or marker to find the periods and circle them. Ask other students to find question marks and exclamation points, using different colors. Remind students how to choose correct end punctuation.

SPELLING Demonstrate for students how to check for misspelled or missing words in the shared text. Have students take turns tracking the print and touching each word as you read the story aloud. Show students that all writers need to recheck their work if they want to become good writers.

ACCELERATED WRITERS

If . . . students are comfortable drawing, writing, or telling about events in the story,

then . . . encourage students to include sentences about reactions to events in the story for each character. Challenge them to include several different reactions or emotions. Then invite them to read or tell their sentences to a partner.

PART 3

Routines and Activities

Part 3 Routines and Activities

Phonemic Awareness Activities

Letter Recognition Activities

Phonics Activities

Writing Routines

Listening and Speaking Routines

Language Routines and Activities: Vocabulary and Conventions

Noun Activities

Adjective Activities

Verb Activities

Sentence Activities

Vocabulary Activities and Games

Read the Words Around You

PURPOSE

Use this routine with the Read the Words Around You Graphic Organizer to help students recognize and learn words that they encounter every day.

PROCEDURE

1. Draw or display a stop sign and ask what it means. Students may answer *stop.* Say: Everywhere there are words and signs that can help us. Point out that the name of the school is on the front of the building. Say: The sign tells people what this building is. It helps people find the school.

2. Display the graphic organizer.

3. Point to a word in the classroom, such as a sign on the door. Model reading the word and figuring out what it means. For example: A sign on this door says P-U-L-L. I know that word is *pull.* This sign tells me how to open the door. Model writing the word *pull* on the graphic organizer in the I Know column.

4. Have students keep a log of the letters, words, and signs they notice and can read throughout the school day.

5. At the end of the day, have students share one word or letter they recognized in a sign, and one they did not. Help students understand the meanings of words they did not recognize.

TEACHING TIPS

- Once you have modeled how to use the organizer, have students complete the organizer independently, in pairs, or in small groups.

- As you discuss students' examples, talk about the information they learn from reading the signs.

- Students can keep a running log of words they see and learn in a notebook to be used as a reference as needed.

- Engage students by asking them each to bring in something from home with words on it that they can read, such as a cereal box, a milk carton, or an advertisement from a magazine.

EXTEND

- Have students organize their letters and words by alphabet or category, such as Foods, Signs, or Rooms.

- Provide advertisements, posters, cereal boxes, and signs. Students can discuss with partners what they learn from reading these examples.

- Create a display. Ask students what information they learn or understand from reading the words on each of these items.

Read the Words Around You

Write the letters or words you see.

Say the letters or words you know.

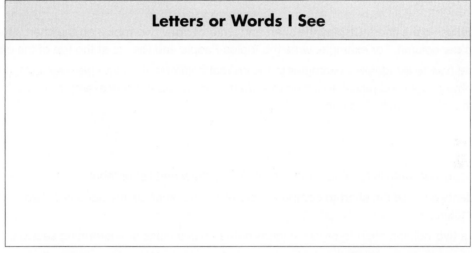

Letters or Words I See

I Know	I Don't Know

Two-Column Chart

PURPOSE

Use this routine with the Two-Column Chart Graphic Organizer. This graphic organizer works well with all types of selections. It can help students explore ideas, story elements, or vocabulary words. Use it to identify and classify characters, settings, and ideas within and across texts.

PROCEDURE

1. Model using the chart. Display the chart and write or draw two topics on the chart, one topic per column. For example, write the topics People and Places at the top of the chart.

2. Model how to list ideas or examples in the correct columns. For example, say: Let's think of some people and places to list on this chart. Our principal is one example; in which column should we list his name?

TEACHING TIPS

- Students can write in the chart, but they can also draw and list or label.
- Students can use the chart to compare story elements, such as the actions of two characters.
- Use a two-column chart to organize ideas gathered in a class brainstorming session.
- Use a two-column chart to explore two vocabulary words. Write the words at the tops of the columns. Then under each word, students can sketch the word.

EXTEND

- Students can work with partners, each partner completing one half of the chart.
- Students can compare two characters by drawing pictures about their physical characteristics or actions.

Two-Column Chart

GRAPHIC ORGANIZER

Three-Column Chart

Use this routine with the Three-Column Chart Graphic Organizer. The graphic organizer can be used to explore or classify ideas, story elements, genres, or vocabulary features. It can also help students recognize comparisons and contrasts or chart ideas within and across selections. This is a multipurpose graphic organizer that is helpful when exploring three concepts. It works well with many selections.

PROCEDURE

1. Display the graphic organizer.

2. Model using the graphic organizer. Choose three simple headings, such as Red, Yellow, and Blue, and write them on the graphic organizer.

3. Point out that this graphic organizer helps organize information. Ask students for details for each heading and record them on the graphic organizer. For example, say: Let's talk about some things that are red, some things that are yellow, and some things that are blue. We can look around this room for ideas. Model how to list ideas or examples in the correct columns.

4. Once you have modeled how to use the organizer, students can complete organizers independently or in pairs or small groups.

TEACHING TIPS

- Students can draw in the graphic organizer as well as list or dictate ideas.

- Students can use the graphic organizer to explore story elements, such as three different characters in a story. They can also compare and contrast the experiences of three different characters across two or more stories.

- Students can use the graphic organizer to organize ideas they generate during brainstorming.

- Students can use the graphic organizer to organize ideas about three different vocabulary words.

EXTEND

- Students can use the graphic organizer to record ideas that follow the pattern of before, during, and after.

- Students can use the graphic organizer to organize ideas in any content area. For example, in social studies, students could list or dictate three different holidays with details about each. In science, students could list or draw three different animals and use the graphic organizer to describe their traits.

Three-Column Chart

Web

Use this routine with the Web Graphic Organizer. This graphic organizer has multiple uses and is appropriate for all levels of learners. Students can explore their prior knowledge as they brainstorm related ideas, recognize concept relationships, and/or organize information. This graphic organizer can help students highlight a central concept and connect it to related words, ideas, or details.

PROCEDURE

1. Display the graphic organizer. Write or draw a central idea or topic in the middle of the web.

2. Ask students for ideas that are related to the central idea. Record those ideas in the circles attached to the middle circle.

3. Point out that the lines show connections. If you wrote, for example, *Things That Go* in the middle oval, you might write *car, bike, airplane,* and *van* in the outer circles. Those are all types of things that go. Explain to students how those objects all connect to the topic Things That Go.

TEACHING TIPS

- Once you have modeled how to use the organizer with the whole class, have teacher-led small groups work to complete the organizer together.

- Provide sentence frames to help students talk about the web: The important idea is ___. Some ideas related to this are ___.

- Use this web to organize and explore information about main ideas and details, character names along with their traits, and vocabulary words and their meanings.

EXTEND

- Students can use the organizer to record ideas about a topic in content area reading or word study, such as Things Plants Need to Grow.

- Have students use the web to record background knowledge about a topic. Use the webs to assess gaps in understanding as you plan instruction.

- Enlarge the graphic organizer so that students can draw in the circles. They can label or write sentences about their drawings.

Web

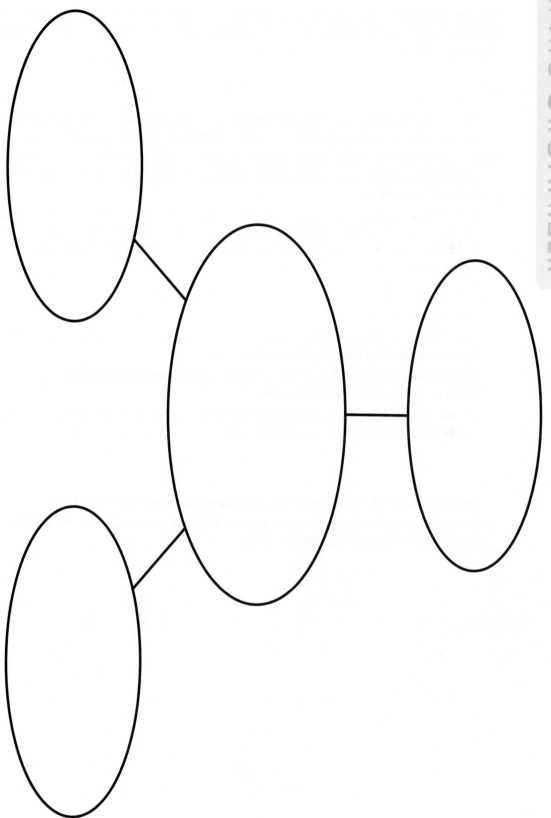

Venn Diagram

PURPOSE

Use this routine with the Venn Diagram Graphic Organizer. Students use this organizer to record similarities and differences between places, ideas, characters, or other elements of fiction or nonfiction.

PROCEDURE

1. Start by comparing and contrasting something simple, such as setting. Write or draw the subjects you are comparing at the top of the circles of the Venn diagram.

2. Point to where the circles overlap. Let students know that in this section, you'll write similarities, or how the two things are alike. Ask: How are the two subjects alike? Record students' responses.

3. Point to an individual circle and let students know that, in this section, you'll write details that describe only what is labeled at the top of the circle. Explain: This is where we can write differences, or the details that belong only to this subject. Ask students to list details as you record them.

TEACHING TIPS

- Ask questions that help students think of details to write in the diagram, such as *Where is the farm located?* or *Describe the weather.*

- Help students with sentence frames: These two things are alike because ___. These two things are different because ___.

- List words that signal comparing and contrasting, such as *alike, different, but,* and so on. Students can point to those words in the text.

EXTEND

- Students can create Venn diagrams to compare characters in fictional texts.

- Students can use Venn diagrams to compare topics in informational texts, such as two plants, two animals, or two different cities.

Venn Diagram

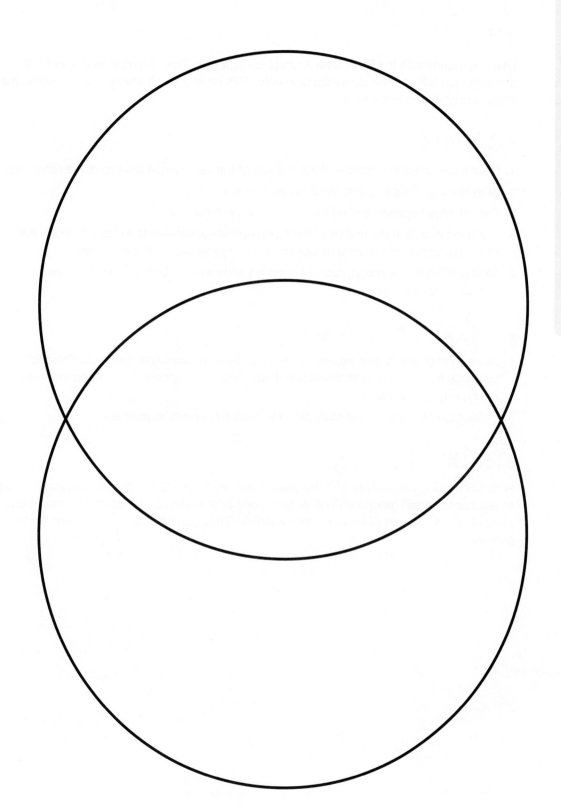

Story Map A

PURPOSE

Use this routine with the Story Map A Graphic Organizer. This organizer works well with any selection with a clear sequence of events. This chart can aid students in recording the sequence of events in a selection.

PROCEDURE

1. Display the graphic organizer. Write the title of the selection at the top of the story map.
2. Start reading. Pause to ask: What happens first?
3. Record what happens first on the top part of the organizer.
4. Focus on events in the middle of the story, pausing for students to identify them. Say: What happens next? Record responses in the middle part of the organizer.
5. As you finish the selection, record important events in the bottom part of the organizer. Ask: How does the story end?

TEACHING TIPS

- Make a list of words that tell time order, such as *after, later, first,* and *next*. Provide sentence frames to help students use them: First, ___ happened. ___ happened next. Afterward, ___ happened.
- Encourage students to use story maps to retell the events to partners.

EXTEND

After completing this activity with the class, have students use the graphic organizer in pairs or teacher-led small groups with other selections or to make up stories of their own. Have students draw pictures of events in the organizer. They can label or dictate words for the pictures.

Story Map A

Title _____

Story Map B

Use this routine with the Story Map B Graphic Organizer. This organizer works well with any selection that has a clear series of events. This chart can help students identify different elements in a story.

PROCEDURE

1. Display the graphic organizer. Write the title of the selection at the top of the story map.

2. Start reading. As you read, pause to think aloud and record information about the characters on the organizer. Ask: Who is in this story? What is this character like? Record these details in the Characters section.

3. Ask: Where does the story take place?

4. Record those details in the Setting section.

5. As you read, pause to think aloud and record information about the sequence of events on the organizer. Guide students to look for clue words, such as *first, in the beginning, next, then, or finally* to help them trace the beginning, middle, and end of the story. Say: Let's talk about what happened in order. How does the story start? Then what happens next? Finally, how does the story end?

TEACHING TIPS

- Model talking about characters and setting: ___ is a (person/animal) in this story. This story takes place ___. (in the future, in the past, today)

- Have students draw pictures of events in the organizer. They can label or dictate words for the pictures to describe those events.

EXTEND

- After completing this activity with the class, have students use the graphic organizer in pairs or teacher-led small groups with other selections.

- Help students think of words to describe characters or setting. Make a list and have students add to it.

Story Map B

Title

Characters	Setting

Events

Main Idea and Details

PURPOSE

Use this routine with the Main Idea and Details Graphic Organizer. This organizer will help students recognize a main idea and distinguish between the main idea and the supporting details. This graphic organizer works especially well with nonfiction selections.

PROCEDURE

1. Display the graphic organizer.

2. Read a selection. Record the main idea in the top box. Define main idea as "the most important idea." For example, *Many things happen in the spring.*

3. Model by recording a detail that supports, or tells more about, the main idea (such as flowers blooming, days getting longer, days getting warmer, animals having babies). Have students supply additional supporting details as you record them. You can use pictures or words to show students that either is acceptable.

4. Once you have modeled how to use the graphic organizer, have students complete the organizer independently, in pairs, or in small groups.

TEACHING TIPS

- Supply a sentence frame about main ideas: The most important idea is ___. Supply a sentence frame about supporting details: One detail about this idea is ___.

- Display part of a selection and model highlighting important ideas. Use different colors to highlight the main idea in one color and highlight details in another color. Ask: What is this text mostly about? This is the main idea. What tells you more information about this main idea? These are the supporting details. Record the important ideas in the organizer.

- Extend or add additional boxes if necessary to include more supporting details.

- Have students draw pictures for the details of the story, and then use their drawings to write or dictate the main idea.

EXTEND

- Have students use the graphic organizer to record ideas for their own writing.

- Have students use the graphic organizer in pairs or small groups to record important ideas from content-area reading, such as social studies or science.

Main Idea and Details

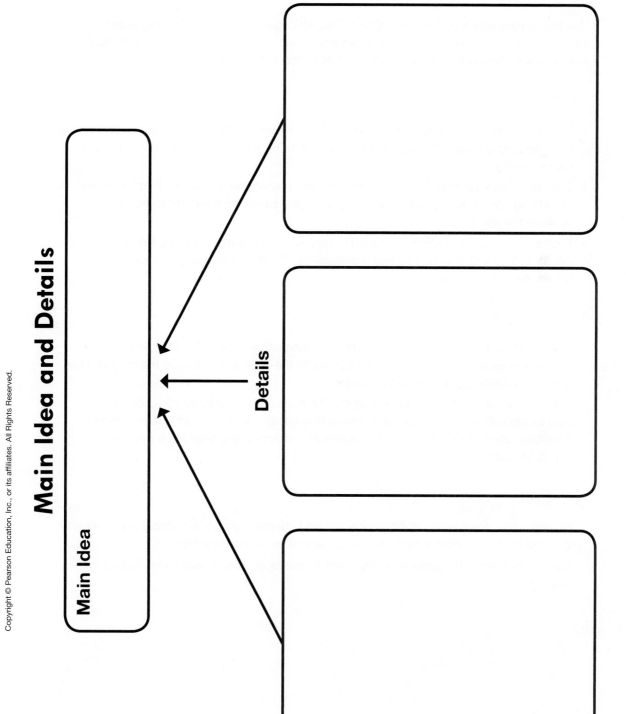

Main Idea

Details

Cause and Effect

PURPOSE

Use this routine with the Cause and Effect Graphic Organizer. This graphic organizer works well with any selection that has clear cause-and-effect relationships. It can help students identify cause-and-effect relationships in either fiction or nonfiction.

PROCEDURE

1. Discuss the idea of an effect with students. Elicit responses from students that something that happens is an effect. Record or draw an effect on the graphic organizer. (I got out my umbrella.)

2. Then ask students: Why did that action happen? Discuss with students that the reason something happens is a cause. Record or draw the cause on the graphic organizer. (It started to rain.)

3. Restate the cause and effect: It started to rain, so I got out my umbrella. Tell students: Cause comes first. It is why something happens. Effect comes next. It happens after the cause.

TEACHING TIPS

- Remind students to ask themselves, *What happened?* and *Why did it happen?* to identify effects and causes. It is usually easier to identify the effects first, before the causes. Use sentence frames: ___ happened because ___.

- List clue words that signal causes and effects, such as *because* and *so*. Look over the clue words with students, but remind them that not all causes and effects in selections have clue words. Help them identify causes and effects in the selections when no clue words are used.

EXTEND

- Students can draw, write, or dictate causes and effects in the informational texts. They can record, for example, causes of thunderstorms or of events in history.

- If students need extra assistance, fill in either causes or effects before distributing the organizer.

Cause and Effect

Cause

Effect

Sound-by-Sound Blending

PURPOSE

Use this routine to help students decode and spell words by systematically teaching them the relationships between letters and sounds.

PROCEDURE

1. Write and say the word. When possible, use visuals or gestures to help convey the meaning. For example, write the word *nap* on the board and make a gesture of a person sleeping.

2. Model blending one sound at a time. Say the first sound in the word, underline and point to the letter(s) that spell that sound. For example, underline *n,* point to it, and say: /n/.

3. Say the next sound in the word, underline and point to the letter(s) for that sound. Repeat for the remaining sounds. For example, underline the *a,* point to it, and say: /a/. Then underline *p,* point to it, and say: /p/.

4. Repeat each individual sound as you point to the letter. Then have students say each sound as you touch under the letter(s).

5. Run your hand from letter to letter as you say the sounds, without pausing between them. Repeat until all sounds have been added and blended. For example, blend /nnnaaa/ and /nnnaaap/.

6. Have students repeat each sound. Then have students blend the sounds with you and then without you as you point to the letter(s).

7. Have students repeat the word several times as you run your hand under the letters quickly.

TEACHING TIPS

- Tell students to watch your mouth as you emphasize the sound of the letter(s).
- If students say an incorrect sound, show them the letter and pictures of items that begin with that letter/sound. Provide students with other words with similar sound-spellings.
- If students stop between sounds, then model how to say the sounds without stopping. Have students blend the sounds again.

EXTEND

- Give students index cards with words, and have them quickly blend the sounds to read the words.
- Have students use alphabet cards to create words, blending the sounds of the letters as they point to each card.

Nondecodable Words

PURPOSE

Use the Nondecodable Words Routine to introduce students to words that are not decodable by helping them recognize the word on sight by identifying familiar letters in words.

PROCEDURE

1. Explain to students that some English words do not sound the way they are spelled. Say: We learn how to recognize these words by remembering the letters. Let's say and spell the words together.

2. Write the word *do* on the board. Point to the word as you read it aloud. Identify the letters in the word, and indicate the number of letters in the word. For example: This is the word *do*. It has two letters. The letters are *d* and *o*.

3. Have students repeat the word, the letters of the word, and the number of letters in the word with you. Then have the students do this by themselves.

4. Remind students to watch how you move your mouth as you repeat the word. Point out any letters that do not follow the standard rules.

5. Use the nondecodable word in a sentence to demonstrate usage of the word. Provide an example that relates to students' experience and uses the word in the same context as the text: *I will do my work now.*

TEACHING TIPS

- Provide pictures, examples, or visual clues to help students understand its usage.
- If students pronounce the word incorrectly, model again the sounds in the word. For example: This is the letter *d*. It makes the sound /d/. The letter *o* in this word is not long or short. It makes the /ü/ sound. Let's try the word again: *do*.

EXTEND

- Have students use the word in a sentence. Provide a sentence frame if necessary.
- Have students use index cards to create flashcards of newly learned words and then practice reading them correctly with a partner.

Parts of a Book

Show students how to hold a book, with the spine on the left and the front cover showing. Point out and explain the title, author byline, and illustrator's name. Turn to the selection pages and read a sentence or two. Discuss how the illustrations go with the text. Page through the book and show how the narrative continues. Point to the text on each page. Then have students practice holding the book correctly, finding the title and author, turning the pages, and pointing to the text on each page.

Letters and Words

Display text in a large format, such as a big book page. Read aloud a sentence, pointing to each word as you read. Then frame one word with your fingers and read it aloud. Explain that it is a word, and point out the spacing before and after the word. Point out the letters within the word, and count the letters. Then invite students to point to other words on the page and to count the letters within the words.

Tracking Print

As you read a book aloud, put your finger on the starting point in the text on each page. Show that you read from left to right by moving your finger along lines of text. Use your finger to show how to sweep back from the end of a line to the beginning of another and how to find the beginning of the text on the next page. Then have students use their fingers to show the correct movement as you read the text aloud again.

Recognizing and Producing Rhyming Words

Pronounce rhyming words for students, and have students repeat them.

> *cat, hat, bat*
>
> *hill, fill, mill*
>
> *pie, sky, my*

Display pictures or use pantomime to help students recognize word meanings. Say: Listen to these words: *cat, hat, bat.* All three words end with *-at.* Then segment two of the words (/k/ /a/ /t/ and /h/ /a/ /t/), and help students hear the same middle and ending sounds. Tell students that these words rhyme. Say: Now I will say three words. I want you to tell me the two words that rhyme: *cat, hop, bat.* After students identify the rhyming words, introduce other words that share the same rhyme, such as *mat* and *sat.* As students learn more words, occasionally have them supply more words that rhyme, such as *at, fat, rat,* and *that.*

Use this routine with other rhyming words, such as *hop, top, pop; hen, ten, pen; sing, ring, thing; cold, old, bold; coat, boat;* or *dizzy, fizzy.* Also provide a word that is easily rhymed (for example, *stop* or *bake*), and invite students to name words that rhyme with it.

Segmenting and Blending Syllables

Gather objects or pictures that represent a meaningful category of words, such as fruits, classroom items, or animal names. Have students identify items one at a time. Repeat each word and clap for each syllable, such as *cray-on, ba-na-na,* or *dog.* Have students clap for each syllable as you repeat each word. Explain that these parts are syllables. For each word, have students say the word, syllable by syllable (clapping for each), and tell how many syllables the word has. Then have them blend the syllables and say the whole word.

Repeat the activity to help students recognize syllables in words of various lengths: *kit-ten, oc-to-pus, coat, bub-ble, five, cat-er-pil-lar, desk, hip-po-pot-a-mus,* and others.

Distinguishing Initial Sounds

Tell students that you want them to listen for words that begin with the same sound. Say: Listen carefully: *dog, dig, dirt.* Say the words with me: *dog, dig, dirt.* Do these three words all begin with the same sound? (Yes.) Now listen carefully: *cat, cup, duck.* Do all of these words begin with the same sound? (No.) *Cat, cup, duck*—which word does not begin like the others? (*Duck* does not begin like *cat* and *cup.*)

Repeat the routine with sets of words such as these: *hot, hand, sad; mug, pack, moon; sock, bug, soap; pan, pipe, race; ant, toy, apple; tape, bog, bib.*

Recognizing Initial Phonemes

Display a simple image of a box. Say: This is a box. The word *box* begins with /b/. Exaggerate /b/ as you say *box* three times. Have students say *box* with you, exaggerating /b/. Repeat with the words *bubble*, *bus*, and *bed*. Then display an image of a fox and say: This is a fox. The word *fox* begins with /f/. Repeat the word *fox*, exaggerating /f/, and have students repeat. Ask which word begins with /b/, *box* or *fox*. Continue teaching the initial /f/ with words such as *fish, fan,* and *face*. Ask if the word *funny* begins with /f/. Use a two-column chart to model sorting words by initial phonemes. For example, write *b* and *f* as column heads, saying each sound, and make marks or draw images in the correct column for each word: *box, bubble, fox, fish, bowl,* and *face*. Have students make marks in the correct columns for words as you say them.

Repeat this activity with other initial phonemes, words, and simple pictures: *cat, corn, coat; hat, horn, happy; apple, ant; pencil, potato, pocket;* and other words.

TEACHING TIP Pictures of items that begin with a target sound will help students associate initial phonemes with words they know or are learning. Use picture cards, teacher-made pictures, or students' simple sketches if appropriate.

English Language Learners Emphasize the sounds in words. English learners often benefit from seeing the letter *b* as they hear /b/ and the letter *f* as they hear /f/ to help them later develop letter recognition and English letter-sound correspondences.

Recognizing Final Phonemes

Adapt the Initial Phonemes activity (above) by modeling final phonemes, such as /b/ in the words *tub, web,* and *cab* and /p/ in the words *mop, cap,* and *top*. As you say the words, exaggerate the final phonemes. If you use the two-column chart, make sure students understand that you and they will make marks (or simple pictures) to sort words by their final sounds.

Repeat with other final phonemes, such as /n/ in *sun* and *moon* and /t/ in *hat* and *dot*.

Distinguishing Medial Phonemes

Say the words *pan* and *pen,* exaggerating the medial /a/ and /e/, respectively. To clarify the word meanings, talk about or draw a pan for cooking and show an ink pen. Ask students to listen for the middle sounds in the words as you repeat them. Then have students say the words, exaggerating the /a/ and /e/. Ask which is used for writing, pan or pen. Model the same medial phonemes in the words *mat* and *met* and *bad* and *bed*. Adapt the activity as the year goes on using other medial phonemes, including /i/ versus /e/ in words such as *pin* and *pen* and /a/ versus /o/ in words such as *hat* and *hot*.

English Language Learners Help ELLs recognize the differences between similar-sounding medial phonemes that may be unfamiliar to them, especially short vowel sounds that are seldom used in certain home languages.

Segmenting and Blending Phonemes

Display a picture of the sun, and say: This is the sun. I will say the sounds in the word *sun:* /s/ /u/ /n/. Have students say the sounds with you. Then say the sounds again, holding up one finger for each sound. Ask: How many sounds are there in the word *sun*? Have students say the sounds, /s/ /u/ /n/, holding up a finger for each. Next, blend the sounds together. Say the sounds in *sun* more quickly, raising each finger as you say a sound. Repeat this several times, having students join you as they pronounce the sounds and hold up a finger for each. Then hold up one index finger as you say /s/, followed by two fingers on your other hand as you say /un/. Say: /s/ /un/, sun. Have students imitate you as they say *sun*. Repeat the activity using words such as *hat, red, mop, pan, pet,* and *wig.* (For *red*, point to a red object, and for *pet*, use a picture of a cat or dog.)

Recognizing and Distinguishing Letters

Write *Aa* on the board, and draw or show a picture of something that begins with *a*, such as an apple. Point to the uppercase letter. Ask: What is this letter? Yes, this is uppercase *A*. Point to lowercase *a*. Say: This letter also is called *a*. Say it with me: *a*. This is an apple. The word *apple* begins with *a*. What letter does it begin with? Have students form uppercase *A* and lowercase *a* on their hands.

Repeat the activity with other letters and pictures. Have students repeat the letters, and ask questions about the letters and pictures.

English Language Learners Help students recognize differences between similar letters, such as *d* and *b*; *p* and *q*; *E* and *F*; or *O* and *Q*. Students whose home languages are not alphabetic (such as Chinese and Japanese) or do not use the same alphabet as English (such as Korean and Russian) often need extra practice with the alphabet. Students whose home languages associate different sounds or tones with familiar-looking letters (such as Vietnamese) also benefit from extra practice.

Recognizing Letters in Context

Write *Aa* on the board, and display a page from a classroom big book that has both an uppercase and lowercase *a* on it. Have a volunteer identify *A* and *a* on the board. Have another student identify an uppercase and lowercase *a* on the big book page that is displayed. Hold the big book page next to the letters on the board. Ask: Do the letters match? (Yes.)

Repeat the activity with other letters and pages in a big book to give students practice with identifying letters.

Recognizing Letters in Words

Display one or more calendars. Have pairs or small groups of students identify uppercase and lowercase *a*. Say: On most calendars you will see the letter *a*. When you find one, raise your hand and tell me whether it is uppercase or lowercase.

Repeat the activity with other letters. Point out names of holidays and other words, besides the names of months. Help students recognize that not every letter appears on a calendar page.

Writing Letters and Numbers

Introduce students to writing all the alphabet letters and to writing numbers. Each time, select two or more letters or numbers for students to identify and practice writing.

Distinguishing Consonant Sound-Spellings

Display pictures of a bag and a doll or hold up a real bag and a real doll. Say: This is a bag. The word *bag* begins with /b/. This is a doll. The word *doll* begins with /d/. What is the beginning sound in *bag*? What is the beginning sound in *doll*? Write *Bb* and *Dd* on the board. Say: The letter for /b/ is *b*. The letter for /d/ is *d*. What is the letter for /b/ in *bag*? What is the letter for /d/ in *doll*? Have students point to the appropriate letter on the board.

Repeat the routine for other pairs of consonant sound-spellings: /p/ *p (pen)*, /m/ *m (mug)*, /f/ *f* (fox), /v/ *v (van)*, /k/ *c (cap)*, /t/ *t (ten)*, /g/ *g (goat)*, /k/ *k (kite)*, /j/ *j (jam)*, /r/ *r (red)*, /n/ *n (net)*, /l/ *l (leaf)*, /w/ *w (wolf)*, /h/ *h (hose)*, /s/ *s (six)*, /z/ *z (zoo)*.

English Language Learners Help students distinguish English sound-letter correspondences that are unfamiliar in their home languages. For example, in Spanish the sounds of *v* and *b* often are indistinguishable, so students at first may not recognize the difference between words such as *best* and *vest*. For students who speak some Asian languages, the distinction between the sounds of *r* and *l* may be unfamiliar. With systematic practice and exposure to English words, children will improve their phonics. Other "confusing consonants" may include *b* and *p*; *k* (or *c*) and *g*; *j* and *ch*; *d* and *th*; *t* and *th*; *ch* and *sh*; and *j* and *y*.

Recognizing Consonant Sound-Spellings in Words

Display a page from a classroom big book that has a word that begins with *b*. Point to the word that begins with *b*. Say: This word (say the word) begins with /b/. What is the beginning sound in (repeat the word)? Write and point to the letters *Bb* on the board. Say: The letter for /b/ is *B*. Point to the word in the big book and identify whether it starts with an uppercase or lowercase *b*. Repeat the word and say: The word (repeat the word) begins with /b/. What is the first letter in (say the word)? (*B*) Say: (Repeat the word) begins with /b/. The letter for /b/ is *B*. /b/, *B*, (repeat the word).

Repeat this routine for other consonant sound-spellings.

Finding Words with Consonants

Write the letters *Bb* on the board and have students name both forms. Using words on a Word Wall or other environmental print in the classroom, help a volunteer find a word that begins with *b* or *B*. (Alternately, display a word that begins with *b*.) Read aloud the word that begins with *b*. Say: This word begins with /b/. The letter for /b/ is *b*. Have the volunteer point to the *b* (or *B*) at the beginning of the word as students repeat the word, the beginning sound, and the letter name.

Then adapt the activity by displaying and reading aloud a word that ends with *b*, such as *cab, tub,* or *crib*. Ask students to point to the letter at the end of the word and say the letter name and the sound. Model segmenting other short words, emphasizing the final consonant, and decoding the words. Have students repeat sounds, letter names, and words, and begin to decode the words as their abilities develop.

Repeat the activity for many other consonant sound-spellings during sessions throughout the year. For words with consonants in final positions, include sound-spellings such as /k/ *ck*, /s/ *ss,* and /ks/ *x*.

More Practice with Consonants

Use classroom items and pictures that show many items to help students practice associating consonant sounds with the letters. Point out objects such as a jacket, a desk, a door, or a shirt that someone is wearing in a picture. For each item, say the word and have students identify the beginning sound and the consonant (or consonant digraph) that represents that sound. Be sure students have had the chance to learn each sound-spelling. Focus on consonants that students have struggled to learn. Adapt the activity as the year goes on to help students practice with final consonants and consonants in the middle of two-syllable words.

Use pictures that show several items or classroom scenes to have students find one or more objects whose names begin (or end) with a particular consonant. Provide help with words and spellings as appropriate.

Recognizing Short-Vowel Sound-Spellings

Display an alphabet book or other big book, and turn to a page with a word that begins with the letter *Aa,* such as *Action* or *Astronaut*. Say the word *action*, and have students repeat it. Say: The word *action* begins with /a/. What is the beginning sound in *action*? Write and point to the letters *Aa.* Say: The letter for /a/ is *a*. This is uppercase *A*. This is lowercase *a*. The word *action* begins with /a/. Here, the word *action* is spelled with uppercase *A*. What is the first letter in *action*? (*A*) Say: *Action* begins with /a/. The letter for /a/ is *a*. /a/, *a*, *action*. Say the word with me: *action*.

Repeat the routine for /e/*e, /i/i, /o/o,* and /u/*u.*

English Language Learners Help students recognize and distinguish English short vowel sounds (and corresponding letters) that are unfamiliar in their home languages. For example, the sound of short *a* does not appear in Spanish, Cantonese, and several other languages. Regularly provide multiple chances for students to hear words with short vowels, see the vowels in the words, say the words, and write these words. Students may need help associating /o/ with the letter *o* because that sound is spelled *a* in Spanish and certain other languages.

Finding Short Vowels in Words

Display pictures of an *ant* and a *map*. Say *ant* and *map* several times, emphasizing the initial and medial /a/. Have students say the words. Then say: The words *ant* and *map* both have /a/. Which word has /a/ at the beginning, *ant* or *map*? Which word has /a/ in the middle, *ant* or *map*? Write the words on the board and ask: What is the letter for the beginning /a/ in *ant*? Have a volunteer circle *a*. Ask: What is the letter for the middle /a/ in *map*? Have a volunteer circle *a*. Say: The letter for /a/ is *a*.

Repeat this routine using the words *egg* and *bed* for /e/*Ee, inch* and *pig* for /i/*Ii, ox* and *top* for /o/*Oo,* and *up* and *sun* for /u/*Uu.*

Practice with Short Vowels

Display a picture of a hat. Ask: What is this? Say the word *hat*, emphasizing the medial /a/. Have students say the word. Ask: What sound is in the middle of *hat*? (/a/) What is the letter for /a/? (*a*) Write the word on the board. Have students check their answer by naming the middle letter in the word. Yes, *a* is the letter for /a/ in *hat*. Continue with the words *jam* and *van*.

Repeat the routine using the words *hen, red,* and *web* for /e/e; the words *pig, six,* and *wig* for /i/i; the words *fox* and *mop* for /o/o; and the words *bus, mug,* and *tub* for /u/u.

More Practice with Short Vowels

Use words for objects shown in picture books (or the colors of some objects) to help students practice associating short-vowel sounds with the correct vowels. Add items in the classroom. Point out objects (or people) whose names have short vowels such as a hat, a cab, a group of men, an inch, a dot, and the sun. Show students the word for each. Have them locate the short vowel, identify it, and learn how to read and write the word. Point out objects that are red, tan, or black, and teach those words. Be sure students have had the chance to learn each sound-spelling. Focus on short vowels that students have struggled to learn.

Use pictures that show several items to have students find one or more objects whose names include a particular short vowel. Provide help with words and spellings as appropriate.

Narrative Writing

Use this routine with the Narrative Writing Graphic Organizer to help students plan and write a narrative story. (See also the Unlock Narrrative Writing lesson in Part 2 of this handbook.)

PROCEDURE

1. Ask students: What is narrative writing? Say: Narrative writing tells a story. The story is told by someone—a narrator. Show examples of stories the class has read recently. Tell students that stories can be true or made up.

2. Explain that every narrative has a beginning, middle, and end. Say: Stories should tell what happens first, then what happens next, and finally, what happens at the end.

3. To begin demonstrating how to write a narrative, use a story starter. For example: Ben and I went outside to play, and we ___.

4. Write the sentence frame on the board and read it aloud. Ask: What do you like to do when you go outside to play? Write their responses on the board. Tell students that all of these activities could be part of a narrative. Choose an activity to write the beginning sentence of a narrative.

5. Display the graphic organizer and model how to fill in the first part with words or pictures, using the beginning sentence you created.

6. Repeat the process with the middle part of the narrative. Ask: What happens next in our story? Guide students in making sure that what happens is a logical progression from the start of the story. Then discuss with students how the narrative might end. The end should follow logically from the sequence of events. Read the narrative you created, pointing to each word as you read it aloud.

7. Now help students complete a sentence starter and use the graphic organizer to tell their own narrative.

TEACHING TIPS

- Read the sentence frames aloud for students several times.
- Talk about stories you have read aloud with students. Ask them to identify what happened in these stories and whether these stories are real or made up.
- Provide additional writing paper so that students can write longer sentences.

EXTEND

Have students share their narratives with a small group or with the class. They may draw pictures to add to their narratives.

Narrative Writing

Draw pictures and then write to show what you did this weekend.

First

Then

Finally

This weekend I _____.
_____

First, _____.
_____

Then, _____.
_____

Finally, _____.

Informative/Explanatory Writing

Use this routine with the Informative/Explanatory Writing Graphic Organizer to help students plan and compose an informative/explanatory piece of writing. Students will inform or explain their topics using drawing, dictating, and writing. (See also the Unlock Informative/Explanatory Writing lesson in Part 2 of this handbook.)

PROCEDURE

1. **Ask students:** What is informative/explanatory writing? **Say:** Its purpose is to explain something or to give readers information about something.

2. Show examples of informative/explanatory writing they've read recently. **Say:** Informative/explanatory writing is nonfiction. That means it's true, not made up. Newspaper articles, magazine articles, and textbooks are examples of informative/explanatory writing.

3. **Say:** In informative/explanatory writing, you first tell the topic or what you will explain. Then you give some information about that topic.

4. Display the graphic organizer. Help students use the graphic organizer to compose their own informative/explanatory piece of writing. Have students decide what they want to explain and then draw a picture of or dictate their topic. Then have them draw or dictate some information they know about their topic.

TEACHING TIPS

- Have students work in pairs to choose a topic and to gather some information about their topic.

- Provide sentence frames to help students get started: I will tell about ___. I can explain how ___.

- Provide simple books on topics of interest to students to help them gather information.

- Ask questions that will prompt students to think more about their topics and how to develop them. For example, if students choose to write about plants, ask: What are some ideas we can explore about how plants grow? What do you already know about them? What would you like to know more about?

EXTEND

Students who are writing can print words instead of drawing pictures.

Informative/Explanatory Writing

My Topic

Information About My Topic

Opinion Writing

PURPOSE

Use this routine with the Opinion Writing Graphic Organizer to help students plan and compose their opinions through dictating, drawing, and writing. (See also the Unlock Opinion Writing lesson in Part 2 of this handbook.)

PROCEDURE

1. Explain that an opinion is how a person feels or what a person believes about something. Say: A fact can be proven to be true. But an opinion cannot be proven true or false because it is not a fact. It is one person's feelings.

2. Give students an example of an opinion statement. Say: Pizza is the best food ever. That is an opinion. It tells what I think about pizza. Explain that different people have different opinions. Say: My best friend doesn't like pizza. She would not have the same opinion as I do. Explain also that opinions are not right or wrong. And then tell students that opinions are stronger when they are backed up by reasons.

3. Explain that a preference about something such as a favorite color or a favorite book can also be an opinion. Say: My favorite color is blue. This is my preference. Point to a student and ask: What is your favorite color?

4. Tell students that when we write about our opinions, we should support them with at least one reason. Say: If I think pizza is the best food, I should ask myself why I think that. Pizza is tomato-y, spicy, and it's fun to eat. Those are my reasons.

5. Display the graphic organizer and help students compose their own opinion or preference about a topic. Have students draw a picture or dictate a topic. Then have them draw or dictate their opinion about that topic.

TEACHING TIPS

- Have students work in pairs to determine a topic and to provide a reason for their opinion about the topic. Help them brainstorm topics and ask questions for them to answer orally first, such as Who is your favorite storybook character, and why?

- Provide sentence frames to help students get started: The best sport is ___.
  ___ is a beautiful color.

EXTEND

Students who are writing can print words instead of drawing pictures.

Opinion Writing

My Topic

Reason For My Opinion

Talk to a Friend

PURPOSE

Use this routine when informal language is used to explain its purpose to students. Say: The words I use depend on whom I am talking to and why I am speaking. I use some kinds of words when talking to adults or people that I don't know well. I use different words when I am talking with my friends or family. When talking to friends or family, I use words that are not serious, such as *okay* or *hi*. I do not always say whole sentences.

PROCEDURE

1. Display the worksheet on the following page. Direct students to look at the picture on the right side of the worksheet. Explain that in the picture, three friends are talking at a party. Say: They are friends having fun at a party. They do not need to speak in a serious way. What do the friends say? *(What fun! Hooray!)* With volunteers, act out the scene in the picture. Model using informal language, such as sentence fragments.

2. Model rating your knowledge of informal language using the rubric at the bottom of the worksheet. Show students how to circle or point to faces after reading the statements together. Model choosing the smiling face when you agree with the statements and the nonsmiling face when you do not agree with the statements.

3. Direct students to look at the picture on the left side of the worksheet. Prompt students to see that this is a young girl having a meal with her family. Again, model informal language with volunteers as you act out the scene. Read aloud the rubric with students and have them tell you whether they agree or disagree with the statements.

TEACHING TIPS

- As students practice, work with them to create a bank of words and phrases that they use when they are with their friends or family. Guide the discussion by asking questions, such as How do you talk about your school day when you are at home? When you want a friend to come over and play, what do you say?

- Have students do a simple activity in which one acts as a child in class and the other acts as a new child who is being introduced to others. The students may use informal English.

- Ask students to work with partners to act out a conversation with a brother or sister. Remind students that this kind of talking is not usually as serious as when talking to some adults or people we don't know well. But these words should not be rude.

EXTEND

- Have students create new scenarios where they might use informal language, and model appropriate language they might use and hear.

- Have students draw another scenario that calls for informal English and use that drawing as the basis for talking to friends.

Talk to a Friend

Say what the people in the pictures are saying.

Tell how you speak with friends and family.
Circle the picture for each sentence.

1. I am polite when I speak to friends or family.   ☺ ☹

2. I know when I can use words like *okay* or *hi*.   ☺ ☹

3. I listen to others before I speak.   ☺ ☹

Talk to an Adult

PURPOSE

Use this routine when formal language is used to explain its purpose to students. Say: The words I use depend on whom I am talking to and why I am speaking. When I am talking with older people or to bigger groups, I use serious language to show respect for the people I'm talking to. When I say someone's name, I say Mrs. or Mr. I don't use words such as hi or okay. Instead, I might say hello or very well. My speech may be slower. I might take more time to think about what I am going to say.

PROCEDURE

1. Display the worksheet on the following page. Direct students to look at the first picture. With two volunteers, act out the scene in the picture. Model using formal language, such as titles. Say: When I speak to a teacher or other adult, I say Miss, Mr., or Mrs. I ask questions using polite words, such as please.

2. Direct students to look at the second picture. Explain that in the picture, a girl is introducing a friend to her grandparents. Ask: Why would she use formal language? (to show respect for her grandparents) What phrase might the friend say? (Pleased to meet you.) With volunteers, act out the scene in the picture.

3. Model rating your knowledge of formal language using the rubric at the bottom of the worksheet. Show students how to circle or point to faces after reading the statements together. Model choosing the smiling face when you agree with the statements and the nonsmiling face when you do not agree with the statements.

4. Have small groups practice acting out the scene in the third picture, depicting a student speaking to a group. When finished, have groups reread the rubric and indicate whether they agree or disagree with the statements.

TEACHING TIPS

- As students practice, work with them to create a bank of words and phrases used in formal English for their reference. Guide the discussion by asking questions, such as How would you ask your best friend's mom if your best friend can have dinner at your house?

- Have partners do a simple activity in which one student plays the role of a student in class, and the other acts as the principal. The student should use formal language while speaking with the principal.

- Ask students to work with partners to introduce themselves in a formal situation, such as a club meeting. Identify phrases that make the speech formal, such as It's nice to meet you.

EXTEND

- Have students create new scenarios where they would use formal language, and model appropriate language they might use and hear.

- Have students draw another scenario that calls for formal English and use that drawing as the basis for role-play.

Talk to an Adult

Say what the people in the pictures are saying.

Circle the picture for each sentence. **Tell** how you speak to adults and a group.

When I talk to adults:

1. I use *Mr., Mrs., Ms.,* and *Miss.*

2. I use *please* and *thank you.*

When I talk to a group:

3. I plan what I will say.

4. I speak slowly and clearly.

Talk to Friends and Adults

Talk to an Adult

PURPOSE

Use this routine when both formal and informal language are used to review with students the differences between the two ways of speaking. Say: When you talk to your friends or family, your language is more casual or relaxed. When you talk to teachers or other adults, however, you do not use casual language.

PROCEDURE

1. Have students name other differences between formal and informal language and give examples of how they speak to friends and how they speak to adults.

2. Then give students an improper example. Say: Hi, teacher. How are ya? What's up? Guide students to change the language so it is more respectful or formal. (Hello, Mr. Thomas. How are you today?)

3. Display the worksheet on the following page. Direct students to look at the first picture. Shake hands with a volunteer to act out the scene. Ask: What language would you use when shaking hands with an adult? (When I speak to a teacher or other adult, I use titles such as Miss, Mr., and Mrs. If I am meeting them for the first time, I might say Hello or It is nice to meet you.)

4. Direct students to look at the second picture. Have them identify if the scene in the picture is a formal or informal speaking situation. Have partners take turns acting out what the children might say to each other while playing. Model using informal language, such as saying Hey! to a friend.

5. Have students draw their own situations in which they would use formal or informal English in the blank boxes. Have partners look at one another's drawings to determine whether formal or informal language would be used, and then role-play words and phrases for the situation.

TEACHING TIPS

- Show students magazine pictures of various settings, such as a business meeting or a family watching television. Ask students to indicate whether the people in the situation would use formal or informal English.

- The use of formal and informal language depends on social context. Help students understand that the type of language is dependent on whom they are speaking to, their familiarity with the speaker, the purpose for speaking, and the larger audience. Give specific examples of situations and ask students to identify whether formal or informal language will be spoken.

EXTEND

- Have students work with partners to talk about a soccer game. The first conversation should be telling a friend about the game. The second conversation should be a recap of the game for the school announcements.

- Give an example of an informal conversation. Have partners repeat the conversation. Then have them practice the conversation again, this time using formal language.

Talk to Friends and Adults

Tell what the people are saying.

Draw more pictures. **Share** with a friend.

Give Directions

PURPOSE

Use this routine to help students understand what it means to give directions in sequential order.

PROCEDURE

1. Give students directions for making a cheese sandwich, but give the directions out of order. Say: Last, eat the sandwich. Next, put the bread slices together. Then, put the cheese slices on the bread. First, take out two pieces of bread and some cheese. Did those directions make sense? What was wrong? (No, they were out of order.)

2. Provide a simple scenario for students, such as giving directions for watering the classroom plants. Have students provide steps as you pantomime or draw them on the board. Help them use sequence (order) words, such as *first, next, then,* and *last,* by asking questions such as What should I do *first*?

3. As students form the directions with you, write sequence words such as *first, next, then,* and *last* on the board for students' reference. Guide students to give clear, sequential directions. Ask: How can we make that direction easier to understand? Can we break that into more than one step? Are those steps in the right order?

4. Display the worksheet on the following page. Model how to use the rubric. Show students how to circle or point to faces after reading the statements together. Model choosing the smiling face when you agree with the statement and choosing the non-smiling face when you do not agree with the statement.

TEACHING TIPS

- On index cards, provide simple pictures for a simple process. Put one step on each card. Give the cards to individuals, partners, or small groups to place the cards in order. Students can say the directions aloud, inserting sequence words to add organization.

- Have partners give directions orally for a simple task, such as sharpening a pencil, folding a sheet of paper, or drawing a triangle. One student can give directions while the other pantomimes or completes the task.

- Have volunteers model proper directions for the class.

EXTEND

- Collect examples of directions, such as recipes or directions for putting something together. Lead a discussion with students about how the various directions are similar. For example, they both contain clear steps and sequence words to keep steps in order.

- Have students work with partners to create a list of additional sequence words with visuals they can use in giving directions, such as *second, third, after that,* and *finally.* Then have them give directions for a simple task, using words from their list.

Give Directions

Read the order words in the box.

Order Words

first   next
then   last

Use the order words to give directions.

Ask a friend to follow your directions.

Tell how you give directions. **Circle** the picture for each sentence.

1. I can give directions with more than two steps.

2. I can use order words *(first, next, then, last).*

3. My directions are clear.

4. I speak loudly and clearly.

Tell a Story

PURPOSE

Use this routine to help students organize their ideas for telling a story or for speaking to a group. Explain: When I am telling a story to a group, the voice I use is different than the voice I use when talking to a friend. I speak clearly and loudly enough so everyone in the group can hear. I look at the group when I speak. I tell the events of the story in order, from beginning to ending.

PROCEDURE

1. Display the worksheet on the following page. Choose a familiar story to model telling, and write the title on the line.

2. Ask students for ideas about how you should tell the story. Then model drawing and labeling the ideas in order on the worksheet.

3. Tell the first part of the story two times. As you tell it the first time, mumble and don't make much eye contact. Ask: Did you understand me? Did you hear what I was saying? Does my story make sense so far? How can I do better? Model rating yourself using the graphic organizer.

4. Tell the story again using the feedback. Call attention to making eye contact and speaking loudly enough so everyone can hear.

5. Review the rubric on the worksheet and have students again provide a rating to demonstrate their understanding of your improved story telling.

TEACHING TIPS

- After you have modeled telling a story, have students draw pictures to plan their stories.

- Have partners take turns using their pictures to tell each other their stories. Allow them to offer each other constructive feedback.

- Give students a chance to plan what they will say. Help them learn words they do not know, using their pictures.

EXTEND

- Have students work on elaborating. Lead them by explaining that stories are more interesting if they use describing words that tell how something looks, feels, smells, or sounds.

- Have students use their drawings to write sentences to read as they tell their story.

- Have students add sequencing words, such as *first, next,* and *last* in their stories.

Tell a Story

Write the title.

Draw what happens in your story.

Tell the story to a friend.

Title: -

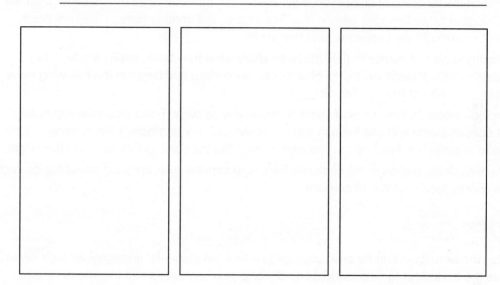

When I tell a story:

I look at others.

I speak loudly and clearly.

My story makes sense.

Tell What You Think

PURPOSE

Use this routine to help students state an opinion.

PROCEDURE

1. Pick up a book that you like and say: I like this book. Point out something about the book that you like, such as the pictures or the story. Display another book that is familiar to students and ask whether they like it.

2. Explain the meaning of an opinion. Say: We tell our opinions to let others know what we think or what we like. One person may like a book, but another person may not like it. People have different opinions, and that is OK.

3. Display sentence frames to help students share what they think, such as telling their favorite color. Provide examples of complete sentences that begin in the following ways: I like ___. I do not like ___. I think ___.

4. Provide students with the worksheet on the following page. Read aloud the examples of opinion words and use them in sample sentences. For example: I like summer. I think walking outside is fun. I do not like loud noise. I like the color yellow because it is bright.

5. Have students complete the sentence frames to express their opinions about topics such as sports, foods, books, or seasons.

TEACHING TIPS

- Use the worksheet first for oral language practice. As students' emergent literacy allows, use the worksheet to help students read words and sentences and to write or dictate short sentences.

- Write sentence frames on index cards, and distribute them to students along with picture cards showing examples of topics, such as colors, seasons, sports, or foods. Have partners choose a picture card and a sentence frame to state an opinion about the picture.

- When calling on students to give oral opinions, have them use phrases such as I like or I do not like, rather than single words. Have pairs ask each other why he or she has that opinion. Report answers to the class.

- Remind students that opinions are neither right nor wrong—they are statements of how someone thinks or feels.

EXTEND

- Have students write statements of opinion and then say them aloud with partners.

- Have students state an opinion to a partner and then elaborate on it by giving reasons for their opinion.

Tell What You Think

┌───┐
│ **Opinion Words** │
│   I think   I like   I do not like   I agree │
│   good   bad   best   worst │
└───┘

Tell what you think.

I like _____

I think _____

I do not like _____

I like _____ because _____

_____

_____

Speak in a Group

PURPOSE

Use this routine to help students understand the importance of being good speakers and listeners in a group discussion. Say: When we work in a group, we talk to each other. We must also listen to each other. This is called having a discussion. We have special rules that we follow when we have a discussion.

PROCEDURE

1. Display and distribute the worksheet on the following page. Have students look at the pictures. Ask them to point to the picture of the teacher reading to the students. Ask: Who is talking in this picture? (the teacher) Who is listening? (the students) One rule for speaking in a group is to have one person speak at a time. We have one person speak at a time so that everyone has a chance to speak. One listening rule is to face, or look at, the person who is speaking. This helps the speaker know that the listeners are paying attention.

2. Have students identify other people in the remaining pictures who are following the listening and speaking rules. Have students discuss their observations of the pictures with a partner.

3. Introduce an easy discussion topic and model discussion behaviors as you speak with a few student volunteers. Pause to think aloud: I asked Lin a question, and then I waited for her to speak. It was my turn to speak first, and now it is Lin's turn. It is important to speak one at a time.

4. Explain that it is also important that the listener understands the speaker. Ask: What can you do if you are the listener and you do not understand what someone has said? (ask questions)

TEACHING TIPS

- Model examples of nonverbal communication skills, such as nodding and making eye contact. Have students mimic you as you model them.

- Consider having students initially work in pairs or small groups to provide multiple opportunities to practice the rules for discussions, as well as to gain confidence in their speaking abilities. As students become more confident through repeated practice, gradually increase the size of the groups.

EXTEND

- Give an example of a conversation that could occur at the lunch table. Have students role-play the scenario. Stress the importance of active listening and behaviors that go with it.

- Have students model discussion scenarios and demonstrate behaviors of listening and speaking for other groups.

Speak in a Group

Look at the pictures.

Discuss them with friends.

Ask Questions

PURPOSE

Use this routine to help students form questions to ask you or their classmates.

PROCEDURE

1. **Explain:** If I don't understand something, I need to ask the person speaking to repeat what he or she said. Then I can understand it. I ask questions to be sure I understand. That is called clarifying.

2. With a student volunteer, role-play a situation in which you would ask a clarifying question. Have the student give you simple directions for doing something, such as how to get your backpack ready to go home at the end of the day. As the student speaks, find an opportunity to ask a question, such as *What does that mean? Can you repeat that, please? How do you do that?*

3. Share the worksheet on the following page with students. Brainstorm with the class some examples of clarifying questions that the students in each of the three pictures might ask. Some examples of clarifying questions include: *Is this right? Can you say that again, please? Can you show me again, please? Will you please help me? What does that mean? Is this correct? How do you say ___ in English?*

4. Ask students to think of an example of a situation, other than those pictured on the worksheet, when they might need to ask a clarifying question. Make a list of suggestions, and have students draw a situation in the blank box.

5. Have partners work together to think of clarifying questions that could be asked in the situation drawn on their partner's worksheet.

TEACHING TIPS

- Have students role-play situations with you in which they ask for assistance for completing a math problem or other classroom task.
- Provide multiple opportunities to practice using clarifying questions.
- Create a classroom poster listing sentence frames for commonly used clarifying questions for students to reference as needed.

EXTEND

Have students work in small groups to identify questions they would ask the teacher, their parents, or other students in a group to clarify their understanding.

Ask Questions

Look at the pictures.

Say questions people are asking.

Draw a picture. **Share** questions with a friend.

Learn New Words
Pairs of Words

PRETEACH

Choose pairs of words that share a relationship. They may have opposite meanings or similar meanings; or two words may rhyme or begin with the same sound. Examples:

OPPOSITES	SYNONYMS	RHYMES	FIRST SOUND
hot, cold	big, large	he, she	dog, duck
up, down	rabbit, bunny	hot, dot	tip, top

Use pictures, actions, or explanations to introduce the words. For example, for *cold* show a wintry scene or shiver, or ask if *cold* has the same meaning as *hot*. Clarify word meanings as needed.

PROCEDURE

1. Show how to associate related words. For example, pantomime or show that washing hands makes them wet; wiping them makes them dry. Say: What is the opposite of wet? (dry) Or say: The words *he* and *she* sound alike at the end. What rhymes with *she*? (he) Write and display each related word pair, reading them aloud and having students repeat them.

2. Monitor students' use of the related words, and clarify word meanings and pronunciation. Provide multiple exposures to the words. As students encounter the words in stories, other selections, classroom conversations, and writing, ask them about word meanings. Acknowledge correct use of learned words.

TEACHING TIP

Have students work in pairs to practice the words using a response activity. For words with opposite or similar meanings, have one student say a word and the other student respond with an antonym or synonym. For rhyming words or words that begin alike, have the first student say a word and the other student respond with a rhyming word or word with the same beginning sound. Provide words as needed.

EXTEND

As students' literacy emerges, help them read and write words and use them in short sentences.

Small Groups of Words

PRETEACH

Choose a small group of words that fit together. Examples:

red, blue, yellow, green	*spring, summer, fall, winter*
hot, warm, cool, cold	*sun, rain, cloud, sky*

Introduce the words by using them orally in daily activities. For example, use color names in a brief coloring activity. A daily look outside provides an opportunity to use weather words.

PROCEDURE

1. Display or provide copies of a simple graphic organizer, such as a word web or a box with spaces for words and students' drawings. Model how to place words in the graphic organizer, explaining words and their meanings. Keep students involved, asking where a word belongs or, for example, holding up crayons and asking which corresponds to each color name.

2. Have students use their copies of the graphic organizers to show the relationships among words. For example, students can begin to copy the word web for colors, writing or dictating the words and coloring the parts appropriately. As their vocabulary and literacy skills develop, students can add new words for colors: *black, white, pink,* and *brown*.

3. Ask students to add to the graphic organizers as new words are encountered. For example, use simple drawings for words such as *sun* and *cloud* or for groups such as *boy, girl, woman, man*. For words such as *one, two, three,* and *four,* students can add numerals to show meanings and improve their skills.

4. Evaluate students' understanding of words and how the words are related. Assess when each student is ready to use vocabulary such as *cat* and *dog* to extend language—for example, learning *kitten* and *puppy* or *pet*. Recognize steps along the way as students learn to use words orally and then in reading and writing, eventually mastering correct spelling and usage.

TEACHING TIP

Students learn new words in relation to other words, not separately. Help students gain familiarity with related words—for example, using a known word (such as *big*) to learn inflected forms of the word (*bigger, biggest*) or to learn a synonym (*large*) or antonym (*small*) or to learn words that can be used with the known word (*elephant, building, hill*). Encourage students to use words together to learn an unfamiliar word by having them answer a question, such as *Is an ant big or small?* Graphic organizers help active learners show relationships and improve their recognition and understanding of words. Display and use a graphic organizer (such as a word web) or provide copies, as this will serve students' vocabulary growth.

Use Classroom Words

Use this routine to help students improve their vocabularies as well as their comprehension of the daily language used in the classroom.

PROCEDURE

1. Introduce the importance of learning classroom words by saying: Every day in class, we communicate with each other. We ask questions and give directions. We work in groups. We listen and ask for help from friends and from the teacher. We have words that we use often in the classroom. It is important for us to know how to use classroom language to get help, work with others, and understand what is happening around us in class.

2. Brainstorm a list of examples of classroom language to illustrate and record on a chart. Ask: What are some phrases or directions that your teacher often says?

3. Display the worksheet on the following page. Using the class chart as a guide, have students provide examples of classroom language that might be said during the activity in the first picture. (*Glue the ___. Cut out the ___. Make/ Draw/ Color ___.*) Add additional examples to the chart as students provide them. Repeat for the second and third pictures on the worksheet.

4. Model rating your knowledge of classroom language using the rubric at the bottom of the worksheet. Show students how to circle or point to faces after reading the statements together. Model choosing the smiling face when you agree with the statements and the nonsmiling face when you do not agree with the statements.

TEACHING TIPS

- Give simple examples of classroom language that require a physical response, such as a teacher asking students to raise their hands.

- While some classroom language is straightforward transactional language that students need to practice in order to learn, other classroom language is idiomatic and may be confusing for students. When you tell students to "line up," for example, they may think of drawing a line. Tell students the meanings of the idiomatic phrases used in the classroom in language they can understand.

- Provide additional pictures on index cards for students to use with a partner while role-playing using classroom words.

EXTEND

Have students create posters to use in the classroom that capture various examples of classroom language. Students can illustrate the posters to show the situations in which they use the classroom language and teach those words and phrases to others.

Use Classroom Words

Look at the pictures.

Act out the conversations with a partner.

Say the words that you would use.

Circle the rating for each sentence. **Tell** how you use classroom words.

1. I can use classroom words.

2. I can help a friend in English.

3. I understand the teacher's directions.

Act Out or Draw Meaning

Use this routine with the Act Out or Draw Meaning Graphic Organizer to help students determine the meaning and significance of a content-area or lesson word that they have recently learned.

PROCEDURE

1. Introduce words from a current selection or from content-area studies. Say: When I learn new words, I want to remember them. Drawing a picture of what the word means helps me remember a word. Acting it out also helps me remember a word. We just learned the new word *roots* in science. Roots are the part of a plant that grows down into the ground. They hold the plant in place.

2. Draw a simple picture of a plant with roots. Place an arrow pointing to the roots. I drew a picture of a plant and drew an arrow pointing to the roots. I can also act out the meaning. As you pantomime, say: I will stand up like a tree and move the top part of my body. My feet are like the roots because they hold me in place on the ground.

3. Place students in small groups and give each group a newly learned word. Have students work together to create a picture and/or gestures to demonstrate the meanings of the words. Have groups present their drawing or gestures for the class to guess their word.

4. Display and distribute copies of the graphic organizer and provide students with a word from the current selection. Model writing the word on the line and drawing a picture in the box.

TEACHING TIPS

- Drawing the meaning of a word such as *wheel* or *smile* helps etch the meaning of that word into the brain, making it a part of our active vocabularies.

- Students may think they cannot draw pictures because they are not artistic. Help them devise symbols or other ways to illustrate meaning when they are "stuck" for picture ideas.

- Have students present their drawings or gestures by explaining the word meanings orally.

- Have students add the words on the cards to their own personal vocabulary notebooks. Assess students' drawings to clear up any misconceptions about the words. Discuss with students how drawing words may help them remember word meanings. Ask: How did drawing the word or acting it out help you remember what it meant?

EXTEND

- Play a guessing game with students. Distribute on index cards words that students have learned in class. Students can take turns drawing pictures or acting out word meanings for other classmates to guess.

- Have students write the word in a sentence to demonstrate understanding of the word's definition.

Act Out or Draw Meaning

Write the word.

Draw the meaning.

Act out the word with a friend.

Word _____

Drawing

Labeling Items and Pictures

Use self-stick notes or slips of paper to label items in the classroom or in pictures. Examples: *mop, mat, bell, pens, box, flag, hats, fish, glass* (on a window), *desk, clock, hands* (in a picture), and *cubby*. Try to include some plural nouns, positioned to clearly identify more than one item. Repeatedly read the labels aloud and have students identify the items. Use the nouns in oral activities. Model making up sentences using them. For example, say: The toys are in a box. Where are the toys? (in a box) Is our state on the map? Have students make up and say sentences using the nouns. As the year continues, help students write nouns and write or dictate short sentences that include the nouns.

Have students draw pictures and tell what people, places, animals, or things their pictures show. Help them write or dictate nouns or noun phrases such as *the bus* to label pictured items. Also invite students to identify items in the classroom or in classroom pictures. As students dictate the nouns, add labels to the items. Read each label aloud so that students need not try to decode words with sound-spellings they have not yet learned. As students' literacy emerges, help them take part more actively in the labeling activity.

Naming People, Places, Animals, and Things

Beginning with nouns for family members (*mom, dad, mother, father, sister, brother,* and nouns for other relatives), have students say nouns for various people. Ask students to draw themselves and other people, and help them label their pictures with their names and nouns, such as *boy, girl, man,* and *woman.* Say the names of people in school, such as your name and the names of other teachers, staff members they know, and the principal. Ask students to name places in the school and other parts of the community. Supply words as needed. Use pictures to list various nouns that name animals and things. With any of the nouns, make up phrases and sentences to model how we use nouns to communicate ideas. Have students make up and say sentences with the nouns. As their emerging literacy permits, help them to read nouns for people, places, animals, and things, and to write or dictate short sentences using familiar nouns.

Use pictures to model how some people, places, animals, and things can be identified by more than one noun or noun phrase. For example, a school building might be called *the school,* (name of school), or *the red brick school*. A picture of a child's dog might be labeled with the pet's name or another noun—*dog, pet,* (breed name), or *animal*. Have students look at pictures and use a variety of nouns or noun phrases to identify what they see.

Use recorded sounds to invite students to identify or guess what they hear, such as a horn, a song, birds, and other nouns or noun phrases.

Recognizing Singular and Plural Nouns

Display a quantity of countable items such as crayons or books, and separate one from a group of more than one. Introduce singular and plural nouns by pointing out and saying *one crayon* (or other kind of item) and, for example, *six crayons*. As you say those phrases, emphasize /z/ at the end of *crayons* (or /s/ at the end of a noun such as *books*). Have students repeat the noun phrases, and listen to help them say the singular and plural nouns correctly. Then draw or display one dot on the board or on paper and say: one dot. Write the word *dot* and read it aloud. Draw or display three dots and say: three dots. Write the word *dots* and read it aloud. Repeat it, emphasizing /s/ and pointing out the letter *s* at the end. Point to the single dot and ask what it is. Point to the three dots and ask what they are. Listen to make sure each student can use the singular and plural nouns.

Repeat the activity with various nouns, using items or pictures. Include nouns whose plural forms end in *-es,* such as *boxes* and *benches*. When students know some regular plural forms, introduce several plurals without *-s* or *-es,* such as *men, women,* and *children*.

Capitalizing Proper Nouns

As students practice writing their names, they learn about proper nouns for people. Extend this concept and the skill of capitalizing by displaying the school name, your city or town name, state name, or other proper names for streets, stores, and other buildings known to students. Ask students for the first names of family members and friends, and model capitalizing the nouns. Show how some proper nouns, such as the name *Ana Luz* or *the United States,* have more than one uppercase letter. During the year, occasionally show a proper noun incorrectly capitalized, and model how to easily correct it.

Display one or more calendars. Have pairs or small groups of students find the names of months and days of the week. Most calendars begin each name of a month or day with an uppercase letter. Have students write the uppercase letter at the beginning of a month name or day name that they find.

Repeat the activity with other letters. Point out names of days and other words besides the names of months. Help students recognize that not every letter of the alphabet appears on a calendar page.

English Language Learners Various alphabetic languages have their own conventions for capitalizing or not capitalizing certain nouns. Help Spanish-speaking students learn the conventions of English, such as always capitalizing names of days and months. Students whose home languages are not alphabetic (such as Cantonese and Mandarin) may be less familiar with capital letters and may need extra practice capitalizing proper nouns.

Building Descriptive Phrases

Use picture cards or pictures and make word cards with three kinds of words:

nouns (such as *ant, bag, cats, hat, man, pals, van, bed, egg, hen, men, kid, lips, wig, box, cow, doll, fox, mop, ox, rock, sock, bugs, bus, cup, duck, pup,* and *tub*)

adjectives (such as *happy, sad, tan, fat, red, wet, thin, big, little, hot,* and *funny*)

articles and number words (such as *a, an, the, one, six, seven,* and *ten*)

Model how to make phrases by putting words in order to create pictures students can imagine: *a little ant, the big bed, six happy pals, a fat hen,* and so on. Read aloud the phrases. Invite students to make many phrases, say them, and draw pictures of the ones they like or think are the funniest.

Repeat the activity with added words as students' decoding skills and vocabulary grow.

English Language Learners In English, adjectives typically come before nouns (*two red socks*), except in a sentence such as *The socks are red*. Students may be familiar with other patterns in their home languages. For example, Spanish adjectives often follow nouns (the Spanish name that means "big river" is *Rio Grande*). Help students recognize the English adjective-noun order by explicitly pointing it out in rhymes (*Old sock, new sock/red sock, blue sock*), songs (*I'm a Little Teapot* or *Happy Birthday*), stories, and descriptions. As students speak and write, model correct adjective use and praise their improving mastery.

Choosing Adjectives That Fit

Use picture cards or other pictures to help students move beyond using a noun alone to identify images. For each picture of a person, place, animal, or thing, have students name it with a noun and add a descriptive adjective. Model by displaying a few pictures and describing what you see: *a tan puppy, a wet turtle, the hot sun*, or *puffy clouds*. Have students take over, describing images in pictures. Help with words as needed.

Repeat the activity with larger, more detailed pictures, such as posters. Invite students to select items to describe.

Writing Short Descriptive Captions

Model writing a short caption for a picture of a person, place, animal, or thing. The caption may consist of a phrase or short sentence. Examples: *A happy girl; A happy girl holds a cat; A red ball; The fast boy runs.* Have students draw pictures and write or dictate short captions that include adjectives.

Repeat the activity as students' reading, writing, and vocabulary develop.

TEACHING TIP Students' early writing may appear more like scribbles than words. They may omit letters, writing *rd* for *red*. As students try to capture sounds of words in writing, they may not achieve correct spelling. Have them tell what their written words say. Model the correct spelling, and provide opportunites for students to practice on their own.

Answering with Opposites

Display and read aloud pairs of adjectives that are antonyms: *happy/sad, hot/cold, big/little, black/white, wet/dry,* and so on. Repeat the words and have students say them with you. Then model saying pairs of phrases that describe opposites, such as *happy kittens* and *sad kittens; hot water* and *cold water; a big hill* and *a little hill; black paper* and *white paper; a wet sock* and *a dry sock.* Use discussion, pantomime, and images to make sure students understand the words and ideas. Then have pairs of students play this game: one student says a phrase with an adjective and a noun, such as *a big dog,* and the other answers with the opposite, such as *a little dog.*

As students' vocabulary grows, repeat the activity with more adjectives. Allow sensible contrasting phrases, even if the nouns differ, for example: *a big truck* and *a little car.*

Demonstrating and Using Verbs

Perform these actions as you narrate, and have students repeat your actions and words: I clap. I walk. I sit. I talk. **Ask:** Which words tell what I do? (*clap, walk, sit, talk*) **Say:** A word that tells what we do is called a verb. Provide other examples of action verbs in brief sentences: I play. You sing. They jump. Dogs bark. Have students repeat each sentence and tell which word is the verb, or the word for the action. Invite students to say other verbs.

Recognizing Verbs That Add -*s*

Help students learn when to add -*s* to a verb. Plenty of exposure to verbs in oral and written language will help establish the pattern. Emphasize the verb endings as you say: She sits here. He sits here. [Student's name] sees me. [Another student's name] sees me, too. Explain that when we tell about one person, animal, or thing doing something now, we add -*s*. The letter *s* at the end of a verb can sound like /s/ or /z/. Say: John hops. Maria runs. A cat sleeps. The wind blows. Have students repeat those sentences and pantomime the actions. Display the verbs *sit* and *sits* and read them aloud. Ask students to finish this sentence with either *sit* or *sits*: A man ___. (sits)

Repeat the activity and include verbs that end with -*es,* such as *Lee brushes the dog* or *Min fixes the cup*. Have students make up sentences with verbs, and monitor the verb forms. As students learn more verbs, model the present-tense forms. Have students say them.

English Language Learners Students of all language backgrounds have much experience hearing about actions, and they can transfer language knowledge to English. Yet, English verb endings and tenses may be unfamiliar or confusing. Speakers of Spanish, Polish, and Russian, for example, use more verb endings that depend on sentence subjects (first-person, second-person, and third-person subjects, as well as singular and plural subjects). Speakers of some Asian languages do not use different verbs for present and past action. Help students understand how English speakers say and write verbs by providing continual exposure to a variety of verbs in sentences. Expect that students may make mistakes such as adding -*s* to verbs that should not end with -*s*. Model correct verb use, and encourage students to produce language, even when they struggle to master verb forms.

Using Verbs for Past Action

Help students learn to say, hear, read, and write regular verbs with *-ed* endings. Say these sentences and display the verbs: I asked her to play. We jumped rope. You called me. I opened the door. Repeat the sentences, emphasizing /t/ at the end of *asked* and *jumped* and /d/ at the end of *called* and *opened*. Model how to write each base verb such as *jump* and how to write each with *-ed*. Show examples of verbs whose past tense ends with *-ed* (*walk, play, jump, call, push, listen, watch,* or *talk*) and read them aloud. Begin a story about children and use a few of the verbs in past tense. Help students add sentences to continue the story, also in past tense. Help them say the verbs correctly. For some verbs, the *-ed* ending is pronounced as a new syllable (*wanted, lifted, melted*). Help students say them.

Repeat the activity from time to time. If students try to add *-ed* to irregular verbs, model the correct forms such as *sat* or *knew,* and tell students that not all verbs have forms with *-ed*. Help students learn verbs whose past forms do not end in *-ed* such as *had* and *grew*.

Using Verbs to Tell About the Future

Provide examples of verbs for future (planned) actions. Say: After school today, I will go home. Tomorrow I will eat a pear. You will play a game. Tell students that verbs for the future, later times, use the verb *will* to help out. Ask students about what they plan to do after school or tomorrow. What will you do? If they use present-tense verbs, model the correct forms: *will go, will visit, will play,* and so forth.

Use pictures of children doing active things—running, hopping, walking, singing—or have students act out or pantomime these actions. Ask them to tell about people who will do the actions tomorrow: I will run, Ella will hop, Mom and Dad will walk, and Daniel will sing. Have students think of other verbs and make up short sentences using those verbs in future tense.

English Language Learners Many English verbs have equivalents in home languages. Students may better understand unfamiliar English verbs if they can relate them to words in their home languages. Often, however, context in English and support such as pantomiming actions will clarify verb meanings.

SENTENCES

Saying and Seeing Sentences

Model a sentence such as: My name is ____. Have each student complete the "My name is" sentence. Write and display the sentence with one name (for example, *Liam*) and read it aloud. Point out that it is a sentence, and say: It tells about the subject of the sentence, *My* name. What does it tell about the name? It tells that the name is Liam. Make up another telling sentence. For example, if a girl in class has a book on her desk, say: She has a book. Have other students tell about something they have. (I have crayons. I have my paper.) Write a few of the sentences, display them, and read them aloud. Point out the subjects such as *She* and *I*. Continue with short sentences about other subjects, such as the following: The door is open. The weather is sunny. This apple is red. A clock is on the wall. Invite students to make up sentences about subjects that they choose.

TEACHING TIP The heart of grammar is sentences—hearing, saying, reading, writing, and understanding sentences that communicate ideas. Students learn the conventions of sentences by hearing and saying many sentences and reading and eventually writing many more. Those activities are greater aids toward success than a teacher spending additional time explaining sentence grammar. Students do not begin with mastery of complete, error-free sentences, but extensive practice and encouragement will promote proficiency. Listen for the idea that they seek to express in each sentence they say. Look for what they are trying to communicate in each sentence they write.

Capitalizing the First Word in Sentences

Use big books or other large displays of text to show students several sentences. Read each sentence aloud, and point out the uppercase letter at the beginning. (Do not use poems or songs in which each line begins with an uppercase letter, even in the middle of sentences.) Tell students that the first word in each sentence starts with an uppercase letter. Have students draw a picture, and help them write or dictate a short sentence about the picture. Have them write an uppercase letter at the beginning of the first word.

Choose a day during which you will take special notice of students correctly beginning a written sentence with an uppercase letter. For example, stick a star or another sticker next to a correct capital letter or have other students give a cheer. Make sure that each student who correctly capitalizes first words of sentences receives the positive attention.

Punctuating the Ends of Sentences

Use big books or other large displays of text to show students several examples of correct end punctuation. Read each sentence aloud and point out the period or other punctuation at the end. (Avoid very long sentences.) Tell students that the last word in most sentences has a period at the end. If there are questions in the text, point out the question mark. If there is an exclamatory sentence, point out the exclamation mark. Have students draw a picture and then write or dictate a short sentence about it. Have them write correct punctuation at the end of the last word.

Choose one or more days during which you will take special notice of students correctly ending a written sentence with a period or other form of end punctuation. For example, stick a star or another sticker next to a correct period or have other students give a cheer. Make sure that each student who correctly punctuates the ends of sentences receives the positive attention.

TEACHING TIP To help students who are struggling to improve their sentence writing, focus on one kind of error (or one need) at a time. Help them make progress incrementally rather than trying to understand multiple corrections at the same time.

Display Good Sentences

After each writing activity, help students display their best sentences. For example, copy an interesting and correct sentence on large paper and post it on a special part of a wall. These sentences can be short or long. If possible, have students and perhaps parent volunteers or aides help prepare the display copies of sentences. Include sentences from as many students as possible during the year.

PREPARE TO READ

Vocabulary in a Flash

Write the vocabulary words for a selection on cards and include pictures that connect to their meaning. Display each card and read the word aloud. Ask students to indicate if they have heard of the word. If some students have heard of the word, ask them to share when they heard it or explain what they know about it. Once all ideas have been shared, challenge students to use the word in a sentence of their own.

Realia and Visuals

For vocabulary words in a selection that can be easily depicted visually, such as *plant* and *seed*, show students physical examples, provide pictures, or pantomime the words' meanings. Say each word aloud as you do so. Have students repeat after you. Then hold up an object or picture (or perform a pantomime) and challenge students to call out the correct corresponding vocabulary word.

Define and Conquer

Have students listen as you say aloud the vocabulary words in a new selection. After saying each word, provide a brief, student-friendly definition, such as the following for *seed:* "something tiny that is placed in the soil to grow." Then ask: What is our new word for something tiny that is placed in the soil to grow? Have students say the word aloud as a class. Repeat for each word. Then challenge students by saying the word and asking them to share what they remember about its definition.

Context Clue Caper

After saying each vocabulary word aloud and repeating its definition, provide a sentence in which it is used correctly in context: The plant needs water to grow. After you have done this for all the words, read another sentence that features one of the vocabulary words: The sunflower is my favorite plant in the garden. Ask students to name the vocabulary word and share something they remember about its meaning.

INTERACT WITH TEXT

Use the Clues!

Identify vocabulary words in a selection that are clearly reinforced by text and picture clues. As you read a text aloud, stop at the first such vocabulary word. Say it aloud and provide a student-friendly definition. For example, you might say the following: squinting: "closing your eyes part of the way because the light is bright." Point out the text and picture clues that reinforce this meaning, such as a picture of a person squinting and holding up her hand to block out the sun. Then have students repeat the word and meaning after you. When you come to the next applicable vocabulary word, repeat the process, but this time ask students to help you identify any text or picture clues that suggest the word's meaning.

Your Turn!

Review the meaning of each word as it is used in the selection. Then ask students to connect the word with their own knowledge and experience. So, for the word *squinting,* ask students to name and describe a time when they found themselves squinting or to imagine and explain an appropriate time in the future when they might need to squint.

Let's Make Conversation!

Review selection vocabulary words and encourage students to use these words when you engage them in conversation about the text. If a student uses a vocabulary word during the discussion, recognize and praise him or her and review the word's meaning as a group.

Picture Dictionary

Assign each student a word from the module that lends itself to a visual representation. On a piece of white paper, have students draw a picture of the word that connects to its meaning. For the word *parched,* for example, a student might draw a drooping flower in the bright sun. Help each student write his or her word on the other side of the paper. Invite students to present their word and picture to the class. Then combine students' pictures into a class picture dictionary that can be added to and referenced throughout the unit and year.

Songs

Adapt the lyrics of popular songs in order to reinforce the meanings of vocabulary words from the selections. For example, you might adapt the lyrics to "The Wheels on the Bus" to reinforce the meaning of the word *temperature:*

The heat from the sun
makes the temperature rise,
temperature rise,
temperature rise.
The heat from the sun
makes the temperature rise,
all through the town.

EXPRESS AND EXTEND

Complete Sentences

Say aloud each of the selection vocabulary words, one at a time. After you read a word, challenge students to be the first to use it in a complete sentence of their own.

Either/Or

Review with students the vocabulary words learned in a selection. Then have them answer the following either/or questions: Which word means "a living thing with roots in the soil," a *plant* or a *seed*? Which word means "a little object that is placed in the soil to grow," a *plant* or a *seed*?

Decorate Your Word!

Have students choose their favorite word from a selection or module. Explain that they will write and then decorate their word in order to show what it means. For example, for the word *shout,* they might write the word in large capital letters and cut and paste from a magazine a picture of a person with his or her mouth wide open, as if calling loudly. Help students, as necessary, to write their word in the center of a piece of paper. Then provide art supplies as well as scissors and magazines. You may choose to play a word-guessing game with students' pictures and then display them around the room.

Word Associations

Choose three selection vocabulary words and say them aloud. Review each word's meaning and give examples. Then challenge students to associate each of the chosen vocabulary words with a presented word or phrase. For example, you might ask: Which word goes with music and listening? (phonograph) Which word goes with hot and cold? (temperature)

Yes/No

Prepare a list of yes/no questions for words in a module. For example, for the words *giggle, enormous,* and *seldom,* you might prepare the following yes/no questions: If something sad happened, would you be likely to giggle? Is an elephant enormous? Is blinking something you do seldom? After students answer each question, ask them to explain in their own words why or why not.

True/False

Prepare a list of true/false questions for words in a module. For example, for the words *murmur, swollen,* and *droop,* you might prepare the following true/false statements: True or false: If my finger is swollen, it is smaller than normal. True or false: If you murmur, you speak very loudly. True or false: If something is firm, it is hard and unbendable. Challenge students to answer true or false and explain why.

Extra Examples

Identify vocabulary words in the module that are verbs. Say each word (for example, *glisten*), review its meaning with the class ("to shine or sparkle"), and provide an example (I watched raindrops on a spider web glisten in the sun). Challenge students to name and describe other examples of the word (a newly washed car, a diamond, an ornament, and so on).

Pantomime

Identify words from the module that lend themselves to pantomime, such as *crunch, smack, plop, sniff,* and *droop.* Say the words aloud and review their meanings as a group. Then assign partners one of the words and ask them to think of a way they could act out or pantomime the meaning of the word for the rest of the class. Provide assistance and feedback as needed. Invite each pair to come to the front of the class or circle to perform while the rest of the class tries to guess the correct vocabulary word.

Making Connections

Identify words in the module that go together, such as nouns, verbs, adjectives, or words that describe a topic. Ask students to tell which two of the three words you will say aloud go together. For example: Which two of the following words are weather words: *drizzle, alley, floods?*

Name That Category

Identify words in the module that go together, such as nouns, verbs, adjectives, or words that describe a topic. Ask students to identify what the words have in common or what category they would fit under. For example, you might say aloud the words *hailstone, rainbow,* and *sunbeam.* Then ask: These words are all examples of what in nature? (weather events, things you can see outside, and so on)

Same and Different

Identify pairs of words from the module that are similar (such as *sparkling* and *glistening*) and pairs that are different (*rises* and *sets*). Say the two words aloud and ask students to tell if they are similar or different and explain why.

It Takes Two

Identify words in a module that can be used together to form a logical sentence. Say the two words aloud (for example, *pollen* and *inside*) and review their meanings with students. Then ask students to create a sentence that uses both of the words correctly. If necessary, provide a sentence frame: The tiny yellow grains we see ___ (inside) the flowers are called ___ (pollen).

Bingo

Help students arrange word/picture cards in a 5 x 5 grid, placing a "free" card in the middle. Explain that you will select definitions from the definition pile and read them aloud. They will place markers on the word/picture cards in their grids that match the definitions. The first student to mark an entire row, column, or diagonal wins the game.

Show Me!

Have students physically demonstrate their knowledge of the meaning of words in a module. For example, you might ask: Who can show me what it looks like to shimmy? Who can show me an example of tromping? Who can show me an example of a good sigh?

Name That Word!

Explain to students that you will read aloud five words from a selection. Then you will give clues about one of these words, and the first student to guess the correct word will win the game. For example, you might provide the following clues for the word *parched*: This word is a describing word. This word describes what you are when you are very thirsty.

Unlock Language Learning

Part 4 Unlock Language Learning

Where Is Home, Little Pip?

Reproduce and distribute copies of the *All About Penguins* student page on page 330. Ask students to look at the picture of the penguin. Point out that a penguin is a bird that lives in very cold parts of our world. You may wish to show a world map to locate where students live and where Antarctica is. Have students tell about the penguin in the picture. Continue with the picture that shows a group of penguins and talk about the ice and snow in Antarctica.

Explain that to understand the story events in *Where Is Home, Little Pip?* students will find it helpful to know about the animals. Have students identify the whale in the next picture. Point out that the whale is swimming in the ocean and there are fish around it. Next, discuss the bird (a gull) and the sled dogs pulling the sled over the ice and snow. Help students tell about the animals, using words such as *fur, feathers, paws, wings,* and *legs.*

Have students work with a partner to complete the sentences in the Team Talk section. Read each sentence and provide students with a model to show how to complete the sentence. Then have partners complete the activity.

TALK ABOUT SENTENCES

For students who need support in accessing key ideas and key language in *Where Is Home, Little Pip?* use the Sentence Talk Routine on pages 408–409 to draw students' attention to the relationship between meaning and the words, phrases, and clauses in the text.

Lesson	Sentence(s) to Deconstruct
1	Pip was hatched in a nest made of pebbles on the cold Antarctic shore.
2	Mama and Papa always said, "Don't wander far, Little Pip."
3	Mama and Papa constantly fished to keep up with Pip's belly.
4	"Where is home?" Pip cried. Nobody answered.
5	Pip frowned. "But that's not *my* home," she said.
6	The tall creature said something, but Pip couldn't make out the words.
7	Tears dripped down her cheek and froze solid.
8	"After such a long, scary day, you must be exhausted, my dear. Let's sleep."
13	Mama and Papa danced and waddled around her.

SPEAK AND WRITE ABOUT THE TEXT

Use the Text-Based Writing Routine on pages 410–411 to model how to speak and write about key ideas and details in *Where Is Home, Little Pip?*

Lesson	Text-Based Writing	Scaffolded Frames
1	On page 2, where was Pip hatched?	• Pip was hatched in a _____. • The nest was made of _____. • The nest was on _____.
2	On page 6, what did Mama and Papa tell Pip to do?	• Mama and Papa told Pip _____. • Pip was not to _____.
3	On page 8, why did Mama and Papa get fish?	• Mama and Papa _____. • Pip needed fish to _____. • Pip ate fish to fill her _____.
4	On page 13, what happened to Pip?	• Pip chased a _____. • Pip got _____. • Pip wanted to go _____.
5	On page 20, why does Pip know it isn't her home?	• Pip does not live in a _____. • Pip knows she lives _____. • Pip does not have a nest in a _____.
6	On page 22, who is the tall creature?	• The tall creature is a _____. • The tall creature has a _____. • The _____ has a _____.
7	On page 26, what did Pip do?	• Pip starts to _____. • Pip's tears _____. • Pip is very _____.
8	On page 30, what did Mama think they should do?	• Mama said Pip should _____ after such a long, scary day. • Mama said she must be very _____. • Mama said Pip should go to _____.
13	On page 29, what did Mama and Papa do when they found Pip?	• Mama and Papa _____ and _____. • Mama and Papa _____. • Mama and Papa moved _____.

EXPAND UNDERSTANDING OF VOCABULARY

Use the Dig Deeper Vocabulary Routine on pages 406–407 to continue to develop understanding of nouns—words that name people, animals, places, or things: *baby, nest, whale, penguin, sea, puppy, ocean.* Use the book cover and point to the penguin. Ask students to name the animal. Point out that the word *penguin* is a naming word. Then say the following sentence: The penguin walks fast. Have students tell the naming word and then tell what the penguin does. Continue with the other naming words, using pictures from the book or other sources.

Name _____

All About Penguins

I see _____.

It has _____.

A House for Hermit Crab

BUILD BACKGROUND

Reproduce and distribute copies of the *Learn About Crabs* student page on page 332. Explain that to understand the story events in *A House for Hermit Crab,* students will find it helpful to know the basic content related to the story. Point to the picture of the hermit crab. Explain to students that a hermit crab lives in the ocean. Point out the pairs of crab legs and explain that the pair by the head has claws called pinchers to grab things. Then review each of the pictures for a shell, a fish in the ocean, a starfish, and pebbles. Have students repeat the name of the object or animal and describe something they see.

Use the Team Talk sentence frames to help students construct sentences. Have students work with a partner to complete the sentences and share their sentences with the group.

TALK ABOUT SENTENCES

For students who need support in accessing key ideas and key language in *A House for Hermit Crab,* use the Sentence Talk Routine on pages 408–409 to draw students' attention to the relationship between meaning and the words, phrases, and clauses in the text.

Lesson	Sentence(s) to Deconstruct
9	He moved right in, wiggling and waggling about inside it to see how it felt.
10	But it was frightening out in the open sea without a shell to hide in.
11	In October, Hermit Crab approached a pile of smooth pebbles.
12	The ocean floor looked wider than he had remembered, but Hermit Crab wasn't afraid.

SPEAK AND WRITE ABOUT THE TEXT

Use the Text-Based Writing Routine on pages 410–411 to model how to speak and write about key ideas and details in *A House for Hermit Crab.*

Lesson	Text-Based Writing	Scaffolded Frames
9	On page 8, what did Hermit Crab do?	• Hermit Crab wanted to find a _____. • Hermit Crab moved into the _____. • Hermit Crab _____ and _____.
10	On page 6, why did Hermit Crab want a home?	• Hermit Crab wanted a _____ place to live. • Hermit Crab felt _____ in the open sea.
11	On page 25, what did Hermit Crab want to do with the pebbles?	• Hermit Crab approached _____. • Hermit Crab needed the _____. • Hermit Crab built a _____.
12	On page 30, where was Hermit Crab and how did he feel?	• Hermit Crab was _____. • Hermit Crab thought the ocean was very _____. • Hermit Crab was not _____.

Name _____

Learn About Crabs

I see _____.

It is _____.

Life in a Pond

Reproduce and distribute copies of the *Look at the Pond student* page on page 335. Ask students to look at the picture of the pond. Ask volunteers to tell what they see or what they know about a pond. Point out that a pond is a very small body of water. It is smaller than a lake or an ocean. Have students tell about the pond in the picture.

Explain that to understand the story events in *Life in a Pond*, students will find it helpful to know about a pond. Have students identify the fish in the picture. Point out that fish can swim in a pond and people can go fishing at a pond. Next, discuss the ducks, frogs, and water lilies. Have students use the picture context to tell some facts about each picture.

Ask students to work with a partner to complete the sentences in the Team Talk section. Read each sentence and show how to complete the sentence. Then have partners complete the activity.

TALK ABOUT SENTENCES

For students who need support in accessing key ideas and key language in *Life in a Pond,* use the Sentence Talk Routine on pages 408–409 to draw students' attention to the relationship between meaning and the words, phrases, and clauses in the text.

Lesson	Sentence(s) to Deconstruct
1	A pond is a small body of still, shallow water.
2	Ponds form in forests, on farms, and in cities.
3	Many kinds of fish swim in a pond.
4	Sunlight reaches plants that grow on the bottom of the pond.
5	Animals find food in ponds.
6	Plants need pond water to grow.
11	Many plants and animals live together in ponds.

Use the Text-Based Writing Routine on pages 410–411 to model how to speak and write about key ideas and details in *Life in a Pond.*

Lesson	Text-Based Writing	Scaffolded Frames
1	On page 4, what is a pond?	• A pond has _____. • A pond is _____. • The water is _____.
2	On page 6, where can you find ponds?	• Ponds can be found _____, _____, and _____. • Ponds can be found in _____. • Ponds can be found on _____.
3	On page 8, what swims in a pond?	• _____ swim in a pond. • Many kinds of _____ swim in a pond. • Fish swim in a _____.
4	On page 18, what does sunlight do?	• Sunlight shines on the _____ at the _____ of the _____. • Sunlight shines on the _____. • The plants are in the _____.
5	On page 20, what do animals find in a pond?	• Animals find _____ in a pond. • Animals find food in a _____. • A pond has _____ for animals.
6	On page 20, what are ponds full of?	• Plants need _____ to grow. • Plants get _____ from the pond. • A pond has _____ for plants.
11	On page 20, what lives together in a pond?	• _____ and _____ live in a pond. • Plants and animals live _____. • Plants and animals live together in a _____.

Use the Dig Deeper Vocabulary Routine on pages 406–407 to continue to develop understanding that words that name people, animals, places, or things are called nouns. Use the following nouns and have students tell whether they name an animal, a place, or a thing: *pond, forest, insect, farm, lake, cattail, water lily.* Use the book cover and point to the pond. Ask students to name what they see. Point out that the word *pond* is a naming word. Have students tell whether the pond is a person, a place, or a thing. Continue with the other words, using pictures from the book or other sources.

Unit 1 Module B

Name _____

Look at the Pond

The pond has _____.

I see the _____.

335

A Bed for the Winter

Reproduce and distribute copies of the *Who Am I?* student page on page 337. Explain that to understand the story events in *A Bed for the Winter,* students will find it helpful to know the basic content related to the story. Point to the picture of the squirrel. Explain to students that a squirrel lives in a tree and collects acorns for food. Have students point to the squirrel, the tree, and the acorns. Then review each of the pictures for the bear and its cave, the rabbit in the field, the toad on the land, and the owls on the branch of a tree. Have students point to the parts of the pictures as they repeat the names of the things they have talked about.

Use the Team Talk sentence frames to help students construct sentences. Have students work with a partner to complete the sentences and share their sentences with the group.

TALK ABOUT SENTENCES

For students who need support in accessing key ideas and key language in *A Bed for the Winter,* use the Sentence Talk Routine on pages 408–409 to draw students' attention to the relationship between meaning and the words, phrases, and clauses in the text.

Lesson	Sentence(s) to Deconstruct
7	The dormouse is looking for somewhere to sleep.
8	A squirrel gathers leaves high in a tree.
9	They huddle together and sleep through the winter.
10	Snug in the tree hole, the dormouse is sleeping.
12	At last she has found her bed for the winter!

SPEAK AND WRITE ABOUT THE TEXT

Use the Text-Based Writing Routine on pages 410–411 to model how to speak and write about key ideas and details in *A Bed for the Winter.*

Lesson	Text-Based Writing	Scaffolded Frames
7	On page 35, what does the dormouse want to find?	• The dormouse wants to find _____. • The dormouse wants a place to _____.
8	On page 36, what is the squirrel doing?	• The squirrel gathers _____. • The leaves are high in a _____.
9	On page 44, what do the bats do?	• The bats _____ through the winter. • The bats _____ together while they sleep.
10	On page 52, what is the dormouse doing?	• The dormouse is _____. • The dormouse sleeps in a _____.
12	On page 52, what has the dormouse found?	• The dormouse has found a bed for the _____.

Name _____

Who Am I?

I am a _____.

I live _____.

Name _____

The Little Penguin

I am a penguin.
I live in the snow.
It is cold.

Name _____

An Animal Home

This is a squirrel.
It lives in a tree.
The tree is by a lake.

Performance-Based Assessment
Unit 1 Module A

Reproduce and distribute copies of the *The Little Penguin* student page on page 338. After completing the Prepare to Write activities on pages 164–165 in Unlock the Writing in Part 2, use the student model to illustrate the features of narrative writing.

Discuss the student model. Point out that the writer has written several sentences that tell about the penguin. Remind students that they read about Pip, the penguin in the story *Where Is Home, Little Pip?* Ask the following questions to review the information on the model: Which animal did the writer write about? Where does the animal live? What is the weather like? What did the writer draw? Then have students look at the sentences. Ask them why there are uppercase letters and lowercase letters. Have students look at the end of each sentence and help them identify what punctuation mark is used. Write a model sentence on the board to review the items discussed and have students identify the features of the sentence. Then have students read the student model story together.

Unit 1 Module B

Reproduce and distribute copies of the *An Animal Home* student page on page 339. After completing the Prepare to Write activities on pages 170–171 in Unlock the Writing in Part 2, use the student model to illustrate the features of informative/explanatory writing.

Discuss the student model. Have students find the squirrel in the picture. Then read the text and have students repeat each sentence after you. Also have them find the tree and lake in the picture. Have students tell about the things they see in the picture and say a sentence that they might use when they write.

Point out the sentences in the text and remind students about the use of uppercase and lowercase letters and the punctuation used in each sentence. As each sentence is discussed, have students name the letter form and the punctuation mark.

Ask students to name the homes for some of the animals in the picture or other animals they know about. Then have students read the student model informative text together.

The Little House

Reproduce and distribute copies of the *A Big Change* student page on page 343. Explain that it will help students understand *The Little House* if they understand the big change that takes place in the story. Make sure they know what the word *change* means. Then discuss the picture sequence with students.

Point to the pictures in the first row. Tell students that these are pictures of the country. What does the country look like? Scaffold with sentence frames such as *The country has _____. I see _____.*

Point to the pictures in the second row. What is happening? Confirm students' understanding by asking them what things people build or construct. Have them complete this sentence frame: *They build _____.*

Point to the pictures in the third row. Tell students that these are pictures of a city. What does a city look like? Scaffold with sentence frames such as *The city has _____. I see _____.*

Have students turn to a partner and complete the sentence frames in Team Talk to tell about the picture sequence, using one sentence for each row. Then have partners read their sentences to explain the big change.

TALK ABOUT SENTENCES

For students who need support in accessing key ideas and key language in *The Little House,* use the Sentence Talk Routine on pages 408–409 to draw students' attention to the relationship between meaning and the words, phrases, and clauses in the text.

Lesson	Sentence(s) to Deconstruct
1	The Little House was very happy as she sat on the hill and watched the countryside around her.
2	The Little House was curious about the city and wondered what it would be like to live there.
3	Now the Little House watched the trucks and automobiles going back and forth to the city.
4	As the Little House settled down on her new foundation, she smiled happily.
10	Time passed quickly for the Little House as she watched the countryside slowly change with the seasons.
11	The air was filled with dust and smoke, and the noise was so loud that it shook the Little House.
13	They rolled along the big road, and they rolled along the little roads, until they were way out in the country.

Use the Text-Based Writing Routine on pages 410–411 to model how to speak and write about key ideas and details in *The Little House.*

Lesson	Text-Based Writing	Scaffolded Frames
1	On page 6, how did the Little House feel?	• The Little House felt _____. • She sat _____. • She watched _____.
2	On page 7, what was the Little House curious about?	• The Little House was curious about _____. • She wondered _____. • What would it be like to _____?
3	On page 13, what did the Little House watch?	• The Little House watched _____. • _____ and _____ went back and forth. • They went to _____.
4	On page 26, where did the Little House settle down?	• The Little House settled down on _____. • After she settled down, she _____. • She felt _____.
10	On page 8, how did time pass for the Little House?	• Time passed _____. • She watched _____. • The countryside changed with _____.
11	On page 17, what shook the Little House?	• The _____ shook the Little House. • It was so _____. • The air was filled with _____ and _____.
13	On page 25, what did the Little House roll along?	• The Little House rolled along the _____ and the _____. • The Little House was in the _____ again.

Use the Dig Deeper Vocabulary Routine on pages 406–407 to continue to develop conceptual understanding of the following nouns: *buds, brook, carriage, cellars, stories, shutters, frost,* and *gasoline.* Review with students that nouns are words that name people, places, animals, or things. Point out that all of these words are nouns and they all name things.

Display and read aloud the following sentence: Trucks and cars traveled on the road. Underline the words *trucks, cars,* and *road.* Explain that these words are nouns. Ask students whether the nouns *trucks, cars,* and *road* name people, places, animals, or things.

Name _____

A Big Change

First it was _____.
Then they _____.
Now it is _____.

Four Seasons Make a Year

Reproduce and distribute copies of *The Seasons* student page on page 345. Explain that knowing about the seasons will help students understand the story *Four Seasons Make a Year.* Point to the first picture. The season is spring. It rains a lot in spring. Continue with the pictures for summer, fall, and winter. Have partners complete the sentence frames in Team Talk. Tell them to use the pictures or their own ideas to tell about each season.

TALK ABOUT SENTENCES

For students who need support in accessing key ideas and key language in *Four Seasons Make a Year,* use the Sentence Talk Routine on pages 408–409 to draw students' attention to the relationship between meaning and the words, phrases, and clauses in the text.

Lesson	Sentence(s) to Deconstruct
5	A year has four seasons—spring, summer, fall, and winter.
6	The pear tree we planted by the porch is covered with white blossoms.
7	On hot summer days I swim in the pond down the road.
8	Cold wind makes bright-colored leaves dance through the air.
9	A bright red cardinal hops onto a snowbank.
12	I'm building a bright white snowman.

SPEAK AND WRITE ABOUT THE TEXT

Use the Text-Based Writing Routine on pages 410–411 to model how to speak and write about key ideas and details in *Four Seasons Make a Year.*

Lesson	Text-Based Writing	Scaffolded Frames
5	On page 30, what are the four seasons?	• The four seasons are _____, _____, _____, and _____.
6	On page 33, what does the pear tree look like in spring?	• The pear tree is _____. • The pear tree has many _____.
7	On page 39, when does the girl swim? Where does she swim?	• The girl swims on _____. • She swims in _____.
8	On page 47, what does cold wind do?	• Cold wind makes _____. • Cold wind makes the leaves _____.
9	On page 54, what does a cardinal do?	• A cardinal _____. • A cardinal _____ onto a snowbank.
12	On page 58, what is the girl doing?	• She is building _____. • It is _____.

Name _____

The Seasons

Team *Talk*

In spring _____.
In summer _____.
In fall _____.
In winter _____.

Farming Then and Now

Reproduce and distribute copies of the *On a Farm* student page on page 348. Explain that to understand the information in *Farming Then and Now*, students need to know about farms. Point to the picture of a farm. This is a farm. Identify the house, barn, silo, fences, and animals. Explain that farmers are people who live and work on farms. Farmers grow food on farms.

Point to and identify the first picture in the first row. These animals are cows. Many farms have cows. Farmers milk cows. Continue with the picture of the sheep, crops, and farm machine, identifying how each relates to farms. (Many farms have sheep. Farmers get wool from sheep. Crops grow on farms. Farmers grow crops such as corn and wheat. Farms have machines. Farmers use machines to help them grow and harvest crops.) Let students share what they know about farms and farmers.

Have students turn to a partner and complete the sentence frames in Team Talk using the pictures. Then have them discuss what they have learned about farms. Scaffold with additional sentence frames such as *A farm has _____. _____ and _____ live on a farm. _____ and _____ grow on a farm. Farmers use _____.*

TALK ABOUT SENTENCES

For students who need support in accessing key ideas and key language in *Farming Then and Now*, use the Sentence Talk Routine on pages 408–409 to draw students' attention to the relationship between meaning and the words, phrases, and clauses in the text.

Lesson	Sentence(s) to Deconstruct
1	There are lots of chores to be done on the farm.
2	Most of the time, farmers get up at daybreak and work until the sun goes down.
3	One hundred years ago, most milking was done by hand one cow at a time.
4	Today, a combine harvester can cut twenty acres of wheat in one hour.
5	One hundred years ago, it took two people to shear a sheep.
6	Life on a farm was hard before there were machines.
12	Some things on the farm never change. Such as getting up at daybreak and working until the sun goes down.

SPEAK AND WRITE ABOUT THE TEXT

Use the Text-Based Writing Routine on pages 410–411 to model how to speak and write about key ideas and details in *Farming Then and Now*.

Lesson	Text-Based Writing	Scaffolded Frames
1	On page 4, what is the first chore on a farm?	• The first chore is to _____. • Farmers have to _____. • They _____ first.
2	On page 4, how long do farmers work?	• Farmers work from _____ until _____. • They start working at _____. • They keep working until the _____.
3	On page 6, how was milking done one hundred years ago?	• Milking was done _____ one hundred years ago. • Farmers milked one cow _____.
4	On page 11, how many acres of wheat can a combine harvester cut in an hour?	• A combine harvester can cut _____ in an hour. • The machine is a _____. • It can cut _____.
5	On page 12, how many people did it take to shear a sheep one hundred years ago?	• It took _____ to shear a sheep one hundred years ago. • _____ sheared one sheep.
6	On page 14, when was life on a farm hard?	• Life on a farm was hard _____. • Life on a farm was hard without _____. • _____ made life on a farm easier.
12	On page 15, what are some things that never change on the farm?	• One thing that never changes on a farm is _____. • Another thing that never changes on a farm is _____. • Today farmers still have to _____ and _____.

EXPAND UNDERSTANDING OF VOCABULARY

Use the Dig Deeper Vocabulary Routine on pages 406–407 to continue to develop conceptual understanding of the following action verbs: *rises, starts, changed, spin, drive, think,* and *travel.* Review with students that verbs are words that tell about actions, or things we can do. Point out that all of these words are action verbs.

Display and read aloud the following sentence: Farmers work hard all day. Underline the word *work. Work* is an action verb. It tells what farmers do. Point out that the words *hard* and *all day* tell more about the verb. *Hard* tells how farmers work. *All day* tells when farmers work.

Name _____

On a Farm

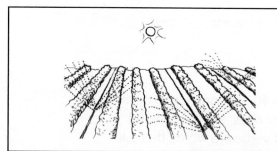

This is a _____.

It has _____.

They can _____.

The Old Things

BUILD BACKGROUND

Reproduce and distribute copies of the *Old or New?* student page on page 350. Explain that understanding the concept of past and present, or old and new, is important to understanding the informational text *The Old Things.* Discuss the first two pictures. Both people are plowing, but one is using a horse, and the other is using a tractor. What is old? What is new? Continue with the pictures of the log cabin and modern house and of the Model T car and modern car. Have partners read the questions in Team Talk and complete the sentence frames using the pictures.

TALK ABOUT SENTENCES

For students who need support in accessing key ideas and key language in *The Old Things,* use the Sentence Talk Routine on pages 408–409 to draw students' attention to the relationship between meaning and the words, phrases, and clauses in the text.

Lesson	Sentence(s) to Deconstruct
7	I play music on my MP3 player. I would like your record player too.
8	This is my old camera. You will need film to take a photo with it.
9	I type on Mom's laptop. But it would be fun to type on your typewriter.
10	Here are my old pen and ink pot. I used them at school.
11	Thank you for all the old things. I will look after them!

SPEAK AND WRITE ABOUT THE TEXT

Use the Text-Based Writing Routine on pages 410–411 to model how to speak and write about key ideas and details in *The Old Things.*

Lesson	Text-Based Writing	Scaffolded Frames
7	On page 5, what does Tom play music on?	• Tom plays music on _____. • Tom has an _____ and a _____.
8	On page 6, what does Gran want to give Tom?	• Gran wants to give Tom _____. • It needs _____ to take _____.
9	On page 9, what does Tom type on?	• Tom types on _____. • Tom uses a _____ and a _____.
10	On page 12, what does Gran want to give Tom?	• Gran wants to give Tom _____. • She used them _____.
11	On page 15, what does Tom do?	• Tom _____ Gran for the _____. • Tom says, "_____."

Name _____

Old or New?

Team *Talk*

What is old? This _____ is old.

What is new? This _____ is new.

Name _____

A Change

Then I did not walk.
Now I run!

Name _____

Life on a Farm?

I would like to live on a farm.
I would have many animals.

Performance-Based Assessment
Unit 2 Module A

Reproduce and distribute copies of the student model on page 351. After completing the Prepare to Write activities on pages 176–177 in Unlock the Writing in Part 2, use the student model to illustrate the elements of narrative writing.

Discuss the first illustration. What does the writer show about something he did when he was younger? When does this event happen? Discuss the second illustration. What does the writer show about what he does differently? When does this event happen? What has changed? If students have difficulty recognizing the change, point out pictures of the Little House on pages 5 and 20 and ask them how the Little House changes over time.

Read aloud the first sentence of the story *A Change*. Why does the writer begin this sentence with *Then I*? What does the word *Then* tell us about when this happened? Which picture does this sentence go with? Continue with the second sentence of the story, the word *Now*, and the connection between the sentence and the second picture. Then have students read aloud the story together.

Unit 2 Module B

Reproduce and distribute copies of the student model on page 352. After completing the Prepare to Write activities on pages 182–183 in Unlock the Writing in Part 2, use the student model to illustrate the elements of opinion writing.

Remind students that opinion writing has three main parts: a topic, an opinion about the topic, and a reason that supports the opinion. Explain that the topic of the opinion piece *Life on a Farm?* is *Would you like to live on a farm?* Read aloud the first sentence. What is the writer telling in this sentence? What is the writer's opinion about the topic? Read aloud the second sentence. What is the writer telling in this sentence? How does this reason support the writer's opinion? Write *topic, opinion,* and *reason* on sticky notes and place them next to the title, first sentence, and second sentence, respectively.

Discuss the illustrations. Point to and name the animals or have students name them. Why did the writer include these pictures? Explain that the pictures show what the second sentence tells: the reason. The writer would have many animals. That is the reason the writer would like to live on a farm.

Come On, Rain!

Reproduce and distribute copies of the *Sun and Rain Effects* student page on page 356. Tell students that to understand the story *Come On, Rain!* they need to understand the effects weather can have on people and things. Explain what the word *effects* means. Then discuss the two sets of pictures with students.

Have students describe the first picture. The hot sun has an effect on plants and people in the story. Have students tell about the next two pictures. Scaffold with sentence frames such as *The sun is _____. It makes plants _____. It makes people _____.* Confirm that students understand the sun's effect on plants and people.

Have students describe the next picture. The cool rain has an effect on people in the story. Have students tell about the next two pictures. Scaffold with sentence frames such as *The rain is _____. Children _____ in the rain. Each mother and daughter _____ in the rain. They feel _____.* Confirm that students understand the rain's effect on people.

Have students turn to a partner and complete the sentence frames in Team Talk. Then have partners read their sentences to explain how weather affects the people in the story.

TALK ABOUT SENTENCES

For students who need support in accessing key ideas and key language in *Come On, Rain!* use the Sentence Talk Routine on pages 408–409 to draw students' attention to the relationship between meaning and the words, phrases, and clauses in the text.

Lesson	Sentence(s) to Deconstruct
1	"Come on, rain!" I say, squinting into the endless heat.
2	I stare out over rooftops, past chimneys, into the way off distance.
3	Jackie-Joyce, in her bathing suit, knocks at the door, and I let her in.
4	Wet slicking our arms and legs, we splash up the block, squealing and whooping in the streaming rain.
5	We swing our wet and wild-haired mammas 'til we're all laughing under silver trinkets of rain.
6	"Absolutely not," Mamma says, frowning under her straw hat.
7	Mamma presses the ice-chilled glass against her skin.
13	I hug Mamma hard, and she hugs me back.

SPEAK AND WRITE ABOUT THE TEXT

Use the Text-Based Writing Routine on pages 410–411 to model how to speak and write about key ideas and details in *Come On, Rain!*

Lesson	Text-Based Writing	Scaffolded Frames
1	On page 6, what is Tessie saying? What is she doing?	• Tessie says, "_____." • Tessie is _____ in the endless heat.
2	On page 9, where is Tessie looking?	• Tessie looks into the _____. • Tessie looks over _____, past _____, and into the _____.
3	On page 16, what is Jackie-Joyce wearing? What does she do?	• Jackie-Joyce is wearing _____. • She _____ at the door.
4	On page 23, what are the girls doing?	• The girls _____ up the block. • They are _____ and _____ in the streaming rain. • The girls are _____, _____, and _____.
5	On page 29, what are the girls and their mammas doing?	• The girls _____ their mammas. They are all _____. • The girls and their mammas are _____ and _____ in the rain.
6	On page 8, what does Mamma say? What does she do?	• Mamma says, "_____." • Mamma is _____ under her straw hat.
7	On page 15, what does Mamma do?	• Mamma presses the _____ against her skin. • Mamma _____ the glass _____.
13	On page 30, what do Tessie and Mamma do?	• Tessie and Mamma _____. • Tessie _____ Mamma, and Mamma _____ back.

EXPAND UNDERSTANDING OF VOCABULARY

Use the Dig Deeper Vocabulary Routine on pages 406–407 to continue to develop conceptual understanding of the following verbs with -s: *sighs, rumbles, murmurs, sparkles, trickles, sniffs, wavers,* and *glazes*. Explain to students that these words are verbs, or words that tell about actions. Point to the *s* at the end of each verb. We use a verb with -s when we use a noun that means one or the word *he, she,* or *it*.

Display and read aloud these sentences: The girl sees clouds. She hopes for rain. Underline *sees* and *hopes*. Circle the *s* at the end of each verb. We use the verb *sees* with the noun *girl. Girl* is a noun that means one. We use the verb *hopes* with the word *she*.

Name _____

Sun and Rain Effects

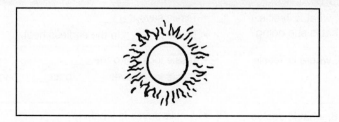

Team Talk

First the sun is _____.
Plants _____. People _____.
Then the rain _____.
People _____ and _____.

The Snowy Day

Reproduce and distribute copies of the *What Does Peter Do?* student page on page 358. Explain that students will better understand *The Snowy Day* if they understand the character's actions. Identify and discuss the pictures. Use them to help students understand that the warm clothes, stick, snow-covered tree, snowball fight, tracks, snowman, and snow angel are parts of Peter's adventure on the snowy day.

Have students turn to a partner and complete the sentence frames in Team Talk. Tell partners to use the pictures to help them.

TALK ABOUT SENTENCES

For students who need support in accessing key ideas and key language in *The Snowy Day,* use the Sentence Talk Routine on pages 408–409 to draw students' attention to the relationship between meaning and the words, phrases, and clauses in the text.

Lesson	Sentence(s) to Deconstruct
8	After breakfast he put on his snowsuit and ran outside.
9	Crunch, crunch, crunch, his feet sank into the snow.
10	So he made a snowman, and he made angels.
11	While he slept, he dreamed that the sun had melted all the snow away.
12	The snow was still everywhere. New snow was falling!

SPEAK AND WRITE ABOUT THE TEXT

Use the Text-Based Writing Routine on pages 410–411 to model how to speak and write about key ideas and details in *The Snowy Day.*

Lesson	Text-Based Writing	Scaffolded Frames
8	On page 35, what did Peter do?	• Peter put on _____. Peter ran _____. • Peter _____ and _____. He wanted to _____.
9	On page 36, what made the sounds crunch, crunch, crunch?	• _____ made the sounds. • As they sank in the snow, _____ made crunching sounds.
10	On pages 46–47, how did Peter play in the snow?	• Peter used the snow to make _____ and _____. • Peter made _____ and _____ in the snow.
11	On page 56, what did Peter dream about the snow?	• Peter dreamed that the snow _____. • The sun had _____ the snow.
12	On page 57, what was happening?	• The snow was _____ and _____. • The snow was _____. More snow _____.

Name _____

What Does Peter Do?

Peter puts on _____.
He goes _____.
He sees _____.
He makes _____.
Peter likes _____.

What Will the Weather Be?

BUILD BACKGROUND

Reproduce and distribute copies of the *Predicting the Weather* student page on page 361. Explain that to understand the text *What Will the Weather Be?* students need to understand the concept of forecasting, or predicting, the weather. Read aloud the question, letting them identify the two kinds of weather shown in the rebus pictures: Will it be (stormy) or will it be (sunny)? We want to know what the weather will be like. People called weather forecasters work to tell us what kind of weather is coming.

Weather forecasters use tools to gather information. They use the information to predict the weather. Here are some of their tools. Identify the first picture in the first row. This tool is a thermometer. A thermometer tells how hot or cold it is. Continue with the pictures of the wind vane, satellite, and map. Then point to the last picture. The girl is watching a weather report on TV. The weather forecaster is using a map to tell about his weather predictions.

Have students turn to a partner and complete the sentence frames in Team Talk using the pictures and discussion. Then have partners share their sentences with the class.

TALK ABOUT SENTENCES

For students who need support in accessing key ideas and key language in *What Will the Weather Be?* use the Sentence Talk Routine on pages 408–409 to draw students' attention to the relationship between meaning and the words, phrases, and clauses in the text.

Lesson	Sentence(s) to Deconstruct
1	The weather forecast was wrong. And people were not prepared for the huge storm.
2	Weather forecasts tell us what kind of weather is coming.
3	After a cold front passes, the sky clears and the weather is colder.
4	Meteorologists, people who study the weather, try to predict where fronts will form.
5	The weather is dry and sunny when the air pressure is high.
6	The maps show the temperature, humidity, and pressure of the air all around the world.
12	Weather forecasts are sent to radio and television stations.

Use the Text-Based Writing Routine on pages 410–411 to model how to speak and write about key ideas and details in *What Will the Weather Be?*

Lesson	Text-Based Writing	Scaffolded Frames
1	On page 7, what happened because the weather forecast was wrong?	• People were not _____. • Because the weather forecast was wrong, people _____.
2	On page 9, what do weather forecasts tell us?	• Weather forecasts tell us _____. • Forecasts tell us about _____.
3	On page 15, what happens after a cold front passes?	• The sky _____, and the weather is _____. • First a cold front passes. Then _____. Finally, the weather is _____.
4	On page 18, what do meteorologists do?	• Meteorologists study _____. They try to predict _____. • Meteorologists are people who _____ and _____ the weather.
5	On page 25, what happens when the air pressure is high?	• The weather is _____ and _____. • When the air pressure is high, the weather is _____ and _____.
6	On page 28, what do weather maps show?	• The weather maps show _____. • The maps show the _____, _____, and _____ of the air.
12	On page 30, where do we find out about weather forecasts?	• Weather forecasts are sent to _____ and _____. • We see weather forecasts on _____. We hear them on the _____.

Use the Dig Deeper Vocabulary Routine on pages 406–407 to continue to develop conceptual understanding of the following nouns: *forecast, temperature, force, liquid,* and *coastline*. Review with students that nouns are words that name people, places, animals, or things. Point out that all of these words are nouns and they all name things.

Display and read aloud the following sentence: Some storms may have thunder and lightning. Underline the words *storms, thunder,* and *lightning*. Explain that these words are nouns. Ask students whether the nouns *storms, thunder,* and *lightning* name people, places, animals, or things.

Name _____

Predicting the Weather

Will it be or will it be 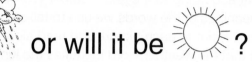 ?

Team *Talk*

Weather forecasters use _____.
These tools tell them _____.
Weather forecasters tell us _____.

Weather Words and What They Mean

Reproduce and distribute copies of the *Words About Weather* student page on page 363. Explain that according to the text *Weather Words and What They Mean,* understanding the meanings of the words we use to tell about weather is key to understanding weather. Point to each picture and read aloud the word. Make sure students understand that the weather word identifies the kind of weather shown in the picture. Model using the weather words in oral sentences. Then have students turn to a partner and complete the sentence frames in Team Talk.

TALK ABOUT SENTENCES

For students who need support in accessing key ideas and key language in *Weather Words and What They Mean,* use the Sentence Talk Routine on pages 408–409 to draw students' attention to the relationship between meaning and the words, phrases, and clauses in the text.

Lesson	Sentence(s) to Deconstruct
7	When the sun sets, the air becomes cooler and the temperature goes down.
8	If the temperature goes below freezing, the dew freezes. Then it is called frost.
9	A rainstorm is when there are strong winds and lots of rain.
10	A blizzard is a very heavy snowstorm.
11	When the wind blows with more and more force, a windstorm develops.

SPEAK AND WRITE ABOUT THE TEXT

Use the Text-Based Writing Routine on pages 410–411 to model how to speak and write about key ideas and details in *Weather Words and What They Mean.*

Lesson	Text-Based Writing	Scaffolded Frames
7	On page 8, what happens to the temperature when the sun sets?	• The temperature _____. • The air becomes _____. The temperature goes _____.
8	On page 13, what happens to the dew when the temperature goes below freezing?	• The dew _____. • The dew _____ and is called frost.
9	On page 20, what two things happen during a rainstorm?	• A rainstorm has _____. • A rainstorm has _____. It also has _____.
10	On page 26, what is a blizzard?	• A blizzard is _____. • A blizzard is a very heavy _____.
11	On page 29, when does a windstorm develop?	• A windstorm develops when _____. • A windstorm develops when _____ with more and more force.

Name _____

Words About Weather

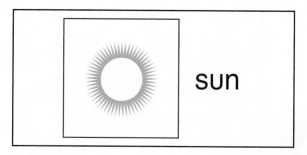 sun

 clouds

 rain

 wind

 snow

The picture shows _____.
The word is _____.
I can use _____ to tell
about _____.

Tessie's First Snow

It snowed last night.
Today Tessie rode on a sled.
She made a snowman.
Tessie had fun.

Unit 3 Module B

Name _____

My Weather Forecast

Today

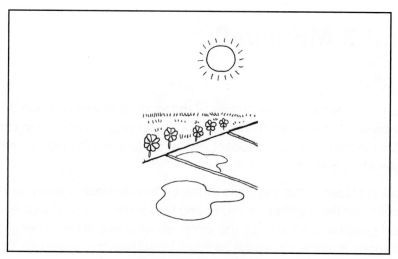

Tomorrow

Today it is raining.
Tomorrow it will be sunny.

Performance-Based Assessment
Unit 3 Module A

Reproduce and distribute copies of the student model on page 364. After completing the Prepare to Write activities on pages 188–189 in Unlock the Writing in Part 2, use the student model to illustrate the elements of narrative writing.

Remind students that the main character in the book *Come On, Rain!* is a girl named Tessie. Read aloud the title of the student model. The title tells us what the story is about. The writer tells about the first time Tessie sees snow. Read aloud the story. What happened first? What happened next? What happened last? Point out that the writer tells about the three events in the order in which they happened: First it snowed. Next Tessie rode on a sled. Last she made a snowman. Explain that the last sentence tells how Tessie reacted to, or felt about, the snowstorm: She had fun. She enjoyed the snowstorm.

Have students tell what they see in each picture. How do these pictures go with the story? Explain that the pictures show something about each of the three events the writer tells about in the story. Have students link each picture to the appropriate sentence. Then have them read aloud the story together.

Unit 3 Module B

Reproduce and distribute copies of the student model on page 365. After completing the Prepare to Write activities on pages 194–195 in Unlock the Writing in Part 2, use the student model to illustrate the elements of informative/explanatory writing.

Remind students that the topic of the informative/explanatory writing is what they forecast for the weather for today and tomorrow. Discuss each illustration using these questions: What does the writer show about the weather in this picture? How does the writer label the picture? Why does the writer use that label?

Read aloud the first sentence of the weather forecast. Why does the writer begin this sentence with the word *Today*? What kind of weather does the sentence tell about? Which picture does the sentence tell about? Continue with the second sentence, asking about the word *Tomorrow,* the kind of weather, and the relationship between the sentence and the second picture. Then have students read aloud the weather forecast together.

I Love Saturdays y domingos

BUILD BACKGROUND

Reproduce and distribute copies of the *Things to Do* student page on page 369. Tell students that to understand the story *I Love Saturdays y domingos* they need to understand activities that families in the story do. Discuss the word *family* with students and point out how families can be similar and different.

Tell students that the pictures show things that families might do. Have students describe the first picture. What is the first family doing? Where are they? Have students tell about the other pictures. Scaffold with sentence frames such as *The family is ___. They are at the ___. They are ___.* Confirm that students understand what the families in the pictures are doing and how the families are similar and different.

Have students turn to a partner and complete the sentence frames in Team Talk using the sentences for each picture. Then have partners read their sentences about families and activities.

TALK ABOUT SENTENCES

For students who need support in accessing key ideas and key language in *I Love Saturdays y domingos,* use the Sentence Talk Routine on pages 408–409 to draw students' attention to the relationship between meaning and the words, phrases, and clauses in the text.

Lesson	Sentence(s) to Deconstruct
1	One Saturday, Grandpa and Grandma play a movie about the circus for me on their VCR.
2	They are always happy to see me.
3	On Saturdays, Grandma serves me breakfast: milk, scrambled eggs, and pancakes.
4	She is glad that now they have a large backyard so she can keep chickens.
5	We sit on the pier and look down at the water.
6	He also tells me about growing up in New York City.
7	*Abuelita* has made me a dress for my birthday party.
8	Finally I blow out the candles and cut the cake.
12	The little birds are singing and the moon has gone to sleep.

Use the Text-Based Writing Routine on pages 410–411 to model how to speak and write about key ideas and details in *I Love Saturdays y domingos.*

Lesson	Text-Based Writing	Scaffolded Frames
1	On page 14, what do Grandma and Grandpa do one Saturday?	• Grandma and Grandpa play _____. • They play _____ for _____.
2	On page 7, how do *Abuelita* and *Abuelito* feel when they see the girl?	• They feel _____. • They are always _____.
3	On page 8, what does Grandma do?	• Grandma makes _____. • The girl's breakfast has _____, _____, and _____.
4	On page 13, why is *Abuelita* happy?	• *Abuelita* has a large _____. • She can raise _____ in the _____.
5	On page 17, where are the girl and *Abuelito*?	• They are on the _____. • They look down _____. • They sit _____ and look _____.
6	On page 20, what does Grandpa tell the girl about?	• Grandpa tells her about _____. • Grandpa grew up in _____.
7	On page 26, what has *Abuelita* made and why did she do that?	• *Abuelita* made _____. It is for the girl's _____. • *Abuelita* made _____ for the girl's _____.
8	On page 30, what does the girl do?	• The girl blows out the _____. • She cuts the _____.
12	On page 32, what are the birds and the moon doing in the song?	• The birds are _____. • The moon has _____.

Use the Dig Deeper Vocabulary Routine on pages 406–407 to continue to develop conceptual understanding of the following nouns: *circus, aquarium, seashore, pier,* and *trail*. Remind students that these words are nouns, or words that name people, places, animals, or things. Point out that these words are nouns that name places.

Display and read aloud the following sentence: Our family went to the beach last summer. Underline *family, beach,* and *summer*. Explain that these words are nouns. Ask students which noun—*family, beach,* or *summer*—names a place.

Unit 4 Module A

Name _____

Things to Do

The family likes to _____.
The family is at the _____.
The family is _____.

Apple Pie 4th of July

BUILD BACKGROUND

Reproduce and distribute copies of the *July 4th* student page on page 371. Explain that students will better understand *Apple Pie 4th of July* if they understand the celebration. Point to the first picture. This is a marching band. The people are playing musical instruments. They are marching in a parade. Use the other pictures to help students understand how fireworks and eating out are related to the story and the 4th of July. Have students turn to a partner and complete the sentence frames in Team Talk. Tell partners to use the pictures to help them.

TALK ABOUT SENTENCES

For students who need support in accessing key ideas and key language in *Apple Pie 4th of July*, use the Sentence Talk Routine on pages 408–409 to draw students' attention to the relationship between meaning and the words, phrases, and clauses in the text.

Lesson	Sentence(s) to Deconstruct
9	I hear the parade coming this way—*boom, boom, boom.*
10	My parents do not understand all American things.
11	and Mother walks through the swinging door holding a tray of chicken chow mein,
13	where we sit and watch the fireworks show—and eat our apple pie.

SPEAK AND WRITE ABOUT THE TEXT

Use the Text-Based Writing Routine on pages 410–411 to model how to speak and write about key ideas and details in *Apple Pie 4th of July*.

Lesson	Text-Based Writing	Scaffolded Frames
9	On page 8, what does the girl hear?	• The girl hears _____. • The _____ is coming this way—*boom, boom, boom.*
10	On page 19, what do the girl's parents not understand?	• The girl's parents do not understand _____. • They do not understand _____ things.
11	On page 24, what does Mother do?	• Mother walks _____. • Mother is holding a _____.
13	On pages 31–32, what does the family do?	• The family _____ and _____. • The family watches _____ and eats _____.

Name _____

July 4th

The people are _____.
This picture shows _____.
On the 4th of July people can _____.

Making Music

Reproduce and distribute copies of the *Let's Play* student page on page 374. Explain that to understand the text *Making Music* students need to understand what musical instruments are and how they are used to make music. Read aloud the title and ask students to look at the pictures. What musical instrument does the first picture show? What sound does this musical instrument make? Use the Internet to find an audio or video clip of the musical instrument being played. Help students associate the instrument with its sound and method of playing.

Continue with the other pictures. Ask students to tell about the picture using these sentence frames: *This is a _____. It makes a sound like this: _____.*

Have students turn to a partner and complete the sentence frames in Team Talk using the pictures and discussion. Then have partners share their sentences with the class.

TALK ABOUT SENTENCES

For students who need support in accessing key ideas and key language in *Making Music*, use the Sentence Talk Routine on pages 408–409 to draw students' attention to the relationship between meaning and the words, phrases, and clauses in the text.

Lesson	Sentence(s) to Deconstruct
1	Most music is made with musical instruments.
2	A group of singers is called a **choir**.
3	The drums are played by hand rather than with drumsticks.
4	Some people write their own music or make it up as they go!
5	Our brains get lots of exercise when we make music.
6	4. Decorate your drum. You can use anything you like.
11	Everyone can have fun when they make music!

Use the Text-Based Writing Routine on pages 410–411 to model how to speak and write about key ideas and details in *Making Music*.

Lesson	Text-Based Writing	Scaffolded Frames
1	On page 4, how is most music made?	• Most music is made _____. • We use _____ to make music.
2	On page 7, what is a choir?	• A choir is _____. • A _____ is called a choir.
3	On page 10, how are these drums played? How are other drums played?	• The drums are played _____. • Other drums are played with _____.
4	On page 15, what are two ways some people make music?	• Some people _____ their own music. • Some people _____ as they go.
5	On page 17, what do our brains get when we make music?	• Our brains get _____. • When we make music, our brains get lots of _____.
6	On page 22, what do you do in Step 4?	• You _____ your drum. • You can use _____.
11	On page 19, when can everyone have fun?	• Everyone can have fun _____. • Everyone can have fun when they _____.

EXPAND UNDERSTANDING OF VOCABULARY

Use the Dig Deeper Vocabulary Routine on pages 406–407 to continue to develop conceptual understanding of the following verbs: *stomp, hum, wrap,* and *decorate*. Review with students that verbs are words that tell about actions, or things we can do. Point out that these words are verbs. They tell about actions people can do. Act out each verb and have students repeat your actions.

Display and read aloud the following sentence: The people clap, shout, and sing together. Underline *clap, shout,* and *sing. Clap, shout,* and *sing* are verbs. They tell what the people do. Point out that the word *together* tells more about the verbs. *Together* tells how the people clap, shout, and sing.

Name _____

Let's Play

I see a _____.
I can play the _____.
I like the sound a _____
makes.

Clothes in Many Cultures

Reproduce and distribute copies of *What to Wear?* student page on page 376. Explain that understanding what people wear and when will help students understand the text *Clothes in Many Cultures*. Point to the first picture and read aloud the title. Make sure students understand that the picture shows people working in an office. Discuss the clothes the people in the picture are wearing and why. Continue in a similar way with the second picture. Then have students turn to a partner and complete the sentence frames in Team Talk using the pictures.

For students who need support in accessing key ideas and key language in *Clothes in Many Cultures*, use the Sentence Talk Routine on pages 408–409 to draw students' attention to the relationship between meaning and the words, phrases, and clauses in the text.

Lesson	Sentence(s) to Deconstruct
7	Around the world, everyone wears clothes for work or play.
8	Parkas keep people warm on cold days.
9	Office workers wear business suits to their jobs.
10	American Indians wear bright colors to dance at powwows.
12	Clothes are different around the world.

Use the Text-Based Writing Routine on pages 410–411 to model how to speak and write about key ideas and details in *Clothes in Many Cultures.*

Lesson	Text-Based Writing	Scaffolded Frames
7	On page 34, what types of clothing does everyone around the world wear?	• Everyone wears clothes for _____. • Everyone wears clothes for _____ or _____.
8	On page 36, what do parkas do?	• Parkas keep _____. • Parkas keep _____ on cold days.
9	On page 40, what do office workers wear?	• Office workers wear _____. • People who work in offices wear _____ to their jobs.
10	On page 46, when do American Indians wear bright colors?	• American Indians wear bright colors to _____. • They wear bright colors to _____ at powwows.
12	What does the text say on page 50? Are clothes around the world the same or different?	• Clothes are _____ around the world. • Clothes around the world are not _____. They are _____.

Name _____

What to Wear?

Time for Work

Time for Play

What do people wear to work?

Some people wear _____.

What do people wear to play?

Some people wear _____.

Name _____

A Day with My Friend

First we sing and dance.
Then we eat lunch.
Last we play a game.
We have a good time.

Name _____

Questions and Answers

What musical instrument do we all have?
We have our voices.
What do ranchers wear to work?
They wear jeans.

Performance-Based Assessment
Unit 4 Module A

Reproduce and distribute copies of the student model on page 377. After completing the Prepare to Write activities on pages 200–201 in Unlock the Writing in Part 2, use the student model to illustrate the elements of narrative writing.

Read aloud the title of the student model. Explain to students that the main characters in the story are the writer and the girl from the story *I Love Saturdays y domingos.* The writer and the girl are friends. The writer tells about what the two friends do together one day. Read aloud the story. What do they do first? Then what do they do? What do they do last? Point to the words *First, Then,* and *Last.* The writer uses these words to tell the order of the events.

Explain that the last sentence tells how the characters react to, or feel about, what they did: *We have a good time.* That tells us that the friends enjoyed their day together. Have students read aloud the story together.

Unit 4 Module B

Reproduce and distribute copies of the student model on page 378. After completing the Prepare to Write activities on pages 206–207 in Unlock the Writing in Part 2, use the student model to illustrate the elements of informative/explanatory writing.

Remind students that the purpose of this informative/explanatory writing is to ask and answer two questions about the topics of the selections. Read aloud the student model. What question does the writer ask about music? What answer does the writer give? Read the question and answer again. Let's look in the selection *Making Music* and see where the writer found this answer to the question. Turn to page 6 and read aloud the text. This text answers the writer's question about music.

Repeat the process with the writer's question and answer about clothing, using the text on page 44 of *Clothes in Many Cultures.* Then have students read aloud the questions and answers together.

The Tiny Seed

Reproduce and distribute copies of the *Growing Seeds!* student page on page 382. Explain that it will help students understand *The Tiny Seed* if they recognize how seeds grow. Make sure students think about seeds being planted and growing. Then discuss the pictures with them.

Point to the first picture. Tell students that this is a picture of the soil. Ask them to describe the soil. Then point to the second picture. Tell students that this is a picture of the seed planted in the soil. Scaffold with sentence frames such as *This is _____. The _____ is planted in the soil.*

Continue with the pictures of the sun, small plant, rain, and bigger plant. Guide students to understand how the pictures show what the plants need and how the plant grows. Point out how each of these items are in the story. Use the discussion to explain what seeds need in order to grow.

Have students turn to a partner and complete the sentence frames in Team Talk to tell about the pictures. Then have partners read their sentences to explain how seeds grow.

TALK ABOUT SENTENCES

For students who need support in accessing key ideas and key language in *The Tiny Seed,* use the Sentence Talk Routine on pages 408–409 to draw students' attention to the relationship between meaning and the words, phrases, and clauses in the text.

Lesson	Sentence(s) to Deconstruct
1	One of the seeds is tiny, smaller than any of the others.
2	Another seed lands on a tall and icy mountain.
3	Finally the wind stops and the seeds fall gently down on the ground.
4	Snow falls and covers them like a soft white blanket.
5	Before the tiny plant has three leaves the other plant has seven!
6	People come from far and near to look at this flower.
7	The flower has lost almost all of its petals.
13	But the wind grows stronger and shakes the flower.

SPEAK AND WRITE ABOUT THE TEXT

Use the Text-Based Writing Routine on pages 410–411 to model how to speak and write about key ideas and details in *The Tiny Seed.*

Lesson	Text-Based Writing	Scaffolded Frames
1	On page 2, what is one of the seeds?	• One of the seeds is _____. • One seed is _____ than the other seeds.
2	On page 6, what does the mountain look like?	• The mountain is _____. It has _____ on top. • The mountain is _____ and _____.
3	On page 12, what causes the seeds to fall down? How do the seeds fall?	• The seeds fall down because _____. • The seeds fall _____ down on the ground.
4	On page 15, what does the snow do? What is the snow like?	• The snow _____ and _____ the seeds. • The snow is like a _____.
5	On page 20, how many leaves does the tiny plant have? How many leaves does the other plant have?	• The tiny plant has _____ leaves. • The other plant has _____ leaves.
6	On page 24, where do people come from? Why do the people come?	• People come from _____ and _____. • People come to _____.
7	On page 30, what is happening to the flower?	• The flower has _____ almost all of _____. • The flower is _____ its _____.
13	On page 30, what does the wind do?	• The wind _____ stronger. • The wind _____ the flower.

EXPAND UNDERSTANDING OF VOCABULARY

Use the Dig Deeper Vocabulary Routine on pages 406–407 to continue to develop conceptual understanding of the following verbs: *sails, drifts, pushes, settle, burst,* and *shakes*. Review with students that verbs are words that tell about actions. Point out that all of these words are verbs.

Display and read aloud the following sentence: The boy picks a flower and gives it to a friend. Underline the words *picks* and *gives*. *Picks* and gives are verbs. They tell what the boy does. Model the actions. I pick. I give. Have students perform the actions with a partner while saying the verbs.

Name _____

Growing Seeds!

I see the _____.

The _____ makes the seed _____.

Jack's Garden

BUILD BACKGROUND

Reproduce and distribute copies of the *What Happens in the Garden?* student page on page 384. Explain that understanding the order of the events in *Jack's Garden* will help students understand the story. Point to the first picture. What happens first? First, Jack puts *seeds* in the *soil*. Continue with the other pictures, emphasizing the order and the words *rain, seedlings, plants, buds, flowers, insects,* and *birds*. Have partners tell about the picture sequence by completing one sentence frame in Team Talk for each picture.

TALK ABOUT SENTENCES

For students who need support in accessing key ideas and key language in *Jack's Garden,* use the Sentence Talk Routine on pages 408–409 to draw students' attention to the relationship between meaning and the words, phrases, and clauses in the text.

Lesson	Sentence(s) to Deconstruct
8	This is the soil that made up the garden that Jack planted.
9	This is the rain that wet the seeds.
10	These are the plants that grew from the seedlings.
11	These are the insects that sipped nectar from the flowers.
12	These are the birds that chased the insects.

SPEAK AND WRITE ABOUT THE TEXT

Use the Text-Based Writing Routine on pages 410–411 to model how to speak and write about key ideas and details in *Jack's Garden*.

Lesson	Text-Based Writing	Scaffolded Frames
8	On page 8, what does the garden have? Who makes the garden?	• The garden has _____. • _____ makes the garden.
9	On page 12, why do the seeds get wet?	• The seeds get wet because _____. • _____ falls on the seeds.
10	On page 16, what do the seedlings do?	• The seedlings grow into _____. • _____ grow from seedlings.
11	On page 22, what gets nectar? Where is the nectar?	• _____ get nectar. • The nectar is in _____.
12	On page 24, what do the birds do?	• The birds go after the _____. • The _____ go. Then the birds go.

Name _____

What Happens in the Garden?

1.

2.

3.

4.

5.

6.

Team *Talk*

First, seeds _____ in the soil.
Then rain _____.
Next, seedlings _____ into plants.
Then buds _____, and flowers _____.
Next, insects _____.
Last, birds _____.

Plant Patterns

Reproduce and distribute copies of the *Find the Pattern* student page on page 387. Explain to students that to understand the book *Plant Patterns,* they need to understand the concept of a pattern. Explain that when something has a pattern, it has a color or shape that repeats, or occurs more than once.

Use the top picture to explain the two kinds of patterns. The white and black flower petals alternate: white petal, black petal. This is a color pattern. All the petals are the same shape. They are arranged in a circle. This is a shape pattern.

Point to the pictures in the first row. What pattern do you see in this row of plants? Scaffold with sentence frames such as *I see a big ___. I see two little ___. The ___ make a pattern.* Guide students to recognize that the pattern is the repeating sets of plants. Then help them find the patterns in the other pictures (repeated pattern with two black plants and one white plant, three white petals and one colored petal, two colored petals and one white petal).

Have students turn to a partner and complete the three sentence frames in Team Talk for each picture in a box. Have partners use their sentences to explain the plant patterns.

TALK ABOUT SENTENCES

For students who need support in accessing key ideas and key language in *Plant Patterns,* use the Sentence Talk Routine on pages 408–409 to draw students' attention to the relationship between meaning and the words, phrases, and clauses in the text.

Lesson	Sentence(s) to Deconstruct
1	Each year, the tree adds a new ring.
2	A pattern is made by a repeated shape or color.
3	Gardeners make patterns by the way they plant different colored flowers.
4	Rows of prickly spines on a cactus make a repeating pattern.
5	Ferns uncurl in a spiral pattern called a fiddlehead.
6	Today, many public gardens grow flowers in patterns for visitors to enjoy.
7	**bamboo** (bam-BOO)—a tropical grass with a hard, hollow stem
12	A sunflower's yellow petals grow in a pattern around the blossom's middle.

Use the Text-Based Writing Routine on pages 410–411 to model how to speak and write about key ideas and details in *Plant Patterns*.

Lesson	Text-Based Writing	Scaffolded Frames
1	On page 18, what does the tree do? When does the tree do this?	• The tree _____ a new ring. • The tree _____ a new ring _____.
2	On page 5, what makes a pattern?	• A _____ makes a pattern. • A pattern is made by a repeated _____ or _____.
3	On page 11, how do gardeners make patterns?	• Gardeners make patterns by _____. • Gardeners plant _____ to make patterns.
4	On page 13, what makes a pattern on a cactus?	• _____ make a pattern on a cactus. • Rows of _____ on a cactus make a pattern.
5	On page 20, what pattern do ferns have? What is the pattern called?	• Ferns uncurl in a _____ pattern. • The pattern is called a _____.
6	On page 28, what do many gardens do? Why do they do this?	• Many gardens grow _____. • Gardeners grow flowers in patterns for _____.
7	On page 30, what is bamboo? What is bamboo's stem like?	• Bamboo is a _____. • The stem is _____ and _____.
12	On page 22, what makes a pattern on a sunflower?	• A sunflower's _____ grow in a pattern. • The _____ of a sunflower make a pattern.

Use the Dig Deeper Vocabulary Routine on pages 406–407 to continue to develop conceptual understanding of the following adjectives: *repeated, single, tropical,* and *hollow.* Review with students that adjectives are describing words. Adjectives are used to describe, or tell more about, nouns. Point out that these four words are used as adjectives in the selection.

Display and read aloud the following sentence: The tall sunflower has yellow petals and brown seeds. Underline the words *tall, yellow,* and *brown. Tall, yellow,* and *brown* are adjectives. They describe nouns in the sentence. Ask students to identify the noun that each adjective describes.

Name _____

Find the Pattern

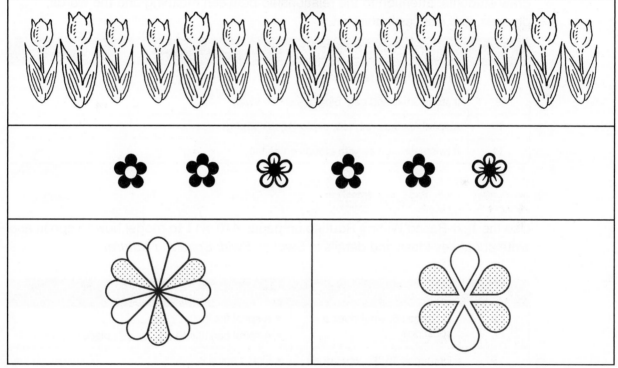

This picture shows _____.

The _____ has a pattern.

The pattern is _____.

Swirl by Swirl: Spirals in Nature

BUILD BACKGROUND

Reproduce and distribute copies of *The Shape of a Spiral* student page on page 389. Explain to students that to understand the informational text *Swirl by Swirl: Spirals in Nature,* they need to understand what a spiral is. Draw a spiral. A spiral goes round and round. It gets bigger and bigger. Then point to and identify each picture. Look for a spiral. Trace the spiral with your finger. Have students turn to a partner and complete the sentence frames in Team Talk for each picture.

TALK ABOUT SENTENCES

For students who need support in accessing key ideas and key language in *Swirl by Swirl: Spirals in Nature,* use the Sentence Talk Routine on pages 408–409 to draw students' attention to the relationship between meaning and the words, phrases, and clauses in the text.

Lesson	Sentence(s) to Deconstruct
8	It fits neatly in small places.
9	It starts small and gets bigger, swirl by swirl.
10	A spiral reaches out, too, exploring the world.
11	It twists through air with clouds on its tail.

SPEAK AND WRITE ABOUT THE TEXT

Use the Text-Based Writing Routine on pages 410–411 to model how to speak and write about key ideas and details in *Swirl by Swirl: Spirals in Nature.*

Lesson	Text-Based Writing	Scaffolded Frames
8	On page 28, what does a spiral do?	• A spiral fits in _____. • A spiral can fit into _____ places.
9	On pages 32–33, what does a spiral do?	• First a spiral is _____. • Then a spiral gets _____.
10	On page 40, what does a spiral do?	• A spiral reaches out _____. • A spiral reaches out to _____ the world.
11	On pages 50–51, what does a spiral do? What does the spiral have?	• A spiral _____ through air. • The spiral has _____.

Name _____

The Shape of a Spiral

Team Talk

This picture shows _____.
The _____ has a spiral.
We see a spiral in _____.

Name _____

My Favorite Book

I choose *Jack's Garden*.
I like this book.
The boy makes a garden.
The garden is beautiful.

Unit 5 Module B

Name _____

Did You Know?

Many plants have patterns.
A rose has petals in a spiral pattern.
A daisy has petals in a ring pattern.
It is fun to look for patterns.

Performance-Based Assessment
Unit 5 Module A

Reproduce and distribute copies of the student model on page 390. After completing the Prepare to Write activities on pages 212–213 in Unlock the Writing in Part 2, use the student model to illustrate the elements of opinion writing.

Read aloud the opinion piece. Remind students that opinion writing has a topic, an opinion about the topic, and one or more reasons that support the opinion. Reread the first sentence. What is the writer telling in this sentence? What is the writer's topic? Which book does the writer choose? Reread the second sentence. What is the writer telling in this sentence? What is the writer's opinion of the book? Reread the last two sentences. What is the writer telling in these sentences? How do these reasons support the writer's opinion?

Discuss the illustrations. Why does the writer include these pictures? Explain that the pictures show the two reasons the writer told about in the last two sentences. The writer likes *Jack's Garden* because the boy makes a garden and the garden is beautiful.

Unit 5 Module B

Reproduce and distribute copies of the student model on page 391. After completing the Prepare to Write activities on pages 218–219 in Unlock the Writing in Part 2, use the student model to illustrate the elements of informative/ explanatory writing.

Read aloud the explanatory text. Remind students that an explanatory text has a topic, facts about the topic, and a conclusion. Reread the title and first sentence. What is the writer writing about? What is the writer's topic? Reread the next two sentences. What two facts does the writer give? How do these facts tell about the topic? Reread the last sentence. This is the conclusion. This is how the writer ends the explanatory text.

Point to and name the flowers in the illustrations. The pictures support the facts. The picture of a rose supports the fact about the pattern of a rose's petals. The picture of a daisy supports the fact about the pattern of a daisy's petals.

On the Town: A Community Adventure

BUILD BACKGROUND

Reproduce and distribute copies of the *What Makes a Community?* student page on page 395. Explain that to understand the story *On the Town: A Community Adventure,* students need to understand the concept of community. Explain that a community has many places to visit and people who work in those places. Then discuss the pictures with students.

Point to the first picture. Tell students that this picture shows a restaurant and the workers in the restaurant. What are the workers doing? Point to the workers, and scaffold with sentence frames such as *The man is ___. The woman is ___.* Explain that the restaurant and the people who work there are part of a community. Places and workers are part of a community. Write *Places* and *Workers* as headings for two lists. Write *restaurant* under *Places* and *waiter and cashier* under *Workers.*

Continue in a similar way with the pictures of the library, grocery store, and doctor's office. Identify the place and discuss who works there and how the workers help people who visit there. Add words that name the places and workers to the lists.

Have students turn to a partner and complete the sentence frames in Team Talk for each picture, using the group discussion to help them.

TALK ABOUT SENTENCES

For students who need support in accessing key ideas and key language in *On the Town: A Community Adventure,* use the Sentence Talk Routine on pages 408–409 to draw students' attention to the relationship between meaning and the words, phrases, and clauses in the text.

Lesson	Sentence(s) to Deconstruct
1	She gave each of the children a black, speckled notebook.
2	Charlie picked up a soda bottle and threw it in the trash can that said "Recycle."
3	"You need a haircut," Mama told Charlie as they left the police station.
4	Then they picked out a thank-you card, and Charlie waved to the man who was behind the pharmacy counter.
5	They left the firehouse and went to the library, where they checked out some books.
6	Louis brought them a pizza—half pepperoni and half mushroom—and they ate it all.
7	"Home!" said Charlie. "I forgot about home!"
12	Then he wrote *My Community* across the front of the book.

Use the Text-Based Writing Routine on pages 410–411 to model how to speak and write about key ideas and details in *On the Town: A Community Adventure.*

Lesson	Text-Based Writing	Scaffolded Frames
1	On page 5, what did the teacher give to each child?	• The teacher gave _____ to each child. • Each child was given a _____ from the teacher.
2	On page 8, what did Charlie do?	• Charlie _____ a soda bottle. • Charlie _____ the soda bottle in the "Recycle" trash can.
3	On page 12, what did Mama tell Charlie?	• Mama told Charlie, "_____." • Mama told Charlie that he needed _____.
4	On page 16, what did Mama and Charlie do? What did Charlie do?	• Mama and Charlie _____ a thank-you card. • Charlie _____ to the man.
5	On page 22, where did Mama and Charlie go?	• Mama and Charlie left _____. • Mama and Charlie went to _____.
6	On page 26, what did Louis do? What did Papa, Mama, and Charlie do?	• Louis _____ a pizza to Papa, Mama, and Charlie. • Papa, Mama, and Charlie _____ the whole pizza.
7	On page 30, what did Charlie say to Mama and Papa?	• Charlie said, "_____!" • Charlie said that he forgot about _____.
12	On page 32, what did Charlie write?	• Charlie wrote _____. • Charlie wrote the title _____ on his book.

Use the Dig Deeper Vocabulary Routine on pages 406–407 to continue to develop conceptual understanding of the following verbs: *explore, writing, polishing,* and *listening.* Explain to students that these words are verbs, or words that tell about actions. Point to *ing* at the ends of three of the verbs. Sometimes a verb has *-ing* at the end.

Display and read aloud this sentence: Mama and Charlie walk through their community. Underline the word *walk*. *Walk* is a verb. It tells what Mama and Charlie do. Point out that the phrase *through their community* tells where Mama and Charlie walk.

Unit 6 Module A

Name _____

What Makes a Community?

This place is a _____.
The workers here help people to _____.
_____ work at a _____.
_____ are part of a community.

Places in My Neighborhood

BUILD BACKGROUND

Reproduce and distribute copies of the *Neighborhood Places* student page on page 397. Explain that knowing what a neighborhood is will help students understand the informational text *Places in My Neighborhood*. Review the definition on page 34 of the text. Then point to the first picture. People live in apartment buildings and houses. They are places in a neighborhood. Continue in the same way with the pictures of the library, grocery store, and playground. Have students turn to a partner and complete the sentence frames in Team Talk.

TALK ABOUT SENTENCES

For students who need support in accessing key ideas and key language in *Places in My Neighborhood,* use the Sentence Talk Routine on pages 408–409 to draw students' attention to the relationship between meaning and the words, phrases, and clauses in the text.

Lesson	Sentence(s) to Deconstruct
8	A neighborhood is a community filled with different places to see.
9	Her apartment is in a building with many other apartments.
10	Carlos visits the fire station in his neighborhood.
11	Justin bikes to the library in his neighborhood.
13	At the grocery store her dad finds fresh grapefruit.

SPEAK AND WRITE ABOUT THE TEXT

Use the Text-Based Writing Routine on pages 410–411 to model how to speak and write about key ideas and details in *Places in My Neighborhood*.

Lesson	Text-Based Writing	Scaffolded Frames
8	On page 34, what is a neighborhood?	• A neighborhood is a _____. • A neighborhood is filled with _____ to see.
9	On page 36, where is Mia's apartment?	• Mia's apartment is in _____. • Her apartment is with _____.
10	On page 40, where does Carlos visit?	• Carlos visits the _____. • Carlos visits the _____ in his neighborhood.
11	On page 46, what does Justin do?	• Justin _____ to the library. • Justin _____ to the library in his neighborhood.
13	On page 48, what does Jen's dad find?	• Jen's dad finds _____. • Her dad finds _____ at the grocery store.

Unit 6 Module A

Name _____

Neighborhood Places

We can go to _____.
We can _____ there.
The _____ is in the neighborhood.

Neighborhood Walk: City

Reproduce and distribute copies of the *In a City* student page on page 400. Explain that to understand the informational text *Neighborhood Walk: City,* students need to understand what a city is. Discuss the definition of the word *community.* Then explain that a city is a very large community.

Point to the top picture. This is a picture of a city. What does a city look like? Scaffold with sentence frames such as *A city has _____. I see _____.* Continue with the other pictures, focusing on what a city has and what makes a city different from other kinds of communities. (A city has many buildings that are close together. Many buildings are tall. A city has lots of traffic—cars, buses, trucks, and taxis. A city has many people. There is always something going on in a city.)

Have students turn to a partner and complete the sentence frames in Team Talk using details in the pictures. Then have partners discuss what they have learned about a city. Scaffold with more sentence frames such as *A city has many _____. _____ live in a city. _____ and _____ are on city streets. A city is _____ and _____.*

TALK ABOUT SENTENCES

For students who need support in accessing key ideas and key language in *Neighborhood Walk: City,* use the Sentence Talk Routine on pages 408–409 to draw students' attention to the relationship between meaning and the words, phrases, and clauses in the text.

Lesson	Sentence(s) to Deconstruct
1	Sometimes, apartments are built in old factories and office buildings.
2	In cities, some people use cars to get from place to place.
3	Others build and repair the roads and buildings that the city needs.
4	Some police officers patrol the city in cars.
5	Most people in cities get their food from grocery stores.
6	In the city hall, government leaders make plans and rules for the city.
7	Most cities have parks, playgrounds, and gardens for people to enjoy.
11	They raise money and run special programs for those in need.

Use the Text-Based Writing Routine on pages 410–411 to model how to speak and write about key ideas and details in *Neighborhood Walk: City*.

Lesson	Text-Based Writing	Scaffolded Frames
1	On page 6, where are some apartments built?	• Some apartments are built in _____. • Some apartments are built in old _____ and _____.
2	On page 8, what do some people use?	• Some people use _____. • Some people use _____ to get from _____.
3	On page 13, what do other workers do?	• Others _____ roads and buildings. • Other workers _____ and _____ roads and buildings.
4	On page 14, what do some police officers do?	• Some police officers _____ in cars. • Some police officers _____ the city in cars.
5	On page 18, where do most people in cities get their food?	• Most people in cities get their food _____. • Most people who live in cities get their food from _____.
6	On page 24, what do government leaders make?	• Government leaders make _____. • Government leaders make _____ and _____ for the city.
7	On page 26, what do most cities have for people to enjoy?	• Most cities have _____. • Most cities have _____, _____, and _____ for people to enjoy.
11	On page 28, what do people in cities do?	• People in cities _____ and _____. • People in cities _____ for people in need.

Use the Dig Deeper Vocabulary Routine on pages 406–407 to continue to develop conceptual understanding of the following plural nouns: *thousands, millions, workers, products,* and *leaders.* Review with students that plural nouns are words that name more than one person, animal, place, or thing. Point out the *s* at the end of each noun that was added to make the noun plural.

Display and read aloud the following sentence: A city has many offices, stores, and restaurants. Underline the words *offices, stores,* and *restaurants.* Explain that these words are plural nouns. Ask students what letter was added to make the nouns plural.

Name _____

In a City

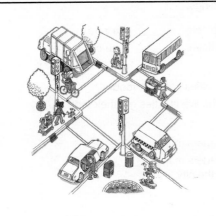

A city is _____.
A city has _____.
People can _____ in a city.

While I Am Sleeping

Reproduce and distribute copies of the *Night Workers* student page on page 402. Tell students that understanding night workers will help them understand the story *While I Am Sleeping*. Explain that most jobs people do at night are also done during the day. Point to the first picture. This worker is a baker. He bakes breads, pies, and cakes at night. Continue in the same way with the pictures of the firefighter, doctor, truck driver, pilot, and police officer. Have students turn to a partner and complete the sentence frames in Team Talk for each picture.

TALK ABOUT SENTENCES

For students who need support in accessing key ideas and key language in *While I Am Sleeping,* use the Sentence Talk Routine on pages 408–409 to draw students' attention to the relationship between meaning and the words, phrases, and clauses in the text.

Lesson	Sentence(s) to Deconstruct
8	While I am sleeping and tucked in my bed at nighttime some people are working instead.
9	Ambulance drivers with sirens and lights rush to help people all through the night.
10	Delivery drivers in trucks and in vans drop papers and food in packets and cans.
12	Grocery store workers fill up the shelves, all laughing and joking amongst themselves.

SPEAK AND WRITE ABOUT THE TEXT

Use the Text-Based Writing Routine on pages 410–411 to model how to speak and write about key ideas and details in *While I Am Sleeping*.

Lesson	Text-Based Writing	Scaffolded Frames
8	On page 3, what is the boy doing? What are some people doing?	• The boy is tucked in his bed and _____. • Some people are _____ instead of sleeping.
9	On page 12, what do ambulance drivers do?	• Ambulance drivers rush to _____ people. • Ambulance drivers _____ all through the night.
10	On page 15, what do delivery drivers drop off?	• The delivery drivers drop _____. • They drop _____ and _____.
12	On page 20, what do grocery store workers do while they are working?	• Grocery store workers _____ while they fill up the shelves. • The workers _____ and _____ while they work.

Name _____

Night Workers

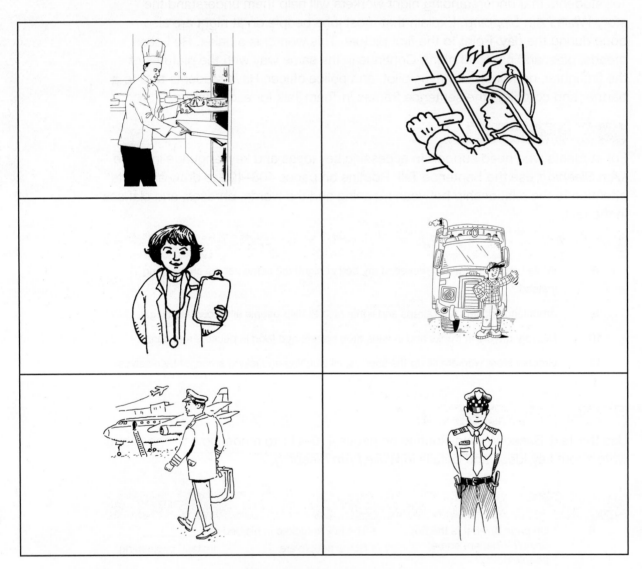

This is a _____.

This _____ works at night.

The job of a _____ is to _____.

Name _____

My Book Review

I choose *Places in My Neighborhood*.
I like this book the best.
I like this book because it has interesting photos.
The neighborhood looks like mine.

Name _____

Visit a Big City!

You should visit a big city.
There are fun things to do in a big city.
You can see tall buildings.
A visit to the zoo is fun.
You can ride on a ferry.
You will have fun in a big city.

Performance-Based Assessment
Unit 6 Module A

Reproduce and distribute copies of the student model on page 403. After completing the Prepare to Write activities on pages 224–225 in Unlock the Writing in Part 2, use the student model to illustrate the elements of opinion writing.

Read aloud the student book review. Explain to students that a book review is opinion writing. Remind them that opinion writing has a topic, an opinion about the topic, and one or more reasons that support the opinion.

Reread the first sentence of the model. This sentence tells the topic. What is the writer's topic? Reread the second sentence. This sentence tells the opinion about the topic. What is the writer's opinion of the book? Reread the last two sentences. These two sentences tell the reasons that support the opinion. What are the reasons that support the writer's opinion?

Point out that the pictures show what the writer's neighborhood looks like. The writer included the pictures to support the opinion and reasons in the book review.

Unit 6 Module B

Reproduce and distribute copies of the student model on page 404. After completing the Prepare to Write activities on pages 230–231 in Unlock the Writing in Part 2, use the student model to illustrate the elements of opinion writing.

Read aloud the student travel brochure. Explain to students that a travel brochure is opinion writing. Remind them that opinion writing has a topic, an opinion about the topic, and one or more reasons that support the opinion.

Reread the title and first sentence. What is the writer's topic? Reread the second sentence. What is the writer's opinion of the topic? Reread the next three sentences. What reasons does the writer give to support the opinion? Reread the last sentence. This is the conclusion. It tells the writer's opinion again.

Point to the illustrations. Why does the writer include these pictures? Explain that the pictures support the writer's reasons. The writer thinks readers should visit a big city because they can see tall buildings, visit a zoo, and ride on a ferry—things the writer thinks they will have fun doing.

Dig Deeper Vocabulary

PURPOSE

Use this routine to help students acquire a more in-depth understanding for select academic vocabulary. Through discussion using multimodal methods, students will unlock the meaning of vocabulary so they can use the words and learn elements of syntax.

PROCEDURE

1. Display the words listed in the Expand Understanding of Vocabulary section. Explain to students that these words appear in the text they are reading and that they are all similar in some way.

2. Model reading the words. Then have students practice saying the words aloud with you. Poll students about their familiarity with each word in order to gauge understanding.

3. Convey the meaning of the words using different modalities such as showing a picture from a magazine or the Internet, drawing a picture, acting out or gesturing, or using realia. Describe each word in context to guide students to associate the new words with familiar vocabulary. For example, show students a picture of a beach with the ocean prominently in view. Say the word *ocean* as you point to the ocean in the picture. Say: The water in the ocean is blue. Briefly describe a visit to the ocean and then ask students if they have been to the ocean.

4. Enrich students with a deeper understanding of each word by creating a list of synonyms. Provide students with one or two examples of synonyms for each word, then proceed to generate a list of additional synonyms with students.

5. Have students turn to a partner and take turns telling a sentence for each word. Use sentence frames as needed. For example: *I like to ___ at the ocean. If I went to the ocean I would ___.*

6. Help students understand how different types of words function in a sentence. For example, share a sentence in which you signal out a specific kind of word or phrase using different colors to write each part of the sentence. Then explain the parts of the sentence and ask students to identify specific words or phrases in the sentence. Look at this example for using nouns:

The *ocean* is very, very big.

Explain that the first part of the sentence names a person, place, or thing. What is the person, place, or thing in the sentence? (ocean) Point out that the rest of the sentence tells more about the ocean. What do you learn about the sentence from the rest of the words? (The ocean is very, very big.)

TEACHING TIPS

- Have students use different modalities to figure out the meaning of words. Doing this will aid their understanding, since they are using different formats to gain meaning.
- Have students write each vocabulary word on separate index cards and add a simple drawing or photograph from the Internet or a magazine that exemplifies the word on the back. Students can work in pairs to look at the picture and then name the word.

EXTEND

Create a word web with students, relating the vocabulary words to other words they know. For example, words can be the same part of speech or have similar affixes, sounds, or meanings. Have students discuss how understanding what words mean can help them better understand stories they read and listen to.

Sentence Talk

PURPOSE

Use this routine to deconstruct complex sentences from the texts that students are reading. Through instructional conversations students analyze key ideas, vocabulary, and sentence structures.

PROCEDURE

1. Identify a complex sentence from the current text. Recommended sentences can be found in the **Talk About Sentences** section of the Part 4 Unlock Language Learning lessons for each Unit/Module. Sentences should include key details or explain a key concept, important vocabulary, and phrases and clauses that merit attention. They may also include figurative language.

2. Decide how to break up the sentence for discussion, focusing on identifying meaning-based phrases and clauses. For example, you could break the sentence below into three parts.

   Pip was hatched in a nest made of pebbles on the cold Antarctic shore.

3. Display the sentence, writing each sentence part in a different color. Prepare conversation starters to focus students' attention on each sentence part. As you discuss each part of the sentence, record students' comments.

   • Why is the word *hatched* an important word? Turn and talk to a partner about what you know about how baby birds are born.

   • What does the second part of the sentence tell you about the nest? Suppose the author was telling a story about a baby bird born in a nest in a tree. What word might replace *pebbles* to describe the nest?

4. Identify key words that may need to be defined in context or have structural significance.

   • What two words does the author use to tell about what it means to be hatched? Yes, Pip was hatched in a *nest* made of *pebbles*. A nest can be made of pebbles, sticks, or leaves. It will protect the eggs and baby chicks from the cold Antarctic shore.

   • Now let's read the entire sentence together. The words *in* and *on* tell me exactly where Pip was hatched.

5. Initiate the activity with students by reading together the page or paragraph in which the sentence appears. Have students turn and talk to a partner about key ideas and details in the text.

6. Then draw attention to the color-coded sentence on display. Use the conversation starters you prepared to focus students' attention on each part of the sentence. Students should take an active role and should be speaking as much or more than you do in this conversation. Periodically, also have students turn and talk to a partner or a small group of peers. Record students' responses during the conversation and reread them at the end of the conversation.

7. Reread the entire sentence and have students discuss or write about what it means. Provide scaffolds as necessary.

   • Pip was _____ in a nest made of pebbles.

   • Pip's nest was on the _____.

   • It was _____ in the place where Pip was hatched.

TEACHING TIPS

• When recording students comments, write each comment in the same color as the sentence part it refers to.

• Create and display a list of key words and phrases from the Sentence Talk Instructional conversations and encourage students to use the vocabulary when they speak and write about the text.

EXTEND

Have students discuss how understanding the meaning of the sentence helps them better understand the overall meaning of the text. Ask: What was the most important thing you learned? What will you keep in mind as you continue to read?

Text-Based Writing

PURPOSE

Use this routine to explore linguistic and rhetorical patterns and registers in writing. Model how to include evidence from text in a written response.

From the section of the text that was read closely that day, present students with a question for guided/shared writing. See the Text-Based Writing column in the Speak and Write About the Text section of the English Language Learners Support lesson for recommended questions.

PROCEDURE

1. Write the question on the board and read it aloud with students. For example: *On page 30, what does the wind do to the flower?* Identify key words in the question and check understanding. Help students determine what the question is asking and what information they need to respond to it. The question asks what does the wind do to the flower. What do you know about wind? *The wind blows _____ seeds and _____.* I can tell from the question that the wind does something to the flower. How can we find out what the wind does? *We can _____ to find evidence in the text about _____.*

2. Locate and read aloud the sentence/sentences in the text that the question refers to. If appropriate, also read the text that comes before/after the sentence. Lead students in a discussion of the text, checking comprehension and explaining key vocabulary and concepts as needed.

   Listen as I reread page 30. How is the wind blowing? *The wind is blowing _____.* What does strong wind do to plants? *Strong wind blow the seeds of plants _____ and _____.* Can seeds travel if there is no wind? *_____, if there is no wind _____.* What is happening to the flower because of the wind? *The flower is _____. The flower's _____ are being _____ by the wind.* Which words tell the reader what the wind is doing to the flower? *The words, "Once more the wind _____ the flower, and this time the flower's _____. Out come many tiny seeds that _____ on the wind."*

3. Guide students to answer the question orally, using the scaffolded sentence frames as needed. Check that students use a rhetorical pattern appropriate to the question. For example, a question that asks *why* something occurred should elicit a response that identifies a cause and effect.

4. Restate the question for students: *On page 30, what does the wind do to the flower?* Model writing a response, talking through the process as you write.

   The wind breaks the flower's seed pod. Then the wind carries the seeds away.

   I will start my sentence with a capital letter. The verbs *breaks* and *carries* tells what the wind does to the flower. What does the wind do to the flower's seed pod? The wind breaks the flower's seed pod. Now I will use text evidence to tell what the wind does to the flower. The wind breaks the flower's seed pod.

Then the wind carries the seeds away. I will add those words to my sentence. I will put a period here to show that this is the end of the sentence.

5. Have students write their answers. For shared writing, have students work with a partner.

6. Give students the opportunity to share their writing with the group. Have students read their answers aloud or write them on the board. Check that students have used appropriate linguistic and rhetorical patterns and included text evidence as needed.

TEACHING TIPS

- Use graphic organizers, such as idea webs and cause/effect charts, to help students organize the text evidence needed to answer the questions.

- As you evaluate students' writing, identify sentences that can be expanded by adding details.

- Encourage students to write in complete sentences to reflect the more formal register of written English.

EXTEND

Ask a second question about the day's close read section and have students work with a partner or independently to discuss and write a response.

Clarifying Key Details

Use this routine to provide frames for conducting accountable conversations that require clarification.

PROCEDURE

1. **Explain:** Sometimes I don't understand what someone says. Maybe the speaker talks very softly. Maybe the speaker uses words I do not know. Maybe the speaker needs to explain an idea. When this happens, I need to ask questions.

2. Explain that sometimes others might have questions about what students say. Remind them that they should answer others' questions and help them understand.

3. Remind students that when they ask questions in a group, they should be polite and not interrupt. Wait until the person finishes speaking. Then say, "excuse me," and ask your question.

4. Share the worksheet on the following page with students. Read the questions aloud, then talk about situations in which they might use the questions. Model completing the sentence frames using a topic that is familiar to students.

5. Have students look at the picture and discuss the following questions. Point to the boy in the middle. This is the speaker. What do you think he is talking about? Point to the boy on the right. The speaker speaks very softly. The boy cannot hear the speaker. What can the boy do? What question can he ask? Point to the girl. This girl does not understand. The speaker uses hard words. What can the girl do? What question can she ask? This is called clarifying.

6. Have students use the questions and frames in a discussion about a selection you have recently read.

TEACHING TIPS

- Have students role-play discussions in which they ask questions for clarification.
- Create a classroom poster listing useful clarifying questions for students to refer to as needed.

EXTEND

Have students think of more clarifying questions and add them to the worksheet. Have them practice asking the questions with a partner or in a group.

Clarifying Key Details

Look at these examples of questions.
Use them when you do not understand something a speaker says.

When you did not hear what the speaker said:
I did not hear you. What did you say?

When you do not understand what the speaker means: _____

- -
You said _____. What do you mean?

When you answer someone's question to you:
_____

- -
I said _____.

_____

- -
I mean _____.

Look at the picture.
Say questions the people can ask.

Clarifying Information

PURPOSE

Use this routine to provide frames for conducting accountable conversations that require elaboration.

PROCEDURE

1. **Explain:** Sometimes I need more information to understand what a speaker means. I can ask the speaker for more details. I can ask the speaker a question, such as, *Can you explain what you mean?* This is called elaborating.

2. **Point out that sometimes students might want to add to a group discussion.** I can give more information in a discussion, too. I can explain my ideas and give information. I can give evidence from the text.

3. **Remind students that when they say something in a group, they should be polite and not interrupt.** Wait until the person finishes speaking. Raise your hand or say, "excuse me." Then, you can speak.

4. **Read the worksheet on the following page aloud to the students.** Then talk about situations in which students might use the questions and statements. Model completing the sentence frames using a topic that is familiar to students.

5. **Have students work as a group to form an elaborating question and answer** in the conversation at the bottom of the worksheet. Write their ideas on the board.

TEACHING TIPS

- Have students role-play discussions in which they ask for and give more information.
- Create a classroom poster listing useful elaboration questions for students to refer to as needed.

EXTEND

Have students role-play the conversation between Sam and Jan, using the frames to ask questions and give more information.

Clarifying Information

Look at the questions and statements.
Use them when you want to clarify information.

When you ask for more information:

_____

Can you give more information about _____?

When you give more information:

_____   _____

-------------------------   -------------------------

I think _____ because _____.

Look at the picture.
Read what Jan says. What can Sam ask? What can Jan answer?

Jan: I really like this book.
Sam: Can you give more information

_____

----

about _____?

_____

Jan: I really like this book because _____.

Reach an Agreement

PURPOSE

Use this routine to provide frames for conducting accountable conversations that require reaching an agreement.

PROCEDURE

1. Explain: Sometimes when I work with a group, my group has to decide something together. My group has to agree about something or make a decision. This is called reaching an agreement.

2. Explain that sometimes when they are in a group, students will need to tell what they think. Tell others what you think. Tell why you think that.

3. Point out that all the members of the group should have a chance to tell what they think. Others will tell what they think. Listen carefully. Ask questions if you do not understand. Remind students to use the frames they practiced on other worksheets.

4. Explain that group members may agree or disagree. You might have the same idea. This is called agreeing. Or you might have a different idea. This is called disagreeing. You can say if you agree or disagree. Tell why.

5. Remind students that it is important to be polite when they disagree. If you disagree, explain why in a nice way. Be friendly when you talk.

6. Explain that to reach an agreement, most of the group members must agree. Find out who agrees. You can vote. Count how many people agree. Count how many disagree.

7. Read the worksheet on the following page aloud to the students. Talk about situations in which they might use the questions and statements. Model completing the sentence frames using a topic that is familiar to students.

8. Have students work with a group to discuss which animal will make the best pet. Have them use the frames to express their ideas and ask questions. Guide each group to reach an agreement.

TEACHING TIPS

- Students can have discussions in which they express ideas and build agreement.
- Create a classroom poster listing useful frames for students to refer to as needed.

EXTEND

Have students work with a group to choose the best activity for a rainy day. Remind them to use the frames on the worksheet to express their ideas and agree or disagree. Ask each group to reach an agreement.

Reach an Agreement

Tell what you think. **Ask** others. **Vote.**

Say what you think: _____

I think _____.

Ask what others think:

What do you think?

Agree: _____

I agree because _____.

Disagree: _____

I disagree because _____.

When you vote: _____

How many think _____?

Choose the best pet. Talk about it.

Bird   **Cat**   **Horse**

Scaffolded Reading/Writing Goals

UNIT 1: MODULE A

Reading Goal: Readers will use both words and illustrations to retell stories.

Emerging	Expanding	Bridging
Readers tell what is happening in an illustration.	Readers use words and illustrations for sentence frames that retell the story.	Readers use story words and illustrations to retell the story in their own words.

Writing Goal: Writers will write a short narrative that includes a drawing and one event.

Emerging	Expanding	Bridging
Writers draw a picture depicting the animal in the whole-group story.	Writers draw a picture depicting the animal in the story and recount the story.	Writers draw a picture for a story about an animal and its home and then write a short narrative.

UNIT 1: MODULE B

Reading Goal: Readers will answer questions about key details in informational texts.

Emerging	Expanding	Bridging
Readers answer questions about text information provided in pictures.	Readers complete frames to answer questions about information in pictures.	Readers use sentences to answer questions about information provided.

Writing Goal: Writers will write a sentence that explains information.

Emerging	Expanding	Bridging
Writers draw a picture to accompany the explanation about an animal's home.	Writers draw a picture for the explanation about an animal's home and tell about it.	Writers draw a picture for an explanation about an animal's home and then write a sentence that explains the information.

UNIT 2: MODULE A

Reading Goal: Readers will retell stories, including characters, settings, and major events.

Emerging	Expanding	Bridging
Readers use illustrations for responding about story characters, setting, and events.	Readers complete sentence frames to identify characters, setting, and story events.	Readers identify characters, setting, and story events.

Writing Goal: Writers will write a simple narrative with two major events.

Emerging	Expanding	Bridging
Writers draw then/now pictures showing how they did something.	Writers draw then/now pictures showing differences in something they can do.	Writers write about something they can do with events from then and now.

UNIT 2: MODULE B

Reading Goal: Readers will ask questions to better understand informational texts.

Emerging	Expanding	Bridging
Readers point to pictures to answer simple questions about text information.	Readers answer simple *what* and *when* questions about the text.	Readers ask and answer questions about the text.

Writing Goal: Writers will state an opinion and draw a picture to show a reason for their opinion.

Emerging	Expanding	Bridging
Writers draw a picture telling what they would or would not like about life on a farm.	Writers draw a picture or dictate a sentence to tell if they would like living on a farm.	Writers write sentences that tell whether or not they would like to live on a farm.

UNIT 3: MODULE A

Reading Goal: Readers will retell stories focusing on character experiences and reactions.

Emerging	Expanding	Bridging
Readers use illustrations to tell how characters respond to story events.	Readers tell how characters respond to events as shown in illustrations.	Readers describe character's experiences and reactions to events.

Writing Goal: Writers will create a simple narrative and include a character's reaction to an event.

Emerging	Expanding	Bridging
Writers draw a picture depicting how the character feels in a snowstorm.	Writers draw, dictate, or write two events in a story about a snowstorm.	Writers dictate or write events that tell about a snowstorm.

UNIT 3: MODULE B

Reading Goal: Readers will ask and answer questions to better understand informational texts.

Emerging	Expanding	Bridging
Readers point to pictures to answer simple questions about weather.	Readers use sentence frames to ask and answer simple questions about weather information.	Readers ask and answer simple questions about weather information.

Writing Goal: Writers will create a simple informative text based on evidence.

Emerging	Expanding	Bridging
Writers draw pictures depicting today's and tomorrow's weather.	Writers draw pictures depicting the weather and tell about the weather.	Writers draw and label pictures depicting the weather and dictate or write sentences.

UNIT 4: MODULE A

Reading Goal: Readers will compare and contrast characters and their experiences in stories.

Emerging	Expanding	Bridging
Readers use illustrations to tell how main characters are alike.	Readers tell how the main characters of the stories are alike and different.	Readers use a story's words and illustrations to compare and contrast characters.

Writing Goal: Writers will write a narrative using the sequence words *first, then,* and *last.*

Emerging	Expanding	Bridging
Writers tell what they would do if they spent the day with the main character of a story.	Writers write what they would do if they spent the day with the main character of a story.	Writers use the words *first, then,* and *last* as they write things they would do with the main character of a story.

UNIT 4: MODULE B

Reading Goal: Readers will use evidence from texts to state and support opinions, ideas, and information.

Emerging	Expanding	Bridging
Readers state opinions, ideas, and information about texts.	Readers state and support opinions, ideas, and information about texts.	Readers support opinions, ideas, and information about texts.

Writing Goal: Writers will compose an informative text that names the topic and includes facts.

Emerging	Expanding	Bridging
Writers draw pictures that answer questions about music and clothes.	Writers use information from the text to fill out sentence frames that answer questions about the text.	Writers ask and answer questions using information in the texts.

UNIT 5: MODULE A

Reading Goal: Readers will identify different types of literary texts.

Emerging	Expanding	Bridging
Readers draw pictures of characters from a story.	Readers recognize characters and events from a story.	Readers distinguish stories from other literary texts.

Writing Goal: Writers will state and support an opinion about a book.

Emerging	Expanding	Bridging
Writers tell which of two stories about plants they like better.	Writers state their book preference and tell one reason they prefer it.	Writers write sentences about which story they like better.

UNIT 5: MODULE B

Reading Goal: Readers will determine the main topic and supporting details in informational texts.

Emerging	Expanding	Bridging
Readers use selection titles and illustrations to tell the main topic.	Readers identify the main topic of a text.	Readers identify a story's main topic and supporting details.

Writing Goal: Writers will write an explanatory text that names a topic and includes facts and a conclusion.

Emerging	Expanding	Bridging
Writers will draw a picture, identify the topic, and make a Did You Know sentence about it.	Writers dictate sentences that tell about a pattern in nature.	Writers will tell about one pattern in nature, and provide a concluding sentence.

UNIT 6: MODULE A

Reading Goal: Readers will use both literary and informational texts to better understand a topic.

Emerging	Expanding	Bridging
Readers find information in the illustrations of a literary and an informational text.	Readers use a literary text and an informational text to respond to questions.	Readers describe communities based on information in texts.

Writing Goal: Writers will write a book review in which they state and support their opinion.

Emerging	Expanding	Bridging
Writers tell which of two selections about communities they like better.	Writers identify which selection they like better and tell their reason.	Writers write sentences and complete the sentence starter I like this book because . . .

UNIT 6: MODULE B

Reading Goal: Readers will ask and answer questions about details in the text.

Emerging	Expanding	Bridging
Readers answer questions about text information in pictures.	Readers use sentence frames to ask and answer questions about text information provided in words and pictures.	Readers ask and answer questions about text information.

Writing Goal: Writers will state and support an opinion and include a conclusion.

Emerging	Expanding	Bridging
Writers use a drawing to show a big city as the writing topic.	Writers use pictures and labels to show a big city.	Writers write sentences about their big city travel.

Linguistic Contrastive Analysis Chart

THE CONSONANTS OF ENGLISH				
IPA*	English	Spanish	Vietnamese	Cantonese
p	*p*it Aspirated at the start of a word or stressed syllable	*p*ato (duck) Never aspirated	*p*in (battery)	*pʰa (to lie prone)* Always aspirated
b	*b*it	*b*arco (boat) Substitute voiced bilabial fricative /ɑ/ in between vowels	*b*a (three) Implosive (air moves into the mouth during articulation)	NO EQUIVALENT Substitute /p/
m	*m*an	*m*undo (world)	*m*ot (one)	*m*a (mother)
w	*w*in	agua (water)	NO EQUIVALENT Substitute word-initial /u/	*w*a (frog)
f	*f*un	*f*lor (flower)	*ph*uʼoʼng (phoenix) Substitute sound made with both lips, rather than with the lower lip and the teeth like English /f/	*f*a (flower) Only occurs at the beginning of syllables
v	*v*ery	NO EQUIVALENT Learners can use correct sound	*V*iệt Nam (Vietnam)	NO EQUIVALENT Substitute /f/
θ	*th*ing Rare in other languages. When done correctly, the tongue will stick out between the teeth.	NO EQUIVALENT Learners can use correct sound	NO EQUIVALENT Substitute /tʰ/ or /f/	NO EQUIVALENT Substitute /tʰ/ or /f/
ð	*th*ere Rare in other languages. When done correctly, the tongue will stick out between the teeth.	ca*d*a (every) Sound exists in Spanish only between vowels; sometimes substitute voiceless θ.	NO EQUIVALENT Substitute /d/	NO EQUIVALENT Substitute /t/ or /f/
t	*t*ime Aspirated at the start of a word or stressed syllable English tongue-touch. Is a little farther back in the mouth than the other languages.	*t*ocar (touch) Never aspirated	*t*ám (eight) Distinguishes aspirated and non-aspirated	*tʰa (he/she)* Distinguishes aspirated and non-aspirated
d	*d*ime English tongue-touch is a little farther back in the mouth than the other languages.	*d*os (two)	*Đ*ōng (Dong = unit of currency) Vietnamese /d/ is implosive (air moves into the mouth during articulation)	NO EQUIVALENT Substitute /t/
n	*n*ame English tongue-touch is a little farther back in the mouth than the other languages.	*n*ube (cloud)	*n*am (south)	*n*a (take)
s	*s*oy	*s*eco (dry)	*x*em (to see)	*s*a (sand) Substitute *sh*– sound before /u/ Difficult at ends of syllables and words
z	*z*eal	NO EQUIVALENT Learners can use correct sound	*r*òi (already) In northern dialect only Southern dialect, substitute /y/	NO EQUIVALENT Substitute /s/
ɾ	but*t*er Written 't' and 'd' are pronounced with a quick tongue-tip tap.	*r*ana (toad) Written as single *r* and thought of as an /r/ sound.	NO EQUIVALENT Substitute /t/	NO EQUIVALENT Substitute /t/
l	*l*oop English tongue-touch is a little farther back in the mouth than the other languages. At the ends of syllables, the /l/ bunches up the back of the tongue, becoming velarized /ɫ/ or dark-l as in the word *ball*.	*l*ibro (book)	cú *l*ao (island) /l/ does not occur at the ends of syllables	*l*au (angry) /l/ does not occur at the ends of syllables

* *International Phonetic Alphabet*

THE CONSONANTS OF ENGLISH

IPA*	Hmong	Filipino	Korean	Mandarin
p	**p**eb (we/us/our) Distinguishes aspirated and non-aspirated	**p**aalam (goodbye) Never aspirated	**p**al (sucking)	**p**ʰei (cape) Always aspirated
b	**NO EQUIVALENT** Substitute /p/	**b**aka (beef)	**NO EQUIVALENT** /b/ said between vowels Substitute /p/ elsewhere	**NO EQUIVALENT**
m	**m**us (to go)	**m**abuti (good)	**m**al (horse)	**m**ei (rose)
w	**NO EQUIVALENT** Substitute word-initial /**u**/	**w**alo (eight)	g**w**e (box)	**w**en (mosquito)
f	**f**aib (to divide)	**NO EQUIVALENT** Substitute /p/	**NO EQUIVALENT** Substitute /p/	**f**a (issue)
v	**V**aj ('Vang' clan name)	**NO EQUIVALENT** Substitute /b/	**NO EQUIVALENT** Substitute /b/	**NO EQUIVALENT** Substitute /w/ or /f/
θ	**NO EQUIVALENT** Substitute /tʰ/ or /f/	**NO EQUIVALENT** Learners can use correct sound, but sometimes mispronounce voiced /ð/.	**NO EQUIVALENT** Substitute /t/	**NO EQUIVALENT** Substitute /t/ or /s/
ð	**NO EQUIVALENT** Substitute /d/	**NO EQUIVALENT** Learners can use correct sound	**NO EQUIVALENT** Substitute /d/	**NO EQUIVALENT** Substitute /t/ or /s/
t	**t**hem (to pay) Distinguishes aspirated and non-aspirated	**t**akbo (run) Never aspirated	**t**al (daughter)	**t**a (wet) Distinguishes aspirated and non-aspirated
d	**d**ev (dog)	**d**eretso (straight)	**NO EQUIVALENT** Substitute /d/ when said between vowels and /t/ elsewhere.	**NO EQUIVALENT** Substitute /t/
n	**n**oj (to eat)	**n**aman (too)	**n**al (day)	**n**i (you) May be confused with /l/
s	**x**a (to send)	**s**ila (they)	**s**al (rice) Substitute shi– sound before /i/ and /z/ after a nasal consonant	**s**an (three)
z	**NO EQUIVALENT** Learners can use correct sound	**NO EQUIVALENT** Learners can use correct sound	**NO EQUIVALENT** Learners can use correct sound	**NO EQUIVALENT** Substitute /ts/ or /tsʰ/
ɾ	**NO EQUIVALENT** Substitute /t/	**r**in/di**n** (too) Variant of the /d/ sound	Only occurs between two vowels Considered an /l/ sound	**NO EQUIVALENT**
l	**l**os (to come) /l/ does not occur at the ends of syllables	sa**l**amat (thank you)	ba**l**am (wind)	**l**an (blue) Can be confused and substituted with /r/

* International Phonetic Alphabet

THE CONSONANTS OF ENGLISH				
IPA*	English	Spanish	Vietnamese	Cantonese
ɹ	*red* Rare sound in the world Includes lip-rounding	**NO EQUIVALENT** Substitute /r/ sound such as the tap /ɾ/ or the trilled /r/	**NO EQUIVALENT** Substitute /l/	**NO EQUIVALENT** Substitute /l/
ʃ	*sha*llow Often said with lip-rounding	**NO EQUIVALENT** Substitute /s/ or /tʃ/	*sieu th*ị (supermarket) Southern dialect only	**NO EQUIVALENT** Substitute /s/
ʒ	*vi*si*on* Rare sound in English	**NO EQUIVALENT** Substitute /z/ or /dʒ/	**NO EQUIVALENT** Substitute /s/	**NO EQUIVALENT** Substitute /s/
tʃ	*ch*irp	*ch*ico (boy)	*ch*ính phủ (government) Pronounced harder than English *ch*	**NO EQUIVALENT** Substitute /ts/
dʒ	*j*oy	**NO EQUIVALENT** Sometimes substituted with /ʃ/ sound Some dialects have this sound for the *ll* spelling as in *llamar*	**NO EQUIVALENT** Substitute /c/, the equivalent sound, but voiceless	**NO EQUIVALENT** Substitute /ts/ Only occurs at beginnings of syllables
j	*y*ou	*ci*elo (sky) Often substitute /dʒ/	*y*eu (to love)	*j*au (worry)
k	*k*ite Aspirated at the start of a word or stressed syllable	*c*asa (house) Never aspirated	*c*om (rice) Never aspirated	*kʰ*a (family) Distinguishes aspirated and non-aspirated
g	*g*oat	*g*ato (cat)	**NO EQUIVALENT** Substitute /k/	**NO EQUIVALENT** Substitute /k/
ŋ	ki*ng*	ma*ng*o (mango)	*Ng*ūyen (proper last name)	pha*ŋ* (to cook)
h	*h*ope	*g*ente (people) Sometimes substitute sound with friction higher in the vocal tract as velar /x/ or uvular /χ/	*h*oa (flower)	*h*a (shrimp)

International Phonetic Alphabet

	THE CONSONANTS OF ENGLISH			
IPA*	**Hmong**	**Filipino**	**Korean**	**Mandarin**
ɹ	**NO EQUIVALENT** Substitute /l/	**NO EQUIVALENT** Substitute the tap /ɾ/	**NO EQUIVALENT** Substitute the tap or /l/ confused with /l/	*r*an (caterpillar) Tongue tip curled further backward than for English /r/
ʃ	*s*au (to write)	*s*iya (s/he)	Only occurs before /i/; Considered an /s/ sound	*sh*i (wet)
ʒ	*z*os village)	**NO EQUIVALENT** Learners can use correct sound	**NO EQUIVALENT**	**NO EQUIVALENT** Substitute palatal affricate /tɕ/
tʃ	*ch*eb (to sweep)	*ts*a (tea)	*cʰ*al (kicking)	*ch*eng (red)
dʒ	**NO EQUIVALENT** Substitute *ch* sound	*D*ios (God)	**NO EQUIVALENT** Substitute *ch* sound	**NO EQUIVALENT** Substitute /ts/
j	*Y*aj (Yang, clan name)	*t*ayo (we)	*j*e:zan (budget)	*y*an (eye)
k	*K*oo (Kong, clan name) Distinguishes aspirated and non-aspirated	*k*alian (when) Never aspirated	*k*al (spreading)	*k*e (nest) Distinguishes aspirated and non-aspirated
g	**NO EQUIVALENT** Substitute /k/	*g*ulay (vegetable)	**NO EQUIVALENT** Substitute /k/ Learners use correct sound between two vowels	**NO EQUIVALENT** Substitute /k/
ŋ	*g*us (goose)	*ang*aw (one million)	*ba*ŋ (room)	*tan*g (gong) Sometimes add /k/ sound to the end
h	*h*ais (to speak)	*h*indi (no)	*h*al (doing)	**NO EQUIVALENT** Substitute velar fricative /x/

* *International Phonetic Alphabet*

THE VOWELS OF ENGLISH				
IPA*	English	Spanish	Vietnamese	Cantonese
i	*beat*	*hijo* (son)	*di* (to go)	*si* (silk)
ɪ	*bit* Rare in other languages Usually confused with /i/ (*meat* vs. *mit*)	**NO EQUIVALENT** Substitute /ē/	**NO EQUIVALENT** Substitute /ē/	*sik* (color) Only occurs before velars Substitute /ē/
e	*bait* End of vowel diphthongized—tongue moves up to /ē/ or short *e* position	*eco* (echo)	*kê* (millet)	*se* (to lend)
ɛ	*bet* Rare in other languages Learners may have difficulty distinguishing /ā/ and /e/ (short *e*): *pain* vs. *pen*	**NO EQUIVALENT** Substitute /ā/	**NO EQUIVALENT** Substitute /ā/	*seŋ* (sound) Only occurs before velars; difficult to distinguish from /ā/ in all positions
æ	*bat* Rare in other languages Learners may have trouble getting the tongue farther forward in the mouth	**NO EQUIVALENT** Substitute mid central /u/ (short *u*) or low front tense /o/ (short *o*)	*ghe* (boat)	**NO EQUIVALENT** Hard to distinguish between /æ/ and /ā/
u	*boot*	*uva* (grape)	*mua* (to buy)	*fu* (husband)
ʊ	*could* Rare in other languages Learners may have difficulty distinguishing the vowel sounds in *wooed* vs. *wood*	**NO EQUIVALENT** Substitute long *u*	**NO EQUIVALENT** Substitute long *u* (high back unrounded)	*suk* (uncle) Only occurs before velars Difficult to distinguish from long *u* in all positions
o	*boat* End of vowel diphthongized—tongue moves up to long *u* or ʊ position	*ojo* (eye)	*cô* (aunt)	*so* (comb)
ɔ	*law* 	**NO EQUIVALENT** Substitute long *o* or short *o* Substituting long *o* will cause confusion (*low* vs. *law*); substituting short *o* will not	*cá* (fish)	*hok* (shell) Only occurs before velars Difficult to distinguish from long *o* in all positions
ɑ	*hot*	*mal* (bad)	*con* (child)	*sa* (sand)
ɑ ʊ	*house* Diphthong	*pauta*	*dao* (knife)	*sau* (basket)
ɔ ɪ	*boy* Diphthong	*hoy* (today)	*ròi* (already)	*soi* (grill)
ɑ ɪ	*bite* Diphthong	*baile* (dance)	*hai* (two)	*sai* (to waste)
ə	*about* Most common vowel in English; only in unstressed syllables Learners may have difficulty keeping it very short	**NO EQUIVALENT** Substitute short *u* or the full vowel from the word's spelling	*mua* (to buy)	**NO EQUIVALENT**
ʌ	*cut* Similar to schwa /ə/	**NO EQUIVALENT** Substitute short *o*	*giờ'* (time)	*san* (new)
ɝ	*bird* Difficult articulation, unusual in the world but common in American English Learners must bunch the tongue and constrict the throat	**NO EQUIVALENT** Substitute short *u* or /er/ with trill	**NO EQUIVALENT** Substitute /i/	*hæ* (boot)

* *International Phonetic Alphabet*

THE VOWELS OF ENGLISH

IPA*	Hmong	Filipino	Korean	Mandarin
i	*ib* (one)	*ikaw* (you) This vowel is interchangeable with /ɪ/; hard for speakers to distinguish these	zuːʃaŋ (market)	*ti* (ladder) Sometimes English /i/ can be produced shorter
ɪ	**NO EQUIVALENT** Substitute /ē/	*limampu* (fifty) This vowel is interchangeable with /ē/; hard for speakers to distinguish these	**NO EQUIVALENT** Substitute /ē/	**NO EQUIVALENT**
e	*tes* (hand)	*sero* (zero)	beːda (to cut)	*te* (nervous) Sometimes substitute English schwa /ə/
ɛ	**NO EQUIVALENT** Substitute /ā/	*sero* (zero) This vowel interchanges with /ā/ like *bait*; not difficult for speakers to learn	thɛːdo (attitude)	**NO EQUIVALENT**
æ	**NO EQUIVALENT** Substitute short *e*	**NO EQUIVALENT** Substitute short *o* as in *hot*	**NO EQUIVALENT**	**NO EQUIVALENT** Substitute /ə/ or short *u*
u	*kub* (hot or gold)	*tunay* (actual) This vowel interchanges with vowel in *could*; not difficult for speakers to learn	zuːbag (watermelon)	*lu* (hut) Sometimes English long *u* can be produced shorter
ʊ	**NO EQUIVALENT** Substitute a sound like long *e* (mid central with lips slightly rounded)	*gumawa* (act) This vowel interchanges with long *u* like *boot*; not difficult for speakers to learn	**NO EQUIVALENT**	**NO EQUIVALENT**
o	**NO EQUIVALENT**	*ubo* (cough)	boːzu (salary)	*mo* (sword) This vowel is a little lower than English vowel
ɔ	*Yaj* (Yang clan name)	**NO EQUIVALENT** Spoken as short *o*, as in *hot*	**NO EQUIVALENT**	**NO EQUIVALENT** Substitute long *o*
ɑ	*mov* (cooked rice)	*talim* (blade)	maːl (speech)	*ta* (he/she) Sometimes substitute back long *o* or *u*
ɑʊ	*plaub* (four)	*ikaw* (you)	**NO EQUIVALENT**	**NO EQUIVALENT**
ɔɪ	**NO EQUIVALENT**	*apoy* (fire)	**NO EQUIVALENT**	**NO EQUIVALENT**
ɑɪ	*qaib* (chicken)	*himatay* (faint)	**NO EQUIVALENT**	**NO EQUIVALENT**
ə	**NO EQUIVALENT**	**NO EQUIVALENT** Spoken as short *o*, as in *hot*	**NO EQUIVALENT** Difficult sound for learners	**NO EQUIVALENT**
ʌ	**NO EQUIVALENT**	**NO EQUIVALENT** Spoken as short *o*, as in *hot*	**NO EQUIVALENT**	**NO EQUIVALENT**
ɝ	**NO EQUIVALENT** Substitute diphthong /əi/	**NO EQUIVALENT** Spoken as many different vowels (depending on English spelling) plus tongue tap /ɾ/	**NO EQUIVALENT**	**NO EQUIVALENT**

* *International Phonetic Alphabet*

Acknowledgments

Photographs

Photo locators denoted as follows: Top (T), Center (C), Bottom (B), Left (L), Right (R), Background (Bkgd)

4 Jill Battaglia/ Shutterstock; **5(TL), 6, 8, 10** Simon & Schuster; **5(BL), 18, 20, 22** Capstone Press; **30** ©Tom Till/Alamy; **56** ©DonSmith/Alamy; **57(BL), 70, 72, 74** HarperCollins Publishers; **57(BR), 76, 78, 80** Holiday House; **82** © Eurasia Press/Photononstop/Corbis; **83(TL), 84, 86, 88** Simon & Schuster; **108** Antoine Beyeler/Shutterstock; **109(TL), 110, 112, 114** Simon & Schuster; **109(BL), 122, 124, 126** Capstone Press; **134** © AfriPics/Alamy; **135(BL), 148, 150, 152** Capstone Press.